THE VIA FRANCIGENA –
CANTERBURY TO ROME

2: The Great St Bernard Pass to Rome

About the Author

A chance viewing of a television programme in the early 1970s led to the author's interest in the Pilgrim Road to Santiago, at that time barely known in Britain. A walker most of her life, Alison had the opportunity to walk the 1000 mile *camino* from Le Puy-en-Velay to Santiago all in one go in 1990, a time which coincided, fortuitously, with Cicerone looking for an author to write an original guide in English to the Spanish section of the route. Since then she has walked and explored many of the pilgrim roads through Europe (France, Germany, Switzerland, Portugal), as well as those she has written about.

Alison is a former teacher of French, German and Spanish to adults, and her other interests include playing the French horn.

Other Cicerone guides by the author

The Way of St James – Le Puy to the Pyrenees
The Way of St James – Pyrenees–Santiago–Finisterre
Vía de la Plata – Seville/Granada to Santiago
The Pilgrim Road to Nidaros – Oslo to Trondheim
The Via Francigena – Canterbury to Rome, vol. 1: Canterbury to the Great
  St Bernard Pass

THE VIA FRANCIGENA –
CANTERBURY TO ROME

2: The Great St Bernard Pass to Rome

Alison Raju

2 POLICE SQUARE, MILNTHORPE, CUMBRIA LA7 7PY
www.cicerone.co.uk

© Alison Raju 2014
First edition 2014
ISBN: 978 1 85284 607 7

Printed by KHL Printing, Singapore

A catalogue record for this book is available from the British Library.
Photographs by Michael Krier unless otherwise indicated.

Dedication

*For all those who begin their journey as a walker and end it as a pilgrim;
and for Graham Scholes, who helped with several of my guidebooks.*

Front cover: Modern relief sculpture of a medieval pilgrim, Bardone

CONTENTS

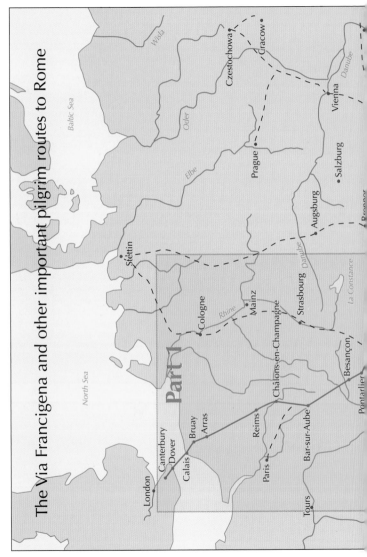

The Via Francigena and other important pilgrim routes to Rome

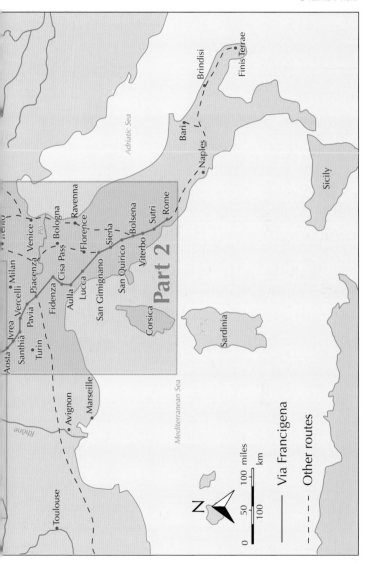

Adriatic Sea

Brindisi

Finis Terrae

Bari

Naples

Sicily

Ravenna

Bologna

Venice

Florence

Milan

Piacenza

Cisa Pass

Vercelli

Siena

Rome

Bolsena

Sutri

Viterbo

Pavia

Ivrea

Fidenza

Aulla

Santhià

Aosta

Lucca

Turin

San Quirico

San Gimignano

Part 2

Corsica

Sardinia

Marseille

Avignon

Mediterranean Sea

Rhône

Toulouse

N

0   50   100 miles

0   50   100 km

—— Via Francigena

– – – Other routes

7

Side street, Pavia (Section 2)

Map Key

———————————	road
——————— - - - -	walk route on road/alternative
— ● — — —	railway/station
—————— - - - - -	walk route/alternative route
～～～～～～	river or canal
— - — - — - — -	regional boundary

•	town/village
▪	habitation
†	cemetery
⌂	cathedral
⚑	chapel/church
Ħ	castle/tower

Abbreviations used in route descriptions

L/R	turn/fork left or right
(L)/(R)	to your left or right (feature described in the text)
KSO	keep straight on
KSO(L)/KSO(R)	keep straight on left or right (at a fork)
FB	footbridge
FP	footpath
VS	via sterrata
VF	Via Francigena
OP	ostello pellegrino (pilgim hostel)
YH	youth hostel
K	kitchen/cooking facilities
rte	restaurant
PO	post office
TO	tourist office
IAT	Informazione d Accoglienza Turistica (TO in large towns)
PS	pilgrim stamp
X	closed/except
CD	cash dispenser
HT	high tension (cables)
AEVF	Associazione Europea delle Vie Francigene
AIVF	Associazione Internationale della Via Francigena
All facilities	a full range of shops, banks, restaurants, hotels, medical centre and public transport
▼	see footnote below (small blue text) for short diversion
❯ ❯❯	route option continues further on at ❮ or ❮❮

Siena cathedral (Section 4)

INTRODUCTION

Admiring the view – looking across the lake from the Great St Bernard Pass into Italy (Section 1)

The Vía Francigena ('the way through France') is a long-distance walk with a difference – a 1900km pilgrimage on foot from Canterbury to Rome. This guidebook, the second half of a two-volume set, describes the route from the Great St Bernard Pass on the Swiss-Italian border southwards through Italy to the 'Eternal City'. (The first volume covers the route through Britain, France and Switzerland up to the Great St Bernard Pass.)

People have been making pilgrimages to Rome since the fourth century. Early pilgrims from Britain usually went across to what is now Germany and then down the Rhine, but from about the eighth century

onwards many of those who started in Canterbury, or passed through it on their way, would have taken much the same route as the one described in this book. This route has become known nowadays as the Via Francigena (pronounced with the emphasis on the 'i' – 'francheegena') and was made a European Cultural Itinerary by the Council of Europe in 1994 (and upgraded to a Major Cultural Route in 2004).

Many people who undertake pilgrim routes such as the Via Francigena, and that to Santiago de Compostela through north and north-western Spain, are not experienced walkers. They have often never done

11

any serious walking in their lives and many will never do any again – for on a pilgrim route, as in the past, walking is a means of transport, a means to an end, rather than an activity for its own sake. And while most long-distance footpaths, in Britain and France, for example, avoid not only large towns but also even quite small villages, the route to Rome, because of its historic origins and the need for shelter, deliberately seeks them out.

Relatively few people make this journey on foot at present, regardless of their starting point, although numbers have begun to increase gradually, and in 2012 some 2500 people walked, cycled or went there on horseback (compared, for example, to the 183,360 who made the pilgrimage to Santiago de Compostela in the same year). However, by no means all of them started in either Canterbury or their own countries. A large number of those who reported their arrival to

the authorities in the Vatican had only done a fairly small section of the route in Italy. To qualify for a Testimonium (certificate of pilgrimage) walkers must have come from at least Acquapendente (151km from Rome), and cyclists from Lucca (375km).

The modern pilgrim

One of the main differences between modern pilgrims and their historical counterparts, whether they walk, cycle or ride, is that very few return home by the same means of transport. The Via Francigena as an early 21st-century pilgrim route has thus become a 'one-way street', and it is unusual today to encounter anyone with either enough time or the inclination to return by the same means as they used on their outward journey.

People today make the pilgrimage from Canterbury (or other starting points in Europe) to Rome for a variety of reasons. For some it is just another

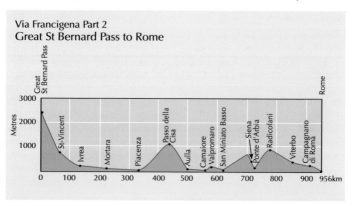

Via Francigena Part 2
Great St Bernard Pass to Rome

Path going down to Bourg Saint-Rhémy (Section 1)

long-distance walk. Many, but by no means all, have already walked or ridden the pilgrim road to Santiago de Compostela (see 'A challenging pilgrim route' below) and would like to experience another of the three great Christian pilgrim destinations (the ultimate one being Jerusalem). For others, however, the journey on foot or by bicycle will be their first pilgrim undertaking, and their motives may be historical, cultural, sporting or religious, or some combination of all of these. For many people it may also be a significant action or event in their lives – to mark their retirement, perhaps, to fill the gap between studying and taking a first job, or the opportunity to take time out to decide which way to go next after a turning point in their lives.

Pilgrims in the 21st century are of all ages, from all walks of life and, nowadays, from all parts of the globe, not just from Western Europe. Some travel alone, some in twos and threes, some (in the Italian section in particular) in quite large groups, usually those on foot. Many complete the entire journey in one stretch, and this is recommended wherever possible, as otherwise the journey tends to become just a series of disjointed holidays, where the walker never really 'leaves home', rather than an actual pilgrimage. Others with more limited time have to cover a section at a time over several years.

Most of those who walk the Via Francigena, like those who have already experienced the Camino de Santiago, and especially those who have been able to do the whole route in one go, would probably agree that it has changed their lives in some way, even if they did not set out with this intention.

A guide for walkers

A cyclists' guide to the route to Rome through Italy is available in English (see Appendix D), and there are several walkers' guidebooks (in Italian) to the route through Italy, but this book, with its companion volume is, at present, the only dedicated walkers' guide in any language to the whole Via Francigena. It addresses primarily the needs of the long-haul pilgrim walking all the way from Canterbury to Rome, and particularly those who undertake the journey all in one go, although it is equally suitable for those with less time, who have to walk the route in sections.

As well as providing route-finding information, a description of places to visit, and information on where to sleep and eat, this guide also contains, in Appendix A, a guided tour on foot of the 23 churches that Sigeric, Archbishop of Canterbury, is reported to have visited during his three-day visit to Rome in 990AD (see 'History' below). Appendix B lists the 48 stages in Italy of the 79 stages in Sigeric's itinerary on his return journey, while Appendix C offers an inventory of

Track near the Cappella di Vitaleta, after leaving San Quirico d'Orcia (Section 5)

Chiesa di Santa Maria Assunta, Monteriggioni (Section 4)

San Rocco churches and iconography along the Italian section of the Via Francigena. There are suggestions for further reading in Appendix D, a glossary of geographical and other terms in Appendix E, and a list of useful addresses and websites in Appendix F. Appendix G gives information on obtaining the Testimonium after completing the pilgrimage. Appendices H, I and J contain, respectively, indexes of maps and principal place names, and a summary of the route with distances between each place.

The 956km journey from the Great St Bernard Pass at 2473m (8114ft) above sea level to Rome will take a reasonably fit person five to six to weeks, allowing for some rest days to visit places of interest along the way or simply to have a break from walking. As indicated above, however, the journey can be undertaken in sections, and information is given in the text as to how to reach (or leave) the main towns along the way. A lot of the walker's route described here is also suitable for cyclists, but they should also consult the Chinn/Gallard guide (see Appendix D for details).

Anyone who is thinking of walking or cycling the Via Francigena should certainly consider contacting the Confraternity of Pilgrims to Rome for advice and membership (see Appendix F for contact details).

HISTORY

People have been making pilgrimages to Rome since the fourth century when, with the Edict of Milan in AD313, the Roman Empire became Christian, unleashing a veritable flood of pilgrims anxious to visit the tombs of Saints Peter and Paul and the early martyrs in the city. These early pilgrims were aided in their undertaking by the well-maintained infrastructure of Roman roads and the network of *mansiones* (inns for travellers) at intervals along the way, as well as by the frequent *termae* (Roman baths) to be found in many places on the route.

Gradually, however, the numbers of pilgrims swelled to such an extent that the existing accommodation no longer sufficed, and as early as the fifth century dedicated pilgrim 'hospitals' (places where hospitality was offered to travellers, both the sick and the well) began to be built. These early pilgrims had no linguistic difficulties, as they were able to convey their needs in Latin (a language later spoken only by clerics). As early as the ninth century, phrase books appeared, with the most important everyday vocabulary provided in the languages of the countries or areas the pilgrim would pass through.

However, with the Barbarian invasions of the sixth and seventh centuries, pilgrim life became much more difficult. Roads and bridges ceased to be maintained, inns and other accommodation were not kept up, and in areas no longer under Christian rule pilgrimage became increasingly dangerous, with pilgrims beset by bands of robbers, barbarian invaders and pirates during sea crossings, to say nothing of storms, wild animals, lack of food and sickness, and the pilgrim

was not at all sure he would reach his destination, let alone return home in one piece.

All these trials and tribulations are well documented in writings from the sixth century onwards, and many pilgrims wrote accounts of their experiences, recounting the everyday happenings as well as the dangers of the route. One of the earliest of these was the English monk Gildas the Wise, who went to Rome in AD530. The two journeys made by Saint Wilfred, in 666 and again in 673, are also well documented, while the first 'tourist guide' to Rome, the *Salzburger Reisebuch*, was produced as early as the seventh century and listed all the places a pilgrim should be sure to visit.

The *Einsiedler Manuskript* of AD750 went a step further, providing the pilgrim, in addition, with ten 'tourist walks' round the town to take in the principal sights of ancient Rome. Modern pilgrims now have access to this guide in English (Howard Nelson, *The Einsiedeln Itineraries* – see Appendix D for details), if they would like to do the same tour when they arrive.

Sigeric and the first 'guidebook'

A detailed route description was left by the Icelandic Abbot Nikolas von Munkathverá, who travelled to Rome in 1154, via Strasburg and Basel, to join the Via Francigena in Switzerland, but the first real 'guidebook' to the route from Canterbury – and the one

Lavoir, Radicofani (Section 5)

which has had the greatest influence on subsequent pilgrim journeys – was made at the instigation of Sigeric, Archbishop of Canterbury, when he went to Rome in AD990.

Like all his predecessors, Sigeric went to Rome to receive his *pallium* – a white woollen stole/scarf with six black crosses on it that formed his seal of office – from the Pope. He went there with a considerable retinue, in 79 daily stages, spent three days in Rome (during which he dined once with the Pope), visited 23 churches (see Appendix A for a walking route to visit these today) and then set off back home. On the return journey he asked his secretary to write up a description of the route, the result of which is a list, in Latin, of these stages and where they spent the night (the manuscript is now in the British Museum).

This 'guidebook' became the basis for future journeys to Rome made by pilgrims from Britain and places along the way, and fixed what is sometimes referred to as the 'Sigeric route', the one which has become known today as the Via Francigena. This is the route described in this book, based on the pioneering investigative work done by the AIVF (Association Internazionale Via Francigena) in the mid-1990s, and it includes most of the stopping places used by Sigeric on this journey through Italy – Aosta, Ivrea, Vercelli, Piacenza, Lucca, Siena, Viterbo and so on. His route used the Roman road network, most of which is now busy main roads, and so quieter, safer alternatives have been provided but in essence, this is the same route as that taken by

17

the late 10th-century Archbishop of Canterbury and his companions on the Italian part of their return journey over a thousand years ago. The numbers of his first 48 stages (starting from Rome) are listed in Appendix B and given throughout the route description.

Alternative pilgrim routes

Until the beginning of the eighth century, however, the route along the Rhine was the one taken by many pilgrims journeying to Rome, but as the area was not yet under Christian rule it was extremely dangerous. The fifth-century English princess Ursula, for example, was returning home from a pilgrimage accompanied by 11 virgins (the numbers swelled to 11,000 in the legend that grew up subsequently) when she and all her retinue were murdered by the Huns as she approached Cologne. By the beginning of the eighth century, English clerics and lay pilgrims had begun to travel through the area that is now present-day France instead.

Under Charles the Great (Charlemagne) things improved dramatically, and pilgrim numbers swelled considerably, but after the end of the Carolingian period pilgrimage became dangerous again as the Saracens moved further and further west. They reached the mouth of the Tiber, threatened to destroy Rome's two most important Christian basilicas, Saint Peter's and Saint Paul's-outside-the-Walls, and invaded the whole Alpine region. Only

when they were finally driven back in the 10th century did the crossing of the Alps over the Great St Bernard Pass become safe enough to use again.

While the dangers of the journey to Rome were sufficient to deter prospective pilgrims, the discovery, in the early ninth century, of the tomb of Saint James in north-western Spain and the establishment of the third important European pilgrimage, to Santiago de Compostela, deprived Rome of its unique position of being the only city to have apostles' graves within its precincts. As the popularity of the Santiago pilgrimage rose, so the one to the tombs of Saints Peter and Paul began to decline, especially given all the practical and political difficulties of this journey.

Holy Years

However, in the year 1300 pilgrimage to Rome received an unexpected impetus when Pope Boniface VIII declared it a Jubilee (Holy) Year, during which pilgrims could receive a plenary indulgence – a complete remission of all sins, something usually obtainable only by taking part in a Crusade. There were conditions attached, and for a complete remission of all sins the pilgrim had to confess on 15 successive days in the basilicas of both Saint Peter's and Saint Paul's (unlike the ordinary citizen, who had to do so on 30 successive days).

So great was the demand for plenary indulgences that over two

St Peter's Square, Rome (Section 5)

million pilgrims went to Rome during the Holy Year in 1300, many in large groups from Germany, France and England. The annals of the hospice at the Great St Bernard Pass for that year recorded 20,000 overnight stays, while for Rome itself the Holy Year was not only a spiritual but also a resounding business success – it was reported that pilgrim donations at the altar in Saint Peter's basilica totalled 30,000 gold florins (some £7 million in today's money) in that year alone.

The next Holy Year was 50 years later and then in the 1400 Jubilee Year there was an outbreak of plague, and large numbers of Roman citizens and pilgrims died. However, in 1450 Pope Nicholas V took in so much gold from pilgrim donations that he was able to start rebuilding Saint Peter's and endow the Vatican Library with precious manuscripts from all over the world. After that Holy Years were declared every 25 years, and pilgrim numbers continued to rise, a pattern which continued until the Reformation, at which point pilgrimages were officially banned in all Protestant countries. Hardly any pilgrims were in evidence in Rome in 1525 and 1550, but with the Counter-Reformation numbers swelled again and Rome, with a population of 100,000 inhabitants, saw some 400,000 pilgrims arrive in 1575 and over 500,000 in 1600.

After that numbers continued to rise consistently each year until, by the end of the 19th century, the arrival of mass transportation started a change which altered the character of pilgrimage from a personal effort made under one's own steam to the phenomenon we have today, whereby large groups of people arrive quickly in Rome by bus, train or charter plane. Pilgrimages in Holy Years continued throughout the 20th century, with television and the mass media making them even better known, and in the 2000 Jubilee Year 25 million pilgrims visited Rome by one means or another. Today's foot pilgrims have therefore swung full circle, making a conscious choice to travel under their own steam and at their own speed, on a journey in which not only the end, but also the means, are of great significance.

Pilgrim street light, Bourg Saint-Rhémy (Section 1)

PILGRIMS THROUGH THE CENTURIES

Who were the pilgrims who made this often perilous journey to Rome? People from all walks of life and strata of society, such as those depicted in the *Canterbury Tales*, more men than women (the latter were often actively discouraged from doing so on 'moral' grounds), the high-born, the low, and all those in between, while among the many prominent persons who made the journey to Rome and back (often more than once in their lifetime) were Wilfrid, Bishop of Ripon, Saint Boniface and, of course, many Archbishops of Canterbury.

But why did people go on pilgrimages? For a variety of reasons – as a profession of faith, for instance, and a quest to save one's soul, as a way of acquiring merit (and thus, for example, reducing the amount of time

spent in Purgatory), and as a search for healing, both mental and physical – although we know nowadays that many who felt themselves to be miraculously 'cured' were very often only in spontaneous remission due to a change of diet, season, climate or place. Pilgrimages were made as a means of atonement too (certain crimes such as the murder of children or a priest could be absolved only by the Pope) or punishment – a system of fixed penalties for certain crimes/sins was in operation during the Middle Ages and a standard sentence for the murder of a bishop, for example, or one's father, the theft of church goods and arson (since almost all houses at the time were made of wood) was a pilgrimage to Rome. For others it was an opportunity to venerate the relics of saints available along way (indulgences were often available to those who visited shrines). Later there were professional pilgrims who would (for a fee) undertake to do the pilgrimage on behalf of someone else who could afford the money but not the time to do it him or herself.

There were some, too, who were just glad of the opportunity to escape their surroundings – from a sense of adventure, or perhaps to shirk family responsibilities. And there were others with very definite ulterior motives – thieves, vagabonds, heretics, army deserters and *coquillards* (pseudo-pilgrims, so named because they would wear the *coquille* or scallop shell to disguise their intentions along the pilgrim road to Santiago) – all of whom were out to exploit the true pilgrim, to rob, steal, and take advantage of the alms and accommodation available

Modern pilgrim sculpture near tourist office, Berceto (Section 2)

to pilgrims of whatever type along the way. Those with the means to do so went on horseback, and some wealthy people made the pilgrimage along with a considerable retinue (Kaiser Friedrich II, for example, is reported to have made the journey in the 13th century accompanied not only by a multitude of servants but 25 camels, five leopards and an elephant!). The majority of pilgrims went on foot, however, and even among the rich there were some who preferred to walk, rather than ride, because of the greater merit they would attain.

Preparing for pilgrimage

Pilgrims in former times were not at all sure that they would reach their destination, let alone return home in one piece, so before setting out (those with honourable motives, at least) they took leave of their family and employer, made their will, gave a generous donation to the poor and needy, and generally put their affairs in order. They obtained their credential (pilgrim passport) – *credenziale* is the Italian term used for this document today – from their bishop or church, which could then be presented in order to obtain food and lodging in the many pilgrim hospitals and other establishments along the way and be stamped there as they went along. This was both a precaution against the growing number of coquillards and a means of furnishing evidence, if needed, that they had made the pilgrimage successfully.

21

Pilgrims had their staff (normally some 2m long and fitted with an iron spike at the end, useful not only to walk with but as a defence against dogs and wild animals) and scrip (small knapsack) blessed in church before setting out (this ceremony is thought to have originated in the blessing of knights before they left for the First Crusade).

They travelled light, carrying little else but a gourd for water. Both male and female pilgrims were easily recognizable by the heavy cloak they wore, made of untreated wool and so reasonably waterproof, and which also served as a blanket at night. Male pilgrims wore wide-brimmed hats, women a shawl or scarf, and both normally walked in sturdy lace-up boots or stout sandals. (Contrary to popular belief, barefoot pilgrims were the exception.)

To distinguish themselves from pilgrims to other destinations, those making their way to Rome bore, on the metal badge they frequently wore stitched to their hat or cloak, either the crossed keys of Saint Peter or the 'Veronica' (the representation of Christ's face on the cloth with which Saint Veronica wiped his face on the way to his death on the cross).

Accommodation

Pilgrims with funds could stay in inns and other publicly available lodgings, but the vast majority probably stayed in the different hospices (lodgings for travellers, usually run by religious orders), 'hospitals' and other facilities provided specially for them. Some of

Former pilgrim hospital, Altopascio (Section 4)

Chiesa di Santa Maria Maddelena, patron saint of the Via Francigena, in Torrenieri (Section 5)

these were in towns, and there were often several in each town (there were 16 in Vercelli, for example). They were located either in the centre or outside the walls to cater both for latecomers and possibly contagious pilgrims, while others were in the countryside, frequently by bridges or at the crossing of important pilgrim feeder roads. These locations are far too numerous to mention here, but they are referred to throughout the route description.

Much of this pilgrim accommodation was provided by religious orders (who also tended those who were sick and looked after them until they were well enough to set out on their journey again), as well as by churches, civic authorities and benevolent individuals. The facilities offered varied considerably from one establishment to another, but surviving records from many of them indicate exactly what was provided for the pilgrim in terms of food, lodging and medical attention – such as *lectum* (bed), *panem* (bread), *vinum* (wine) and *ignem* (firewood) – often specifying the quantities per pilgrim as well.

Routes to Rome

Although the name Via Francigena has now become synonymous with the pilgrim route from Canterbury to Rome, as described in this guide, this route is not (and never was) the one and only 'real' pilgrim road to Rome, but simply one of many taken by those who came from Britain or places along the way. Pilgrims from the Iberian Peninsula, for example, would have followed the coast through southern France to get to Italy, while those from other parts of France

23

would have crossed the Alps not by the Great St Bernard Pass but by the Montcenis or Montgenèvre passes. German pilgrims and those from further afield may well have taken the Brenner or Sankt Gothard passes into Italy, while others would have made their way overland to Venice and from there to Rome. And there were other routes, too, taken by pilgrims approaching the Eternal City from the south, some of which are being cleared and investigated today. There was thus a whole network of routes to Rome, and the journey began, at least until the 20th century, from each and every pilgrim's own front door. 'Omnes viae Romam perducunt', as the well-known saying goes – 'All roads lead to Rome'.

There were also variations in the route taken even by pilgrims from the same starting point, depending on their mode of transport. Those on foot or on horseback, for instance, could take the shortest, most direct route, while the well-to-do, who rode in carriages heavily laden with luggage, would have to resort to larger roads. The route chosen also depended on how safe or dangerous a particular section was reported to be. In general, the pilgrim routes to Rome remained more or less static until the advent of mass transportation in the late 19th century, when the old pedestrian/riding routes began to disappear as pilgrims began to take first the train, then the bus/coach and finally the charter flight to reach their destination.

The length of time away from home changed too, making the modern conception of pilgrimage very different from that of the past.

The account above is only a very brief introduction to a vast subject, just enough to put modern pilgrims 'in the picture' a little as regards the background to their undertaking. For an introduction to pilgrimage in general the Sumption book (see Appendix D) is highly recommended, but at present, unfortunately, there is no book on the history and background of the Via Francigena as a whole (as opposed to individual places along the way) available in English.

PILGRIM SAINTS

San Rocco (Saint Roch)

Saint Francis of Assisi is known to have made the pilgrimage to Rome many times, as well as to Santiago de Compostela and Jerusalem, and Saint Christopher (frequently represented carrying a child on his shoulder) is well known as the patron saint of travellers in general. However, the real patron saint of pilgrims is Saint Roch ('San Rocco' in Italian), the one most in evidence on the Via Francigena in Italy.

San Rocco was born around 1295 in Montpellier in the south of France into a well-to-do family (his father was the governor of that city), and at his birth he was found to be marked with a red cross on his chest, which

Free-standing sculpture of San Rocco as pilgrim, Chiesa di San Rocco, Gropello Cairoli (Section 2)

On his return journey San Rocco visited Parma, Modena, Mantua and other towns along the way, but when he reached Piacenza he himself was stricken with the disease. This left him with an unsightly sore on his thigh, so to warn people to keep away from him he kept the front flap of his coat turned up to reveal it, pointing it out to all he came across. He then withdrew to live in isolation in a forest near Piacenza and, so the story goes, he was brought a loaf of bread every morning by a dog, stolen from its master's table in a large house nearby.

San Rocco continued living in this way for some time, but after a while the dog's owner, Gothard (Gotardo) Palastrelli, became curious as to where his dog disappeared to every morning and one day decided to follow it. When he discovered where the saint was living he took him to stay in his home until he recovered (some say because the dog licked his wound; others because he was cured by an angel).

increased in size as he grew. His parents died when he was only about 20 years old, at which point he decided to hand over the governorship of the city (which he had inherited) to his uncle, distribute his wealth to the poor and needy, and set off on a pilgrimage to Rome. He stopped for a while in Acquapendente on his way, a town stricken by the plague at the time, and devoted himself to looking after its victims, curing them by making the sign of the cross. He then visited other neighbouring cities before reaching Rome, where he remained until 1371, and everywhere he went he was able to cure plague victims in the same way.

After that San Rocco set off back home again to France, on foot, but when he reached his native Montpellier he refused to reveal his identity and was taken for a spy disguised as a mendicant pilgrim. He was imprisoned by order of the then governor (his uncle in some versions of the story), where he remained until he died five years later in 1327, barely 30 years old. It was only then, when the red cross on his chest was discovered, along with some papers

Fresco of San Rocco, Cappella San Rocco, on leaving Santhià (Section 1)

they are still to be found. His feast day is celebrated on 16 August.

In his short life San Rocco worked along much of what has now become known as the Via Francigena in Italy, and today he is still very much in evidence in various forms. There are some extremely large and grandiose churches dedicated to him along the way, such as the 18th-century Chiesa di San Rocco in Gropello Cairoli, but the majority of buildings bearing his name are quite small, simple affairs, more like large chapels, frequently by the roadside, and often at the entrance/exit to a large population centre. Many of these date from the 17th century, when the plague was particularly rife, and were built, often by the local population or some private benefactor, in thanksgiving for their survival. Many hospitals and confraternities of San Rocco were also founded, one or two of which still exist today.

In addition to the churches and chapels dedicated to San Rocco (sometimes jointly with another saint, such as the Chiesa di San Rocco e San Bernado in Ponticello or the Chiesa di San Rocco e San Sebastiano in Campagnano di Roma), in the Italian section of the Via Francigena there are also innumerable representations of the saint in sculpture (both free-standing and relief), frescoes on the outside of buildings and paintings inside all the way from the Alps to Rome. As a saint he has a halo, is often dressed in the Italian style of the period in

in his possession, that his true identity was revealed, after which he was given a public funeral and numerous miracles occurred, attesting to his sanctity. Thus, if the first 20 years of his life are discounted and the five years he spent in prison at the end of it, San Rocco's period of 'active service' was remarkably short in view of the enormous number of plague victims he was able to cure in that limited space of time – only seven or eight years. His relics were taken secretly to Venice in 1485, where

which the work of art was created, and has the flap of his (usually knee-length) coat turned up, with his index finger pointing to the exposed wound on his thigh. At his side is the faithful dog (frequently with a loaf of bread in his mouth) and sometimes a child or angel too. However, legend has often confused San Rocco with Santiago Peregrino (Saint James the Pilgrim), and he not infrequently appears in a 'pilgrim version' as well, with added hat, staff, bag and one or several scallop shells on his clothing, wearing boots or stout sandals. He also exists in a 'hybrid' version too, with halo instead of a pilgrim hat, but with one or more scallop shells on his coat or cape.

A list of the known San Rocco churches, chapels and iconography along the route through Italy is given in Appendix C.

San Pietro (Saint Peter)

Those who have already made the journey to Santiago de Compostela, particularly along the Camino Francés, will have been struck by the sheer number of churches and chapels dedicated to Saint James along the way in Spain, and by the numerous statues, stained-glass windows, paintings and other representations of the saint in his different guises – aspects of the route which arose after the pilgrimage became popular. Pilgrims who make the journey to Rome will not find the same number of references to Saint Peter ('San Pietro' in

Italian) along the way, despite the fact that, in the past at least, the goal of their undertaking was to visit his tomb in the Basilica in Rome (as well as the final resting places of Saint Paul and other Early Christian martyrs).

There are a number of churches and chapels dedicated to Saint Peter along the Via Francigena en route to Rome, but these exist because this has always been a popular church dedication in many countries, and not because they were on an important Christian pilgrimage route. Where known, the presence of these is indicated in the text, as are representations of Saint Peter in sculpture,

Saint Peter, side altar, Aosta cathedral (Section 1)

27

stained glass and so on. There are also one or two churches along the way dedicated to San Pietro in Vincoli (Saint Peter in Chains), referring to the chains that bound him while he was imprisoned in Jerusalem and which were preserved afterwards as relics.

Saint Peter is represented chiefly as an older person, frequently (although not always) seated, and recognisable by his keys (to the Kingdom of Heaven). He is also often accompanied by a model of a boat (recalling the fact that he was a fisherman before he became an apostle) and/or by a cockerel, reminding the viewer of Peter's threefold denial of Christ. More is known about the life of Saint Peter than that of any of the other apostle, and we are told, for example (although only in the Apochryphal New Testament), that his martyrdom took place by crucifixion – but upside down, so as not to be equated with his master. The feast day of Saints Peter and Paul is celebrated on 29 June.

GEOGRAPHY

Italy is divided into 20 *regioni* (its biggest administrative unit), and the Via Francigena passes through seven of them – Val d'Aosta, Piemonte, Lombardia, Emilia Romagna, Toscana, Liguria (very briefly) and Latium. Each *regione* comprises a variable number of *provincie*, which are in turn sub-divided into *comuni*, each made up of many individual *frazione* (hamlets). These distinctions are visible on notice boards and signposts in Italy, beginning with the bilingual (French and Italian) Val d'Aosta.

After leaving the **Great St Bernard Pass** and going along the side of the lake into Italy, the modern pilgrim starts the 1890m (6201ft) descent into Aosta. From above the tree line, with its rocky peaks, you begin to make your way down the valley, steeply at first and then less so, with wonderful views on a clear day. First of all you reach Bourg Saint-Rhémy, go past the entrance/exit to the road tunnel under the pass, through Saint Oyen,

Looking down on San Gimignano from the Torre Grande (Section 4)

Path leaving Saint Oyen (Section 1)

Etroubles (with its open-air museum spread all round the village), then Gignod with its tower, and through Variney to **Aosta** itself.

Here the pilgrim 'turns left' through the valley, with the Dora Balthea (river) along its bottom. Traditionally the left-hand (*adret*) side of the Val d'Aosta was the most inhabited as it faced the sun and so was better suited to agriculture, vineyards, cereal production and so on than the right-hand (*envers*) side, which was steeper, darker, damper, more subject to flooding in the spring and only really suitable for lumber and livestock. The upper slopes of the valley, particularly on the left-hand side, were densely populated by people engaged in subsistence farming – cultivation of wheat, barley, oats and potatoes – and who rarely came down to the valley below. Houses were built of stone, but this was not dressed in the early days in houses located high up, except at the corners and over archways, as these dwellings were used only in the summer months (wood was only used for balconies). However, from about 1700 onwards many began to be used for permanent living and so were gradually improved.

The land was divided into *colline* – prime agricultural land with grape vines, chestnut and walnut groves, and fruit orchards, the whole area being irrigated by an elaborate system of *rus* (canals channelling water from the rivers along the hillside to supply water to the fields). The system was set up largely between the 13th and 15th centuries and originally included the irrigation of very small plots of land, but nowadays only the bigger

29

ones are still intact (and in working order). Pilgrims will frequently walk alongside them, high up and on the level, for long stretches and with good views, or walk over the top of the rus when the water has been piped underground. Most of these canals simply served to irrigate the fields, although some, such as the Ru de Chavianaz (above Chambave), were used to power the oil, flour and saw-mills common in the area. Most villages had communal ovens (like the ones in the Montjovet area) and oil and wine presses, of which you will see a few restored examples as you walk along.

Another very striking feature of the Aosta valley, particularly on the left-hand side, is its numerous castles. Built for military and strategic purposes, some of the castles later became elaborate residences (the Castello di Fénis on the right-hand side, for example). Located on prominent hilltops and hillsides these castles formed a long line, so that at least two or three of them were visible from each one and they could communicate with each other by a system of fires, smoke signals, courier pigeons or semaphore. Pilgrims will pass (or pass near to) several along the way, and many are open to visit.

As regards religious architecture, many of the old (11th and 12th century) churches in the Aosta valley still retain their original bell tower (*campanile*). These are free-standing, separated from the rest of the church, as most of the churches were rebuilt or restored during the 18th and 19th centuries. Also along the way are numerous *edicole*, *sacelli votivi* and *oratorietti* (wayside shrines, crosses and tiny chapels). They are located

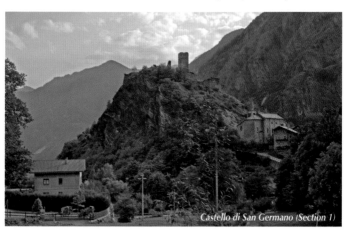

Castello di San Germano (Section 1)

Farmhouse, Bardone (Section 2)

at the beginning of routes, by bridges and crossroads, and over steep drops and precipices, being places to stop and say a prayer for protection from adversity. Other features seen regularly in the Val d'Aosta are sundials on both public buildings and private houses. Pilgrims will also come across many drinking fountains on this part of the Via Francigena (unlike many parts of the route further on), most of which, if running continuously, are safe to drink (*potabile*).

As pilgrims make their way through the Val d'Aosta the valley becomes gradually wider and the hills lower, and at Caremma (just after Pont Saint-Martin) the regione of Piemonte ('foot of the mountains' – ie the Alps) is entered. So by the time you reach Ivrea and the area known as the Canavese the land round about is more or less dead flat and the mountains have receded into the distance.

Ivrea today is an industrial town, set in motion when Camillo Olivetti set up his first typewriter factory in 1908, together with a large section of workers' housing for his employees (along the lines of the philanthropic Cadbury establishment in Bourneville in the UK). Today the Olivetti firm has moved on from making the original *macchina da scrivere*, and then adding and calculating machines, to producing state-of-the-art IT equipment. From here to **Santhià**, **Vercelli** (after which the regione of Lombardy and the Pô valley are entered), **Pavia** and **Piacenza** the region is flat. It was originally a large malarial swamp, but the landscape of the Lomellina section of Lombardy, in particular, altered when Cistercian monks from France reclaimed the land in the Middle Ages. They established the dense network of irrigation channels still seen today that make possible the large-scale production of rice (the area's main crop – this is where risotto originated) as well as the plantations of poplar trees.

The style of the farmhouses and buildings has also changed by now, and the *cascina* (farmstead) often resembles a barracks. It comprises a series of buildings accessible to the outside via a single entrance and built round a central, usually rectangular, courtyard with a threshing floor for drying rice, a well, cowsheds, barns and storage buildings. Historically, the owner's house was on a grand scale, whereas those for wage earners and seasonal workers were a lot smaller. Other types of farms and their buildings from here onwards, as seen particularly in their names (on signposts, notice boards and so on), are the *tenuta* (estate) and *podere* (farm).

After **Piacenza** (shortly before leaving the Lombardy regione and entering that of Emilia Romagna), Fiorenzula d'Arda and Fidenza, the landscape begins to change again and – gradually – becomes hillier as pilgrims approach the foothills of the Apennines and start to climb, slowly but steadily, up to the **Passo della Cisa** at 1040m. Here you enter Toscana (Tuscany), through which a very long section of the Via Francigena passes – **Lucca**, **San Gimignano**, **Siena** and **San Quirico** – until shortly before Acquapendente (apart from a brief foray, near **Aulla**, into Liguria and then back again).

The landscape in Tuscany reflects its volcanic origins, being dotted about with hills, big and small, round or pointed, and almost all of them have something perched on top – be it a town, a village, a hamlet, a

Cappella di Vitaleta, after leaving San Quirico d'Orcia (Section 5)

castle or even just a farm. The landscape, with its dry climate, often looks brown and parched, but perhaps one of the most striking features, for the outsider, is the quality of the Tuscan light – clear, bright, with no haze at all and casting everything into sharp perspective. There are splendid views as the route goes up and downhill and along the ridges, through Lucca, San Gimignano and San Quirico, frequently with vineyards and olive groves to either side.

Shortly before reaching Acquapendente pilgrims enter the region of Lazio and pass the **Lago di Bolsena** (the largest lake of volcanic origin in Europe), going through hilltop towns of Etruscan origin built on tufa rock – Montefiascone, **Viterbo** (and the thermal springs on the way there), Vetralla, Capranica, **Sutri**... After that, as pilgrims approach **Rome** itself, the landscape flattens out and becomes more densely populated, built up and industrial as the route makes its way through Campagnano di Roma, La Storta and the suburbs of the 'Eternal City' to the Vatican. The land is only 25m above sea level now – so 2448m lower than at the snowy heights of the Great St Bernard Pass.

However, despite the many and varied landscapes and places through which the Via Francigena passes in Italy, there is one feature which you will notice all along the route, from the first example in Fonteinte, 2.5km below the Swiss border, all the way to the outskirts of Rome – the former case cantoniere (road-builders' houses). Some are extremely large, others are very small indeed, while many are somewhere in between – but all are painted the same dark red colour and all bear the road name and number on which they are situated. They are still all the property of ANAS (the Italian national road maintenance service), but many have quite different uses today, including two (one in Cassio, the other 2km below the Passo della Cisa) which are now *ostelli*, providing simple dormitory-style accommodation for walkers, cyclists and other travellers.

ROUTE DESIGN AND TERRAIN

Route design

Whether pilgrims are walking all the way from Canterbury to Rome in one go or tackling the route in sections, this guide aims to describe a safe route, preferably quiet, which will lead pilgrims as directly as possible to their destination of St Peter's Basilica – but without missing out any of the important sights, any of the Sigeric halts (where they still exist), or any places of great religious or historical significance along the way. The route in this guide follows, in the main, the one proposed by the AIVF in their pioneering *vademecum* in 1994, but there are various factors that have influenced the course it takes.

From the time that Sigeric made his journey to Rome in AD990 until

Colle di Val d'Elsa (Section 4)

the late 19th century, pilgrims would have travelled by foot or horse on the network of Roman roads. With the advent of motorised transport, these roads became the basis of the modern Italian road system, carrying ever-increasing quantities of fast-moving vehicles. They are now completely incompatible with the needs of the modern foot pilgrim and alternatives have therefore had to be sought, although not without their inconveniences.

Many Italian roads (such as the SS2 in Section 5) pass along the bottom of steep-sided valleys that have few, if any, minor roads running parallel to them that could easily be used as an alternative by the 21st-century foot pilgrim. Instead, minor roads are frequently at right angles and so involve very lengthy loop-shaped detours with a lot of 'zigzagging' that adds many

kilometres to the pilgrim's journey. At other times the landscape may be flat (between Santhià and Vercelli in Section 1, for instance), but because there are so many very large *cascine* (farms) and few villages there are very few minor roads or public tracks to use as an easy, safe alternative to the traffic whizzing along on the SS11.

Another complicating factor is that much of the waymarking on these minor roads has not been done by local pilgrim associations (as it has been on the Camino de Santiago in Spain), whose members have already walked the route in question and have waymarked it with the long-haul pilgrim in mind. Instead, the Via Francigena has been waymarked by walking organisations such as the CAI (Italian Alpine Club), whose members are generally only out walking for the day and thus have very different needs. The day walker, for example, has only a small rucksack, brings all his/her food and drink for the day (so does not need to go shopping or find a bar for a drink), and probably welcomes a few extra kilometres to take in scenic detours and panoramic views. The day walker can stay at home in bad weather, whereas the long-haul pilgrim has to keep on walking and so needs safe routes in case of snow, torrential rain or poor visibility.

The 21st-century pilgrim is rarely an experienced hill-walker either – something that is often forgotten in route design – and carries (probably) 10kg or more on his/her back, and so needs a decent surface to walk on. While tarmac is not ideal, walkers also need a route that is not unduly uncomfortable underfoot – not kilometres of very narrow footpaths

covered in loose rocks, shale or gravel, such as are experienced, for example, on the 16km mountain stretch between Aulla and Sarzana (Section 2), which makes it very difficult to get any sort of rhythm going.

In instances where routes have not been designed with the long-haul pilgrim in mind, and where routes would not be safe in all types of weather, this guide provides alternatives.

The high-level route through the Aosta valley (Section 1) and the mountain option down from the Passo della Cisa (Section 3) are examples of this problem. They make use of existing footpaths and are spectacular routes in clear, bright weather, but the former is longer than the original AIVF itinerary and contains a lot of climbs and descents to reach the many rus (ancient irrigation channels) that are

Looking down over Berceto (Section 2)

then walked along on the level. The high-level route down from the Passo della Cisa is also considerably longer than the minor road alternative via Gravagna and goes up and down constantly until the last 5 or 6km before Pontremoli. Neither of these two high-level options requires a good head for heights, but both would be slippery in wet weather, dangerous in bad light and high winds, as well as very tiring with their constant changes of level. This guide describes both a high-level route waymarked by the local walking association and a more direct, lower level (although maybe less interesting) option for use in bad weather, short hours of daylight or for the pilgrim who is extremely tired. These different options are clearly differentiated in the relevant route-finding descriptions.

Another issue is that the course taken by the Via Francigena in Italy is still in evolution in several sections, with the result that the waymarking continues to change due to problems of terrain, local factors and rights of way. The author of this guide has gone to great pains to seek out the most recent waymarking, checking and rechecking on numerous occasions, but the user may find variations which have been set in place since this book was published, something over which the author has no control and for which she can take no responsibility. The advice in such cases is to follow the waymarking if this appears reliable and consistent, but otherwise to follow the directions given here, as these will always lead the pilgrim to his or her destination for that particular day.

A final problem concerning route design is the existence of two main pilgrim associations in Italy, the Association Internazionale Via Francigena (AIVF) and the Associazione Europea delle Vie Francigene (AEVF), although the original pioneering work was undertaken by the Perugia-based Confraternitá di San Jacopo. The AIVF was founded in 1997 by Adelaîde Trezzini, who got it classified (like the Camino de Santiago) as a European Cultural Itinerary in 2004. The AEVF was founded later and is chiefly concerned with what has now become known as the 'official' route, broadly following the one taken by Sigeric but concentrating more on the cultural aspects of the route. Both associations provide accommodation information to pilgrims on the Italian part of the Via Francigena, but neither appears to concern itself with the spiritual/reflective (as opposed to strictly religious) reasons why a pilgrim would want to make such a journey.

The AIVF is still busy investigating and opening up the strictly historical route, and is gradually beginning to waymark it with their own signage, such as the southern option between Ivrea and Santhià (described in Section 1 of this guide) that passes to the south (rather than to the north, as does the 'official' route) of the Lago di Viverone. Some sections will end up longer than the presently waymarked route. One in particular, between San Miniato and Gambassi Terme (Section 4), that the pilgrim is obliged to do all in one day because there is no accommodation in between, will increase the present 30km (hilly) stage with no facilities en route by another 10km in order to pass Sigeric's 22nd halt, San Genesio.

San Gimignano, street surface (Section 4)

Paths, tracks and streets

From the Great St Bernard Pass to Rome the Via Francigena leads pilgrims through woods, on ridges and along valleys by a variety of paths and tracks – including small, quiet tarmacked roads, *vie sterrate* (unsurfaced roads), *strada bianca* (gravel roads), occasionally a *strada privata* (private road), grassy paths and small footpaths. Sometimes they are on private land, where the landowner has given permission. There are also, occasionally, unavoidable short sections on busy roads (but with pavements or cycle tracks in the main). There are some sections of Roman roads with the original paving (*basulata romana*) intact – shortly after Montefiascone, for example, on the stretch between there and Viterbo (Section 5). It will also be necessary, from time to time, to ford a number of streams and small rivers (see below).

The names of the roads (and/or their numbers) and streets are given, where known, in the route description. If you don't find the name of a street when you turn into it, you can often find it on house-number tiles or, in towns, on the names of bus stops.

Cobbles, Monteriggioni (Section 4)

Some of the Italian street names may surprise you. There are a lot named after famous writers, public figures and so on – innumerable Vie Giacomo Matteotti (an early 20th-century socialist politician), Garibaldi, Dante Alighieri and so forth – as well as the dates of famous events in Italian history (XXVIII Febbraio, XXI Aprile, I Maggio and XXIV Maggio, to name but a few). The linguistically minded pilgrim will also spot more than one Via de Bonhumore, streets named in memory (of those who fell (*caduti*) not only in war, in the army, the air-force and so on, but also of people who died in accidents at work (Via dei Caduti del Lavoro...). And yet more unusual, to the outsider, are those named in honour of blood donors

Street-name sign for 'Blood and organ donors' square' near the church in Pont Saint-Martin (Section 1)

(Via dei Donantes de Sangre) and, near the church in Pont Saint-Martin, even a Piazza Donatori del Sangre e di Organi ('other organs').

Crossing rivers and streams

In several places pilgrims will have to ford small rivers or big streams that are dry in late summer and autumn but probably full of water in the spring time. Sometimes it is possible to get across via stepping stones, but often the water is too deep or there aren't enough stones, so look around to see if there is a better place to cross. Check first, however, to see where you will 'land' on the other side – not a vertical bank, for example!

If you do have to ford a stream or river you should **never**, under any circumstances, attempt to do this in bare feet. With a heavy rucksack you are likely to lose your balance, but additionally the water may be dirty and there may be sharp items under the water, so that if you cut yourself you would run the risk of getting seriously

infected feet. Rubber/plastic sandals are useful in such circumstances.

Note A *fiume* is a large and important (and often very long) river (such as the Dora Baltea, the Pô or the Tevere/Tiber), while a *torrente* is a smaller one that may well be dry in summer but in full spate in spring and autumn.

PREPARING FOR YOUR JOURNEY

Read up as much as you can about the route – its history, art, architecture and geography – as well as other people's accounts of their journeys. Suggestions for further reading are given in Appendix D, but there is almost no information about the route as a whole (as opposed to the individual places) in English at present. However, the Confraternity of Pilgrims to Rome's *Newsletter* has some interesting articles on various aspects of the pilgrimage, as does also the twice-yearly (bilingual – Italian and English) *Via Francigena* magazine.

If you are not used to walking or carrying a rucksack day in, day out, or have not already walked (without back-up transport) other long-distance routes, then make sure you get in plenty of practice before you go. Consider joining your local rambling club at least six months in advance and go out with them as often as you can. Most clubs have walks of different lengths and speeds so you can start with shorter, slower ones if you need to, and gradually build up your speed and stamina. In this way you can benefit from walking with other people (usually friendly) and having someone to lead who knows the way and suitable places to go (which you may not), and you can also practise walking in hilly places (which you will need).

Then start increasing the amount of weight you take out with you until you can carry what you need. After that go out walking on at least two consecutive days on several occasions, in hilly places, carrying all your proposed gear with you – walking 30km on a 'one-off' basis is a very different matter from getting up again the following morning, probably stiff and possibly footsore, and starting out all over again. In this way you should have an enjoyable journey, with trouble-free feet and back. Remember too, however, that several sections of the route through Italy are on tarmac (which will be hot in summer), so get in plenty of practice on this type of surface too, as well as on stony tracks and loose gravel.

Once you are in Italy don't expect anybody – anybody at all – to speak English! Assume you will have to speak Italian all the time (or French in the section through the bilingual Val d'Aosta) for everything you need, however complicated. So if you are not already fairly fluent, consider a year's evening classes or home study in your preparations – you will find yourself extremely isolated if you are unable to carry out practical transactions and converse with the many local people you will meet along the way. And make sure that, even if you don't achieve much else, you have mastered the numbers and can recognize them at speed in prices, distances, telephone numbers, and so on. (The BBC's Italian book in its 'Get by in…' series is recommended for complete beginners – see Appendix D for details.)

Decide what type of footwear you will be taking – walking shoes, lightweight boots, heavy (thick-soled) trainers, and so on – and break them in well before you go.

Pack your rucksack well ahead of your departure, leave out anything which 'might come in useful' and which you would only be using occasionally, and remember that you will have to allow space for food and water.

CHOOSING YOUR COMPANIONS

Two-legged

Unlike the busy Camino de Santiago the Via Francigena at present is not a route for people who cannot cope with extended periods of only their own company. So, unless you plan to go with someone you already know well and have walked with before, think very carefully about any companion you might consider going with, especially if you feel that you would rather go with anyone else rather than be alone. (In Italian there is an expression which alerts you to some of the possible dangers – 'Meglio soli che male accompagnati' – better alone than in unsuitable company.)

Some issues are obvious – does the other person walk at the same speed as you, for example, or do the same sort of daily distances? Others, however, are less so. Consider, for example:

- do you prefer to walk non-stop until you reach your daily destination, or take rests and sit down to admire the view?
- do you get up at the crack of dawn and start immediately or find it difficult to get going in the morning?
- do you want to stay in hotels or in pilgrim refuges, parish accommodation, youth hostels or other economical accommodation?

- do you enjoy eating out in restaurants or doing your own cooking where possible?
- do you/your companion speak fluent Italian while the other one is monolingual English?
- does one of you chatter non-stop all day long while the other prefers to walk mainly in silence?
- do you both – something that is often overlooked until it is too late – both have the same level of funds available?

If walking speed, rhythm and rests are the only problem, these can often be resolved by walking separately during the day and meeting up in the evening (with plenty to talk about). Other differences are more difficult to resolve, but all these issues can make or mar a pilgrim journey in the constant company of another person. It

Pilgrim refuge next to the Chiesa di Santa Margherita, Sivizzano (Section 2)

Piazzetta Castello, San Miniato Alto (Section 4)

will help, though, if you discuss these issues in advance.

Four-legged

Do not be tempted to take your dog with you.

- You will meet local dogs along the way who are on their own territory and do not take kindly to strange ones.
- You may have problems finding accommodation.
- You may have transport problems returning home.
- Most dogs, although used to going out all day long, are not accustomed to continuous long-distance walking and may experience problems with their feet.

PLANNING YOUR PILGRIMAGE

The Great St Bernard Pass to Rome can be walked comfortably in five to six weeks by anyone who is fairly fit, and this includes plenty of time to visit places of interest along the way.

However, be generous with your timings when planning your itinerary, especially if you are not an experienced walker. Start with fairly short stages, if accommodation allows, and always stop before you are tired. You can increase the distances as you get fitter and into the swing of things. In addition, allow plenty of time and flexibility for unforeseen circumstances (pleasant or otherwise).

It is advisable to include short days and rest days in your schedule – where and how many is up to you. On a short walking day you can arrive at your destination during the late morning, ideally, and have the remainder of the day completely free. However, because of the lack of accommodation in some stretches, it may be difficult to include such short days in your programme, so you will probably need to take a whole day off if you want to have a rest.

If you are extremely tired, or having trouble with your feet, a complete day off works wonders (particularly in a small place with no sights to be visited), and is well worth the disruption to your schedule that it might initially seem to entail. If you are walking all the way to Rome in one go consider taking days off at least in Aosta, Lucca and Siena as you make your way, slowly but surely, towards the Eternal City.

A CHALLENGING PILGRIM ROUTE

Comparing the Camino de Santiago and a Cammino per Roma

As many, although by no means all, of those who decide to walk the Via Francigena today have already made the pilgrimage to Santiago de Compostela, usually along the route from the Pyrenees known as the Camino Francés, what follows is intended to alert them to some of the many differences between the two routes. As a consequence, this section highlights some of the possible difficulties involved in undertaking a Cammino per Roma, but is certainly not intended to discourage prospective pilgrims.

In the 'old days' (before the early 1990s) pilgrims needed to be physically fit to walk the Camino Francés and capable of covering 35–40km a day, if necessary, carrying all their supplies with them. They would have to sleep on the floor in uncomfortable places, often without a shower, in the sparse infrastructure of available refugios (unless, of course, they stayed in a hotel), then get up again the following morning to start all over again. Nowadays things have changed, and pilgrims need walk only 10km (or even less) each day and find accommodation (often inexpensive) and there are services/facilities at very frequent intervals along the way.

On the Via Francigena, pilgrims will need to be fit before they start. Although the Pô valley is flat, the preceding Val d'Aosta is full of ups and downs, the Passo della Cisa rises to 1041m above sea level, and Tuscany is distinctly hilly. The distance between places to sleep is greater in Italy, especially for those on a tight budget; while the Camino Francés has dedicated pilgrim refuges at frequent intervals along the route, a similar network in Italy is at an earlier stage of development.

Siena, general view (Section 4)

On the Camino Francés pilgrims can turn up at a refuge (usually open and waiting for you) and frequently find another English-speaking pilgrim to 'show you the ropes', even if the person in charge of the establishment speaks only Spanish. You will also frequently find plenty of other English-speaking pilgrims to talk to. On the Via Francigena, on the other hand, pilgrims need a reasonable level of Italian to cope with the mechanics of finding accommodation, especially since this involves telephoning ahead.

However, in contrast to the Camino Francés, where pilgrims are now so commonplace as to no longer attract the attention of local people, on the Via Francigena you do meet people who are curious to know where you are going, what you are doing (and often why), and who like to chat

to you. If your linguistic skills are up to it, this can be a very enjoyable and enriching part of your experience, although it also brings with it a sense of being an 'ambassador', paving the way for the pilgrims who follow, and the responsibility that goes with it. So unless you stay exclusively in the kind of up-market establishments where you can book up everything in advance on the internet you will need enough Italian to do more than 'get by' ordering food and drink – the parish accommodation, for example, needs prior (and tactful) telephone contact.

You are unlikely to meet many other pilgrims going to Rome on the Via Francigena at present, although things are improving year by year, so there is not yet much of the 'fraternity of the road' that exists along the Camino Francés, where you get to know people as you go along. So you need to be very self-reliant if you decide to walk to Rome. The hardest part of the whole enterprise is not, however, the actual walking, but the mental effort needed to find somewhere to sleep, night after night after night, especially if you are doing the journey on a tight budget, unlike on the Camino Francés with its well-known and easily located network of dedicated pilgrim refuges. It can often be difficult to remember that you are a pilgrim, too, on the Via Francigena at present, even in Italy, and not just a walker, as not only are you on your own much or all of the way, but even if you go to church and/or stay in religious houses from time to time there are no dedicated pilgrim masses, other services or pilgrim discussion groups as there are now, increasingly, on the Camino Francés.

Hotel/pension-type accommodation in Italy is more expensive than Spain, and pilgrims rarely find the bar-restaurants with rooms that are often encountered along the route in Spain. There is also no equivalent of the very good-value all-inclusive Spanish *menú del día* (three courses with wine) in Italy, and few places at present where you can do your own cooking – although this is improving.

There is a very great deal more road walking on the Via Francigena than there is now on the Camino Francés where, for the benefit of both pilgrims and other road-users, much of the Spanish Camino has

been re-routed onto newly cleared old tracks and paths. It is therefore, at present at least, more difficult to 'switch off' as you walk along the Via Francigena, although the route is now, in the main, well waymarked,

One other way in which the two pilgrimage routes differ, and already mentioned above, is the relative paucity, on the road to Rome, of anything comparable to the very extensive Jacobean iconography to be found on the Camino Francés. In Italy you will find numerous depictions of the patron saint of pilgrims, San Rocco (statues, friezes, paintings and so on), and many small churches and chapels dedicated to him, but fewer references to Saint Peter.

So why, the reader might well be wondering, and given all these difficulties, would anyone actually want to walk to Rome?

There are all sorts of reasons, of course, ranging from the sheer physical challenge of such a lengthy undertaking, through cultural/historic considerations to spiritual aspects in the widest sense. There is also the build-up of inner strength that takes place as one day unfolds before the next – seeing new places, meeting new faces, the simplicity of life on a camino pared down to its bare essentials, solitude – and each or a combination of them will be personal to each pilgrim, just as they combine to resemble the reasons that led him/her to walk the Camino Francés.

EQUIPMENT

What to take

- **Passport**
- **EHIC** (European Health Insurance Card) Make sure it is up-to-date
- **Rucksack** At least 50 litre capacity if carrying a sleeping bag
- **Footwear** Both to walk in and a spare pair of lightweight trainers/sandals. (*Tip for cold weather* – wear sock-liners or trainer socks inside your main pair of socks to keep your feet warm, but without the added bulk of two sets of cuffs round your ankles.)
- **Waterproofs** Even in summer it may rain and a poncho (a cape with a hood and space inside for a rucksack) is far more useful (and far less hot) than a cagoule
- **Pullover or fleece jacket** Parts of the route are high up and it can get cold at night, even in summer
- **Scarf and gloves** According to season
- **Sun hat** Ideally with wide brim
- **Sunglasses** You will be walking south/southeast most of the time, with the sun in your face all day
- **Sleeping bag** Essential if you are camping or staying in parish-type accommodation
- **Thin pillowcase** Useful in parish-type accommodation (or tent) to hold clothes when pillows are not provided
- **Towel** Essential if you are camping or staying in youth hostels or parish-type accommodation
- **Ear plugs** Essential if sleeping in dormitory/communal accommodation
- **First aid kit** (including a needle for draining blisters). The type of elastoplast sold by the metre is more useful than individual dressings. Scissors. High-factor sunscreen if you burn easily. Crêpe bandage.
- **Torch**
- **Large water bottle** At least 2 litre capacity for July and August
- **Stick** Useful for fending off/frightening dogs, testing boggy terrain, and propelling you along more quickly in hilly places
- **Guidebook**
- **Maps**
- **Compass**
- **Small dictionary/phrase book** Unless your Italian is very good
- **Mug, spoon, plate and knife**

If you have to have a hot drink in the morning a **Camping Gaz-type stove** is a great advantage, even though it will add extra weight to your luggage. Alternatively, if you just want to heat water for a drink, an electric plunger/mini-boiler type of heater (with continental adaptor) is useful.

In general, travel as light as you can, not just for the weight but because of the hills and, according to the season, the heat.

What not to take

- Anything 'that might just come in useful'
- Too many spare changes of clothing
- Reading matter unassociated with the pilgrimage
- Shampoo/toiletries in large or glass bottles

GETTING THERE AND BACK

Great St Bernard Pass Buses from both Martigny (train from Geneva airport) and Aosta (June to September only)

Aosta By train to Turin and then to Milan via Chivasso. Budget airlines from several UK airports have flights to Milan-Bergamo. By Pullman (long-distance coach) to Milan. The Paris–Milan

Eurolines coach service runs four times a week and stops in Aosta.

Vercelli By train to Milan or Turin; TGV (Paris-Milan) stops in Vercelli

Lucca Short train ride from Pisa (budget flights from several UK airports)

Siena Train to Rome (change in Chiusi-Chanciano). Pullman from Rome (direct).

Rome By TGV to Paris. Eurolines coach Paris/London. Budget flights from Rome (Ciampino) to several UK airports; other airlines fly from Roma Fiumincino.

ACCOMMODATION

There are different types of accommodation along the route, including campsites, youth hostels (*ostelli*,

Ostello Via Francigena at Cassio (Section 2)

whether they are part of the Italian youth hostel association – AIG – or independently run) and hotels/ *alberghii*, although there are few of these in the one- or two-star categories. (If you have already walked or cycled one of the Caminos de Santiago do not confuse the Italian word *albergo* – another term for 'hotel' in Italy – with the Spanish word *albergue* (hostel); 'hostel' is *ostello* in Italian.) Also look out for the term *foresteria*, which refers to either the guest quarters in a convent, school or monastery or to youth-hostel type accommodation (a *forestiero* is a stranger or foreigner in Italian). Note that many of these smaller establishments – in common with bars and restaurants – are regularly closed on one fixed day a week (indicated in the text where known – 'X Mon', for example, means that it is closed on Mondays). A number are also *chiuso per ferie* (closed for holidays) in July and August.

There are also an increasing number of *affittacamere* (rooms for rent) in towns, often with use of the kitchen (ask about the availability of these in tourist offices), as well as B&Bs in country areas in particular. (Note that an *agriturismo* is not a B&B, although it may sometimes offer this as well, but is primarily an establishment for the bulk sale of local products – wine and olive oil, for example – to the general public directly from the producer.) There is also some accommodation available in religious houses.

Each year an increasing number of parishes offer basic accommodation (sleeping bag required) for one night only in church halls, parish rooms and so on for pilgrims with a *credenziale* (pilgrim passport); some of these have a fixed charge while others operate on a donation basis (you should always offer to leave a donation – or put one in the box if they refuse). Remember that other pilgrims will be coming after you, and although you will not be required to attend services you may feel it is courteous to do so. You should phone ahead if possible to make sure somebody is there when you arrive; and try not to arrive too early or too late (by 7pm, for example). The existence of these parish-type facilities is indicated in the text as 'OP' (*ostello pellegrino*).

It is essential to phone ahead for all types of accommodation, apart from campsites, and a reasonable level of spoken Italian is therefore necessary. This includes the OP facilities as, unlike on the Camino de Santiago, where the refugios are open and waiting for pilgrims, on the Via Francigena the people who own or run this type of accommodation have other jobs, are not on the premises all the time, and do not see pilgrims every day. It is usually enough to book one or two days ahead, and in this way you are not tied down to too rigid a timetable, leaving no flexibility for unforeseen circumstances.

The Italian Confraternità di San Jacopo runs three pilgrim refuges on the Via Francigena, in Radicofani, in Abbadia Isola and in Rome itself.

Prices have not been indicated for each individual accommodation entry in the guide, but in general, in 2012, hotels in Italy cost between 50€ and 70€ for a double room (without breakfast). B&B is slightly less expensive, while prices in youth hostels vary (15€–20€) according to whether you are in a dormitory or a single or double room.

PLANNING THE DAY

In Italy there are many places well worth visiting along the route of artistic, architectural, cultural or religious interest, and they are open at convenient times for the walker – usually 10am–12pm and 4 or 5pm–7pm.

In July and August in particular it can be extremely hot in Italy during the day, with temperatures well up into the 90s (F) or high 30s (C). The best way to avoid walking in the heat is to get up before it is light and set out, if you can, at daybreak. When walking in hot weather it is important to avoid becoming dehydrated by drinking plenty of water before you feel thirsty, as once you realise you feel thirsty it is too late to do anything about it, even if you have supplies with you (top up your water bottle whenever you can). If you can drink at least half a litre of water as soon as you get up in the morning (as well as any tea/coffee available) you will find the hot weather affects you much less.

Tip A large quantity of very cold *acqua gassata/frizzante* (sparkling mineral water) is probably the best way to quench your thirst in hot weather. It can be bought very cheaply in supermarkets, but it will not be cold. However, bars sell not only the small (50cl) bottles, which will be on display, but also large 1.5 litre bottles, which are kept in the fridge under the counter. So ask if you don't see what you want.

It is a good idea, in large towns and other places of any size, to go for

Countryside before Torrenieri (Section 5)

a walk in the evening and check your onward route, so as not to waste time or get lost the following morning. And it is always useful to read through the following day's walk the night before!

OTHER PRACTICAL INFORMATION

Road numbering SS (*strada statale*) followed by a number (such as 'SS2') refers to the number of a main road. SR and SP respectively refer to *strada regionale* and *strada provinciale*, roads maintained by, respectively, the regione and the provincia.

Italian roads are not only numbered but also have marker posts every kilometre (such as 'SS2 KM89'). Each kilometre is also subdivided into 100m sections, each with its own marker post. So if a post has on it 'KM89/iii', it is 300m before or after the KM89 post (depending on your direction of travel). The numbers on the posts are referred to in the route instructions in this guide. They are also often seen in addresses – of a hotel or restaurant, for example, located on a main road between two towns or villages.

Road walking Except for places such as bends, where it is obviously dangerous to do so, walk on the left-hand side of the road, facing any oncoming traffic.

Street names There are a lot of inconsistencies in the names of places on road signs in Italy, so a street name, for example, may appear in one form at the start of the street and in another at the end. This guidebook follows the spelling as it appears on the signs.

Railways Trenitalia is the name of the Italian state railway system. Be warned that there are often lightning strikes (*sciopero*) on the railways, especially at peak times and around public holidays.

Public holidays There are public holidays (*giorni festive/feste nazionale*) in Italy on: 1 Jan, 6 Jan, Good Friday, Easter Sunday and Monday, 25 April, 1 May, 2 June, 15 Aug, 1 November, 8 December, 25 and 26 December. Shops, including those for food (but not bars, restaurants or bakeries), banks and offices are closed on these occasions.

Changing money There are cashpoints (*bancomat*) in all reasonable sized places in Italy, including fairly small towns, and these accept Visa, cash cards bearing the Cirrus/Maestro logo, and so on. Bank opening hours are normally from 8.30am until about 3–4pm, sometimes with a break for lunch, Monday to Friday only, and it is often possible to change money in post offices and large railway stations.

Shops Pilgrims who have already walked all the way from Canterbury will find life much easier in Italy as regards shops and cafés. A *supermercato* is normally a fairly large concern, often open all day long, with a wide variety of goods for sale and considerably cheaper than an *alimentari*. The latter is a grocer's shop, more like a delicatessen, and as they often stock only top-of-the-range products they are frequently an expensive option. Large supermarkets in shopping centres are usually open all day long (and often on Sunday mornings), while the alimentari closes for lunch. Bakeries (*panettaria*) open early in the day and many sell hot drinks, especially in small places.

Meals In Italy meals are available in restaurants between 12–2pm and 7–9pm (although if you are a vegetarian you will probably find life difficult if you want to eat out, except in pizzerias). Many places provide a *menu fisso* (fixed-price meal) or a *pranzo di lavoro* (worker's lunch) at lunchtime, while in busy areas many bars now offer their customers one hot dish (changed daily) – a *primo piatto* – at midday.

Cafés and bars These usually open as early as 6am, particularly in towns and if they are run by bakeries, but note that you have to pay for your drink before you are served, often at a separate till, and will always be given a receipt. Remember, too, that many establishments, including restaurants and small hotels, are often closed on a particular day of the week (these are indicated in the text where known.)

50

Post offices These (*Posta*) are open from 8am in large places, 9am in small, until as late as 7pm (12.30 or 1pm on Saturdays), and many of them have cash dispensers.

Telephones Phone boxes (*cabina telefonica*) are found in many public places, although many of them are out of order and many do not accept coins (even though phone cards are no longer available in Italy, many public telephones accept nothing else!). The international dialling code for Italy is +39, and phone numbers (landlines) consist of a four-digit area code plus either five (the older numbers) or six digits for the subscriber. Mobile phone numbers all begin with the figure '3' and consist of a three-digit prefix (the provider) plus a seven-digit customer number.

The **emergency numbers** in Italy are 112 for the Carabinieri (who have both civil and military powers), 113 for the police (for criminal matters), 115 for the fire brigade (*vigili del fuoco*) and 118 for an ambulance.

Mobile phones While mobile phones (*cellulare*) are useful for emergencies and phoning ahead for accommodation (although they frequently do not work in rural areas, where there is no coverage), you will probably find it better to leave it switched off except for a very limited time each day. You will find it a much more 'pilgrim' journey if your friends and relations back home cannot contact you at all hours.

Internet/Cybercafés These are not always easy to find, and as their availability changes frequently they have not been systematically listed in this guide. (Tourist offices should be able to tell you where to find one locally.) Note that before using them you almost always have to show your passport as proof of identity.

Drinking water/fountains When these are running continuously, or when you see local people using them, they are generally safe to drink from.

Stamps for pilgrim passports Modern pilgrims who want proof of their pilgrimage carry pilgrim 'passports' or 'credentials' (*credenziale* in Italian), which they have stamped (with a *timbro*) at regular intervals along the way (in churches, tourist offices, town halls, post offices and so on), and which they then present to the authorities in the Vatican when they arrive in Rome to help them obtain their Testimonium (certificate of completion of pilgrimage) – see Appendix G. More information about pilgrim 'passports' is available (to its members) from the Confraternity of Pilgrims to Rome (see Appendix F).

Churches Many churches in Italy are open all day in large towns, particularly 'touristy' towns with important cathedrals and artistically significant churches, but in smaller places they are usually firmly shut except at service times. (Note that you should be

suitably dressed to visit churches – no short shorts, for example.) Masses are often held at about 6pm during the week, with several on Sundays and holidays.

There are far too many churches along the way to describe them all in detail, so only the main ones are mentioned in the route description. However, nearly all the historic and other noteworthy churches in Italy have information boards outside, frequently in three or four languages.

For pilgrims who attend mass and who would like to be able to join in at least once during the service, the Lord's Prayer is given below in Italian:

Padre nostro, che sei nei cieli,
sia santificato il tuo nome,
venga il tuo regno,
sia fatta la tua volontà,
como in cielo così in terra.
Dacci oggi il nostro pane quotidiano,
e rimetti a noi I nostro debiti
come noi li rimettiamo ai nostri
debitori,
e non ci indurre in tentazione,
ma liberaci dal male.

Medical assistance Make sure that you obtain an EHIC (European Health Insurance Card) before leaving home. This is a Europe-wide document entitling you to free or reduced medical (but not dental) treatment. In Britain the card can be obtained free of charge from the NHS website (www.nhs.uk). (If you already have one, check its expiry date before departure.) Note, however, that the EHIC does not cover transport home, for which you will need separate insurance. Pilgrims from countries outside Europe will need to organise their own health and/or travel insurance.

If you wear glasses, take either a spare pair or the prescription with you.

Beware of the dog

Dogs Italian dogs are usually (although not always) tied up, hear you ages before you have any idea of where they are, and are often enormous (although the small ones are, in fact, a greater nuisance, as they have a nasty habit of letting you pass by and then attacking from behind, nipping you in the back of your ankles). A stick is very useful – not to hit them with, but to threaten. Be warned!

Italian abbreviations In Italian the middle of a word is abbreviated, so 'Cascina', for example, becomes 'C.na', 'Corso' becomes 'C.so', 'Fratello/Fratelli' becomes 'F.llo/F.lli'. You will often see these on street names and in the names of shops and businesses.

Striking clocks Clocks on churches and public buildings strike the relevant hour (for example, ten times for 10 o'clock) twice on the hour (the first set serves as a warning that the second will follow shortly). If the clock in question also strikes the half-hours, then at that point it strikes the relevant hour followed by a 'ping' (on a completely different note), which indicates that it is now, for example, half past 10. The whole sequence is then repeated a second time a minute or two later. (So if, at 12 o'clock, you happen to find yourself in a place with several such clocks in close proximity, but not all synchronised, the different strikes may continue for nearly ten minutes!)

Sign outside the Chiesa di Santa Maria Maddelena in Torrenieri (Section 5)

Selection of Via Francigena waymarking, old and new

USING THIS GUIDE

Waymarking

In general the Via Francigena is well and clearly waymarked in Italy, although the style, design and colour of the signs varies quite a lot. Along much of the way is seen the red and white adhesive tape of the 'official' route, marked with a black pilgrim silhouette to distinguish it from other long-distance footpaths (which are also marked in red and white). In other places are seen the older markers with either a yellow or a brown and yellow pilgrim carrying a bundle on his back, as well as the yellow and white stickers (also depicting a pilgrim), the brown 'Via Francigena' signposts (although many of these are not for walkers but people touring the area by car), the newer waymarks bolted to posts, and yellow arrows like those found on the Camino in Spain (although some of these are also white). The historic routes waymarked

53

by the AIVF have their own blue and white signage.

The waymarking may often be in both directions, as much of the Via Francigena through Italy is also used – in reverse – by Italian and other pilgrims bound for Santiago. There is thus quite a variety of styles of waymarking in evidence, as the photos here show, but this is not as confusing as it might seem, and you should have no trouble finding their way.

Maps

Except for a few mountainous areas (that surrounding Mont Blanc, for instance) there are no maps of Italy available to the general public (only the army) covering the whole country at a scale of 1:25,000, 1:50,000 or 1:100,000 – in other words, at a scale you can walk from. This means it is not possible, as you can in Britain, for example, or France, with its excellent IGN maps, to go into a general bookshop and purchase a map of the areas through which the route passes at any of these scales. There is therefore no uniform mapping to work from, so sketch maps of the route at a consistent scale (1:200,000; 1cm = 2km) are included in this guide and route-finding information is therefore extremely detailed, with turn-by-turn directions.

There is, however, from Vercelli (at the start of Section 2) onwards, a set of specially prepared maps for the Via Francigena by Monica D'Atti and Franco Cinti; designed to accompany their guidebook, the maps are also sold separately (see Appendix D for details). These, at the somewhat unusual scale of 1:30,000, include heights, distances and GPS coordinates, and are in the form of three very large sheets designed to be separated into long perforated strips. Each strip depicts one daily stage (with the next one on the reverse), and they are very easy to walk from. They have been updated since they were first produced in 2007, and the third edition was published in November 2012. It is highly recommended that you buy them (they are available from general bookshops in Italy, from www.amazon.it, from Stanfords in London and The Map Shop in Upton-on-Severn – see addresses in Appendix F), as even if they vary slightly from the current waymarking you will always know where you are. Make sure, however, that you get the latest edition.

Route description

The text is divided up into five main sections, which start at the Great St Bernard Pass, Vercelli, the Passo della Cisa, Lucca and Siena. With the exception of the Cisa Pass these are all places where walking pilgrims can reach or leave the route easily by public transport, if they need to complete the journey in shorter stages.

Each of the main places along the route appears in a box, with its name in bold, preceded by the distance walked from the previous place. The box also contains a description of the facilities available there, a brief

Romanesque bridge, Echallod (Section 1)

history, where applicable, and an indication of the places of interest to visit. (Pilgrims wishing to spend time in any of the larger towns should obtain information brochures and a street plan from the tourist office, which frequently has leaflets for self-guided walking tours as well.)

The figures in parentheses after each box heading indicate both the distance in kilometres from the Great St Bernard Pass and the distance remaining to Rome. In the case of large towns such as Vercelli the distances are to/from their centres, normally at either the cathedral or the town hall (*municipio*). Note that because the alternative routes described in this guide are rarely the same length as the 'main' route, the boxes for places along the alternative routes do not give the distance from the Swiss border or to Rome.

In addition the boxes give, where known, the population and the altitude in metres above sea level. 'All facilities' indicates that there is a full range of shops, banks, restaurants, hotels, medical centre, public transport and so on in the place concerned, while 'shops etc' indicates that normally there are one or two bars, a food shop, pharmacy, restaurant and, usually, a bank machine.

The text in the guide is deliberately not divided up into daily stages, so that you can decide the distances you would like to cover each day. (You could go through the text in advance and highlight possible overnight stops.) Key place names appear in the text in **bold type**, as do other names that help in wayfinding, such as street names, the names of prominent buildings, rivers and so on. Note that in many parts of the route it is

55

B&B sign, Bolsena (Section 5)

often difficult to find somewhere to sit down for a short rest, so 'seat' is often mentioned in the text, in italics, as are other brief notes and indications of facilities as you pass them.

In the route description the symbol ▼ points to a blue paragraph in smaller type (below) with information about a short alternative to the main route. The symbol ❯ indicates that the route description for a particular route option stops at this point and is picked up again further on, at the point shown by ❮. The symbols ❯❯ and ❮❮ are used as a pair in the same way, to differentiate between overlapping options.

Unlike pilgrimages to Lourdes, Fatima or other locations where miracles are sought and help for specific problems requested, and where being in the pilgrim destination itself is the most important factor, on the Via Francigena, like the Camino de Santiago, it is the journey itself that is the pilgrim's principal concern, the arrival in Rome being only a conclusion to the rest of the undertaking. It is not a 'map and compass route', either, although the walking is sometimes strenuous. Timings have not

56

been given from place to place, but 4km per hour, exclusive of stops and except in very hilly places, is often considered average, especially when carrying a heavy rucksack. However, a comfortable pace may often be more than this – a fit walker may well be able to maintain a speed of 5–6km or 3½ miles per hour.

The route through Italy is practicable for most of the year, although not necessarily recommended. However, if you are walking all the way from Canterbury to Rome in one go or are starting from the Great St Bernard Pass you will need to plan your journey to take into account the altitude and weather conditions at 2473m (8114ft) above sea level. Under no circumstances should you consider crossing the Great St Bernard Pass in winter, when it is accessible only on skis or snow shoes (or by helicopter). The pass is normally free from snow from late May to late September, although snowfalls can occur at night even during July and August (and snow remains during the day). If you are starting in Aosta, or further on, in the winter, early spring or autumn, you may be able to avoid the heat in Italy for a substantial part of your journey, although the advantages of cooler weather will be offset by shorter hours of daylight.

But now, all your preparations made, it is time to set off on your journey…

Buon cammino!
Tanti auguri!

GREAT ST BERNARD PASS TO VERCELLI

Terraced vineyards near Pont Saint-Martin

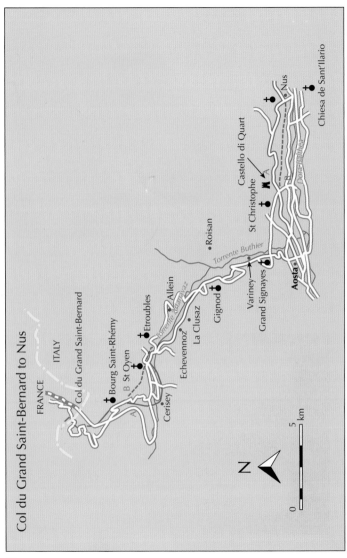

Col du Grand Saint-Bernard to Nus

FRANCE
ITALY
Col du Grand Saint-Bernard
Bourg Saint-Rhémy
B St Oyen
Etroubles
Cerisey
Echevennoz
La Clusaz
Allein
Gignod
Roisan
Torrente Buthier
Variney
Grand Signayes
Aosta
St Christophe
Castello di Quart
Nus
Chiesa de Sant'Ilario
Dora Baltea

N

0   5   km

Col du Grand Saint-Bernard (0/956) 2473m

The col is slightly more than the halfway point on the journey from Canterbury to Rome. It is likely to be very cold here at night, even in mid-summer, when you can also expect snow. The road route up to the pass is open only between late May/early June and mid-October. From June to the end of September there is a bus service three times a day from Martigny up to the col and down to Aosta on the other side and back, but at other times the only way to get up (or down) from here (to either Bourg Saint-Pierre on the Swiss side or Saint-Rhémy-en-Bosses in Italy, after which you can take the bus through the tunnel under the col) is on skis or with snowshoes. There are also a lot of avalanches in this area, so if you do encounter snow, fog or mist at any time of the year you should stick to the road, even though it is considerably longer than the path route which shortcuts the road's many loops and long hairpin bends.

The Roman road up to the Mont Joux pass was built in 12BC, under Emperor Augustus, but there had been a track up and over the col since pre-historic times, and it was used first by the Celts and then by the Romans as a

Hospice, Great St Bernard Pass

rapid passage between northern Italy and their provinces in Gaul and along the Rhine. The Romans built a temple to their god Jupiter (Jove) in AD50, along with two other buildings (*mansios*) that served (like inns) to accommodate travellers passing by. The Swiss section of the current road was first opened in 1892, and the Italian part in 1905.

The Hospice du Grand Saint-Bernard was founded about 1050AD by Saint-Bernard d'Aoste (Saint Bernard de Menton) to accommodate pilgrims and other travellers and has been in continuous use for nearly 1000 years. It has never closed in all that time, unlike most other hospices which, although they still exist, have had interruptions in their activity. Today it is run by the *chanoines reguliers* (not monks, but priests active in the surrounding community) who follow the rule of Saint Augustine, plus a relay of lay volunteer help in the summer months, and has dormitory-style accommodation plus some single and double rooms for walkers and others who want to spend a few quiet days there. Mass Sat 8.30pm, Sun 10.30am. Monastic offices daily (held in crypt chapel) – *liturgie* and *lecture*, *laudes*, *prière du midi*, *vêpres*, *complies*. The hospice also has a small treasury and offers video presentations (in French, German, Italian and English) about its history and work. It is recommended that you phone in advance if you want to stay there (027.7871236).

The Hôtel de l'Hospice across the road is owned by the hospice, which opened it in the early 20th century an as overflow facility to deal with the increasing number of travellers that they were unable to accommodate in their main building. It is closed in the winter months, but when the hotel is open the hospice provides accommodation only for those who arrive there under their own steam (on foot, by bicycle, horse riders, people on skis). Any other visitors (as well as walkers, cyclists and so on who prefer hotel-type accommodation and meals) who wish to spend the night on the Swiss side of the col will therefore need to stay either in this hotel (cheaper rates during the week than at weekends, 027.7871153) or in the Hotel Italia on the Italian side of the lake (see below). However, apart from the Café/Resto Montjoux, a tourist office (summer only) and souvenir shops there are no other facilities at the col and no cash machine. Look out for ibex and marmots sunning themselves on the hillsides to either side of the road.

The Musée/Chenil de l'Hospice gives the history of the Saint Bernard dogs, but these are no longer used for rescue purposes. Despite being very strong, they are both extremely heavy – to transport in a helicopter, for example – and difficult to train, so today German Shepherds are used instead.

These are much lighter, so that two can be taken (in a helicopter) at a time if needed, and are easily trained. The Saint Bernard dogs are still bred, though; they live in the *chenil* (kennel) at the col in the summer (in the winter they are taken down to Martigny), where you can see them either resting in their very large cages or being taken for long walks each day in the surrounding area. However, one or two are still trained and used for avalanche rescue, as they have an extremely acute sense of smell. Visitors can also accompany them on their daily walks (two levels – both 'sportif' and shorter/slower – ask in the tourist office if you are interested).

Whether you have already walked from Canterbury or somewhere else along the route through France or Switzerland, or are starting your pilgrimage here, consider staying for two nights either here or in Aosta to rest up before continuing and/or to collect your thoughts a little before setting off down through Italy.

To leave the hospice and set off for the Italian border go under the bridge linking the hospice to the hotel, and 100m later, halfway along the lakeside, cross the border into **ITALY.** At the other end of the lake reach ***Hotel Italia** and bar, 1/6–25/9 (0165.780908, closed in winter), and another bar/restaurant.

From here to Aosta there is a descent of 1890m (6201ft), from 2473m (8114ft) at the Great St Bernard Pass to only 583m (1913ft), and as the route goes down the temperature rises correspondingly.

You are now in the Valle d'Aosta, a bilingual province, so all signs and notices are both French and Italian. People working in shops, offices and hotels speak both languages, although you will mainly hear Italian spoken. So if you have already walked all the way through France and Switzerland, it will give you time to get used to the names of public buildings, directional signs and so on in Italian before you move into the next area, Piemonte, from which point everything is in Italian only.

Continue on road, veering L past the Hotel Italia, and then, just before the road enters a *galleria* (covered section), fork L down a paved slope leading to a wide FP (103), *marked in black and yellow 'lozenges' – you will follow this long-distance walking route all the way down to Aosta. When the route is marked with signposts as well, these bear the Via Francigena (VF) logo with the figure of a small pilgrim.*

Continue on a grassy track, then 200m later, before a small stone house, turn L downhill. KSO, KSO(L), continue downhill, cross a wooden FB and reach the road again. Cross over, continue on the other side and reach the road again at

2.5km Fonteinte (2.5/953.5) 2200m

The Cantine d'Aosta is a building of Roman origin and was formerly a small hospice for pilgrims and other travellers, dependent on the one at the Great St Bernard Pass. It was founded in 1258 and in use until 1791. After that it became a customs post, due to its commanding view of the area, and was manned by border guards. It is now a B&B with a café (335.5810075).

The small chapel belonging to the hospice, Notre-Dame des Neiges (Our Lady of the Snows), on the left, next to the dark red casa cantoniera (former road-builders' accommodation), fell into disrepair and by the beginning of the 19th century it was used to house animals. It has now been restored, is used for worship once again, and is normally open.

Cross over and continue ahead on well-waymarked track then, when path divides, take the RH (lower) option, which becomes a narrower path. *The exit from the road tunnel is visible below, with several kilometres of gallerias running along the hillside.*

KSO on path, descending all the time. Pass memorial stone to 'Gli zingari stagnini', referring to a mountain tragedy in which many gypsies died. KSO, and after 2km reach a T-junction with a bigger rough track coming from the R. Turn L along it. After crossing several concrete water channels the FP becomes a wide grassy track and leads down to the road when it comes level with a deserted farm on the hill opposite. Continue on road for 300–400m more then, 100m past a large wayside cross and a water treatment plant, both on R, turn hard R and then immediately hard L onto a FP that continues downhill below the road and to the LH side of the river. 700–800m later enter the small village of

4.5km Bourg Saint-Rhémy (7/949) 1600m

**Hotel/Resto Suisse, Via Roma 26 (0165.780906). Eglise Saint-Rhémy.
 Stage XLVIII (Sce Remei, 48) in Sigeric's itinerary.

KSO(R) ahead down pedestrianised street, passing church, to junction of FPs by bus stop, where you have a choice of routes. *The waymarked Via Francigena (Option A) goes to the RH side of the river, via Saint-Rhémy-en-Bosses and Cerisey, while the shorter route (Option B, waymarked as FP 14C and easy to follow) passes to the LH side.*

Looking down on Bourg Saint-Rhémy

OPTION A – SAINT OYEN VIA SAINT-RHÉMY-EN-BOSSES AND CERISEY

Turn R at the end of the pedestrianised street, cross a wooden vehicle bridge over the river and then turn L on the other side onto a wide track. KSO for 1.5km and reach a T-junction with a stop sign at the beginning. Turn L, reach another stop sign, cross a minor road and fork R on the other side along a narrow street. Go under the road and go down narrow cobbled street on other side to main street and church in

2km Saint-Léonard 1521m

PO, *osteria* opposite church of Saint-Léonard, B&B La Vieille Cloche (0165.780927) and La Thuillettaz (335.5243008). 15th-century Château des Seigneurs de Bosses, now an exhibition hall.

Cross road, pass to RH side of church, then turn L down behind it on a grassy FP downhill. KSO. Turn R alongside a fence and an irrigation channel and then L, through woods, with a wall to LH side most of the time. FP varies in width. KSO. Cross a wooden FB, then a bigger sturdy one over the river. Turn R on other side, veering L, then R down small street to junction by road bridge in the small village of

1.5km Cerisey 1400m

Turn second L at T-junction onto bigger road, with river to R, down towards a T-junction with another road, but 50–60m before it turns L down tarmac lane to hamlet of **Barral**. Continue on path past houses and then on path through fields, with woods above you to your L and river to the R. 700m later continue on FP with wooden railings to RH side. KSO, fairly level most of the time, with irrigation channel to your LH side. Another path joins from back R, and 150m after that a path is signposted as forking R to the road below and marked 'Saint Oyen'. Do **not** take this, but continue ahead on FP 103, and 500m later reach the SS27 again at the entrance to **Saint Oyen**.

OPTION B – DIRECT TO SAINT OYEN

At the bottom of the pedestrianised street in Bourg Saint-Rhémy KSO(L) ahead here (as if you were going back uphill on the main road) then, at the first hair-pin bend, KSO ahead (there are several FP signs) on a wide gravel track, slightly uphill, along the side of the hill. 500m later fork R, downhill, on route marked '14C'. This continues as a wide gravel track to start with (*splendid views on a clear day*), gently up and down, but shortly after passing under HT cables veer L and

enter the woods where it becomes a FP. KSO on semi-shaded path, down-hill all the time, then zigzagging more steeply until you reach the road (SS27) below by a lay-by. Cross over and then turn hard L down grassy slope, hard R and then hard L again onto a grassy lane on top of an embankment. *Handy seat near start. Views over to Saint Oyen and Etroubles below.* Continue ahead, and 700–800m later rejoin houses at start of village. 100m before you reach the road the path waymarked as the Via Francigena joins you from back R to become the **Chemin de la Vieille Montée**.

Stained-glass window of Saint Oyen

Both routes

Turn R onto the SS27 (pavement) and continue to the church and the centre of

5km Saint Oyen (12/944) Pop. 190, 1373m

Ospizio Château Verdun, Rue de Flassin 3 (0165.78247), has accommodation, **Hotel Rte Mont Velan, Rue du Grand Saint-Bernard 13 (0165.78524), Campeggio Vecchio Mulino, Rue de Flassin 13 (0165.78119), Campeggio Pineta, Rue de Flassin 19 (0165.78114). Alimentari/general stores behind church, Rte Chez Felice, opposite church.

The village of Saint Oyen originates from the 11th century, when travel over the Great St Bernard Pass had begun to increase considerably, after the founding of the hospice there. The original date of the church (useful very large FP map on wall outside), dedicated to San Eugendo (ie Saint Oyen, 449–510), is not known. Château Verdun was a building given to the Canons of the Great Saint Bernard Monastery in 1137 by Amedeo III of Savoy. Halfway between the Col and Aosta, it has been attached to the hospice at the Great St Bernard Pass ever since and took the name 'hospitalis' (ie accommodation for travellers over the pass). Today Saint Oyen is also the location of a Benedictine convent, 'Regina Pacis' (a closed order).

To continue, with your back to the church turn hard R opposite it down the **Rue de Verraz**, then fork L down **Rue de Condemine** between houses. Turn L down slope along **Rue de Flassin**, passing **Château Verdun** at No 3. Continue to end of Rue de Flassin, cross main road onto the **Route pour Barasson** on other side, but then turn R immediately by wayside cross down tarmac slope and then KSO(L) ahead on clear FP with railings to RH side. This then widens out to become a grassy track. KSO.

Cross the start of the **Rue de Vachery** by a wayside shrine, pass to its RH side and continue down slope to main road at entrance to Etroubles, by a junction with a wooden statue at a hairpin bend. Continue down street ahead (**Rue Albert Deffayes**), then turn first R down **Rue du Velan** (*No 9, on RH side, was a hospice until the end of the 18th century*). Turn R at the bottom to go through a passage under the main road, and turn L on other side to cross the covered wooden footbridge over the **Torrente Artanavaz** in

2km Etroubles (14/942) Pop. 450, 1264m

Shops etc, TO Strada Nazionale G S Bernardo 24 (by petrol station, 0165.78559, etroubles@turismo.vda.it), bars, rtes. Ospitalità Religiosa Casa Alpina Sacro Cuore, Strada Nazionale G S Bernardo 34 (on main road at entry, 0165.262138), ***Hotel Col Serena (0165.78218), ***Hotel Beau Séjour (0165.78210), B&B La Maison d'Ulysse, Piazza E Chanoux 1 (near church; 0165.781269 (at meal times) or 328.4265035). Campeggio Tunnel, Via Chevrières 4 (0165.78292).

Polychrome terracotta relief sculpture, pharmacy building in Etroubles

Village already in existence in Roman times (Restapolis). Chiesa del Assunto (Assumption) originally dated from 12th century, but the present building is from 1814. Hospice built in village and opened on 13 Dec 1317, along with a *lazaret* (isolation hospital for people with infectious diseases, especially leprosy or the plague), which became a customs barracks later. Bell tower of church built 1480. Musée en Plein Air, open-air museum of sculptures and other art works located in different parts of the village (TO has walking tour leaflet).

On the other side of the river turn L into **Rue Saint Roch** (*seats, shade*), above and parallel to main road, passing to R of cemetery on wide gravel track, uphill at first and then down (*orange arrows in this section*). Return to road 800m later, continue on its RH side and then KSO(R) ahead, just before the stop sign, on grassy FP above it, alongside water channel, into small village/hamlet/frazione of

2.5km Echevennoz (16.5/939.5) 1233m

B&B L'Abri (0165.789646, 347.9680595), Dortoir Ostello, 11pl. in 3 rooms, cooking facilities for groups, all year (Marietty Silvana, 0165.78225). Bar/ Trattoria by road.

Chapel (*chiesetta*) del Assunto with outside murals (frescoes). The original building dated from 1440 and was on the other side of the (main) road. It was demolished in 1770 and rebuilt on its present site. Frescoes (outside) date from 1886. Inside the church is a painted and gilded wooden altar depicting the Coronation of the Virgin and Souls in Purgatory (L'Incoronazione della Vergine e le animi del Purgatorio).

Continue on road above village and above minor road below then, at a bend (*B&B L'Abri to R, 0165.789646*) continue ahead on FP by water channel, cross FB and continue ahead on LH side of channel. *(Note frescoes on outside of church, below L.)*

Join road briefly by houses in hamlet of **Chez-les-Blancs-Dessus**, 1249m, then turn R and immediately L, veering L behind long building to rejoin water-channel path again (you follow this nearly all the way to Gignod). This is shady all the time and gradually clears, gets wider and becomes a track by concrete water channel (below L, with a FP leading down to the road at **La Clusaz**, 1200m. *The building next to the road that is now an albergo (hotel) (0165.56075) was formerly a pilgrim hospital. It dates back to 1234 and is one of the oldest in the Valle d'Aosta.* KSO ahead here.

When the path splits 200m later take the lower one, steeply downhill (a FP again), then 100m later, at hairpin bend in gravel track, fork R uphill. Shortly afterwards fork L steeply downhill at junction of paths. KSO, cross sturdy FB over a stream and continue with water channel on RH side.

Path and watercourse near Chez-les-Blancs

1km later reach minor road at hairpin bend. KSO(R) ahead at first, but then fork L immediately down gravel track between the two parts of the 'hairpin'. KSO ahead along side of hill, level, with splendid views on a clear day. This is the **Ru Neuf**, a 15km path that started in Echevennoz, following the course of a 14th-century water channel.

The whole of the Aosta valley was irrigated in this way from the 14th century onwards, with a very elaborate system of rus (water channels) that took water to even the smallest of fields, while the larger canals are still in use today. You will see many of them in the section after the town of Aosta, if you take the higher-level route, and will walk alongside them for many kilometres, on the flat, once you are up there, often with splendid views.

800m later, at fork (*railings to L*) KSO(L) ahead, still on the level, shadier, with trees to L. Reach sturdy FB, turn L over it, and pass grotto 'Je te salue' with statue, holy water stoop to L and flowers planted in front. Path continues with water channel to L and trees on both sides.

500m later reach junction of other FPs by hairpin bend in minor road. Fork L downhill, steeply on green lane with wall to R and then Gignod golf course to L below.

KSO downhill, but on reaching a clearing with a large pile of rocks to R and an earth track (forking R) going steeply uphill to the road above KSO(L) ahead (*not signed at first*) to L of telegraph pole. After this the route becomes a clear lane, walled to RH side, descending all the time.

500m later, when track bends L, there is a plunging view of Gignod church and Aosta below. Reach minor road, cross over, continue steeply downhill on other side then turn hard L 100m later, downhill again. Veer R, continue on wide granite staircase and then FP to road at **Le Cau** (1045m) (*fountain to L*).

Cross over and continue ahead on other side, downhill steeply on FP that turns R by railings to RH side of houses. Continue down RH side of small field to road. Continue ahead, short-cutting two hairpin bends then, on reaching a bigger minor road, cross over and KSO down street (no name plates), fountain on R, to church (*priest's house at No 3 opposite*) in

7.5km Gignod Chef-Lieu (24/932) Pop. 1310, 936m

**Hotel Bellevue, Ressaz 3 (0165.56392). Camping Europa (0165.56444). Shop, bars, PO (with CD).

Torre di Gignod/Tour Carrée, 11th century. Chiesa parrocchiale di Sant'Ilario (who was one of the first saints to bring the gospel to Gaul); church building stood next to ruins of De Gigno's family castle in 14th–15th centuries. Parish church of Sant'Ilario built in 15th century, in place of smaller, older building. Repairs done in 1895, including rebuilding the facade, interior decoration and demolition of Rosario altar. 15th-century frescoes in R nave depicting Pietà (Deposition) scene and prophets. Rose window had 16th-century glass (representing Santa Nicola, Santa Caterina and San Ilario), but this is now in the museum. Square tower dates from 12th–13th centuries.

Turn R here, veering R downhill to main road, then KSO ahead (pavement on R). Pass campsite (L), cross road by underpass, turn R on other side then turn L down road past **municipio/Maison Comunale** on R and PO. *Torre Gignod to L of road below.*

Follow road downhill past **Hotel Bellevue** (on R). Pass entry board for **Cré Gignod** (910m), then turn hard L downhill, veering R (*you are still on FP 103*). Pass signboard for **Courtil** (Gignod, 876m). Then, by group of houses and just before roadside shrine (on L, with frescoes), after house No 61B, turn R down lane, steeply, downhill (*fountain on L*). At next group of houses (**Chez Henry**, 845m), with another fountain (*where a thoughtful person has left a glass for you to use*), KSO downhill.

Pass another fountain, after which tarmac stops and lane becomes gravel track, veering R to minor road. Turn L and then immediately R onto another minor road, past modern building on R, rising gently and veering R to meet another minor road coming from back R.

Turn L here along it, downhill, then veer L, then R 500m later to meet a bigger minor road (*seat to R*) by **Chez Roncoz**, 778m). Turn R, following road round (*bar and shop on R*). Enter Variney. KSO, passing covered seating area on L opposite school and another bar and then, by roundabout and entrance to a road tunnel, KSO(L) ahead down street, passing small church, **Chapelle de Saint Suaire** (*fountain on L*).

3.5km Variney (27.5/928.5) 785m

*Hotel Papagrand, Variney 31 (0165.56076) on main road.

KSO ahead past church then fork L shortly afterwards, gently downhill all the time and pass the entry boards to Aosta. 300m later join main road (*alimentari to L, telephone box*) in **Signayes** (733m). KSO ahead on main road (path to L of crash barrier), passing **Chiesa di San Rocco** 500m later on L.

Facade has frescoes with portrayals of Santa Caterina, Saint Bernard de Menton, Saint Grat, the Virgin Mary, Pope Innocent V and San Rocco. Here Saint Roch has two scallop shells on his short shoulder cape, two on his hat slung behind his head, halo, stick, scrip, wound on L, dog and boots (ie the 'pilgrim version' – see 'Pilgrim saints', Introduction, and Appendix C). Saint Joconde, another saint associated with pilgrimage, often accompanies him in frescoes too.

Wayside shrine with Saint Grat, near Verrès (holding the head of Saint John Baptist)

You will see many representations of Saint Grat in the Aosta valley, in paintings, frescoes, sculptures and so on. He is the patron saint of the diocese of Aosta, so his feast day, 7 September, is a public holiday in the whole region. Saint Grat (Gratus) was of Greek origin, but fled to Rome to escape the persecutions of the East and was sent as an emissary to Charlemagne. A vision experienced in the Pantheon sent him to Aosta, where he converted many pagans. He was then sent – by divine command – to the Holy Land to find the head of Saint John the Baptist, which he found concealed in Herod's palace. He smuggled it out of Jerusalem, returned with it to Rome where, so the story goes, all the church bells there pealed of their own accord in celebration of this event. Saint Grat presented the Baptist's head to the Pope, but in handing it over the jawbone is said to have remained in the saint's hand. This was seen as a sign, and he was allowed to take the relic back to Aosta with him. As a result Saint Grat is very frequently portrayed in art holding Saint John the Baptist's head in his hand.

Walk on LH side of road then, 100m later, go down slope to minor road. Return to road at 'stop' sign (cross by *lavoir* – pubic clothes-washing facility), then fork R up minor road marked 'Grand Signayes'. Pass electricity substation then continue (L) ahead between houses in **Grand Signayes**. Follow road round to R, then 500m later, just past a small chapel (on R) and when tarmac stops, fork L steeply downhill on a track with a wall to its RH side. Turn hard L at the bottom by house, veering R to continue on tarmac lane down to minor road.

Cross over, KSO downhill on other side, reach another road (*petrol station to R, bar and shop opposite*), cross over and KSO downhill again. Turn R at 'stop'

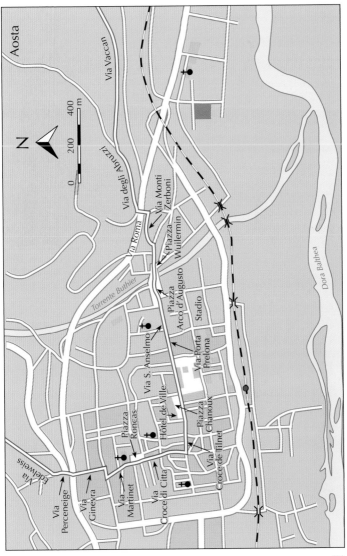

Aosta

Via Vaccan

Via degli Abruzzi

Via Roma

Via Monti Zerboni

Piazza Wuillermin

Torrente Buthier

Piazza Arco d'Augusto

Stadio

Via S. Anselmo

Via Porta Prelona

Dora Balthea

Via Edelweiss

Via Perceneige

Via Ginevra

Via Martinet

Via Croce di Città

Piazza Roncas

Hôtel de Ville

Piazza Chanoux

Via Croce de Tillnet

N

0   200   400
m

sign, then at junction with main road (**Rue des Bouleaux**, *campsite to L*) cross over and turn R behind crash barrier into **Via Eidelweiss**. KSO, downhill all the time, to a roundabout at the bottom. Cross over (**Via Parigi/Rue de Paris**) and continue ahead on **Via Ginevra**, passing hospital on R.

If you want to go to the OP accommodation offered by the Parrocchia Saint Martin de Corléans (0165.555373, 329.0845757) at the extreme west end of the town turn R at the next junction along the Via Saint Martin de Corléans, and KSO for nearly 1km. The parish house is at No 201, next to the modern church; the (smaller) old church is across the road (presently being restored).

Continue ahead along **Via Martinet** and **Via Croce di Città** then turn L into **Via Le Tiller** and reach **Piazza Chanoux** and the **municipio/Hôtel de Etats** (Hôtel de Ville) in

5.5km Aosta (33/923) Pop. 36,000, 583m

All facilities, TO Piazza Porta Praetoria (0165.236627). Hotels in all price brackets, including **La Belle Epoque, Via d'Avise 18 (0165.262276), **Excelsior, Via Chambery 206 (0165.41461), **Mignon, Viale G S Bernardo 7 (0165.40980), **Mochettaz, Corso Ivrea 107 (0165.43706), **Monte Emilius, Via G Carrel 11 (0165.230068), **Sweet Rock Café, Via O S Bernardo 18–20 (0165.553251), *Mancuso, Via Voisin 32 (0165.34526), *Al Camminetto, Via Canonica J Bréan 33 (0165.555313). OP in Parrocchia Saint Martin de Corléans (see above).

Street scene, Aosta

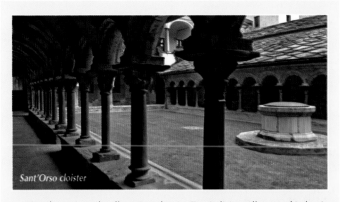

Sant'Orso cloister

Coach service ('il pullman') and train (Trenitalia) to all parts of Italy via Torino (Turin), coach to Milan, as well as a daily bus services up to the Great St Bernard Pass in summer (mid-June to mid-September only) and Martigny (via the tunnel all year, but with no stops between Saint Rhémy-en-Bosses and Bourg Saint-Pierre). A place with more sights to see than you might expect for a place of its size.

Situated at the centre of the Aosta valley the town (Augusta Praetoria) was founded by the Romans under Emperor Augusta in 25BC at the junction of the major roads leading to France and Switzerland. The Christianisation of the Valle d'Aosta dates from the fifth century AD, and Saint Anselm (1033–1109, saint and doctor of the church, born in house No 66 on the Via Sant Anselmo) was Bishop of Aosta and later Archbishop of Canterbury. This street was also the location of the Hospice de Porte Saint-Ours, founded in the 12th century, which provided shelter for pilgrims until it closed in 1782. The town's main sights are from both Roman and medieval times and include the Teatro Romano, capable of holding up to 4000 spectators, the Porta Praetoria/Porte Pretorienne, Arco d'Augusta, Roman bridge, Roman villa, the cathedral, the Early Christian basilica and church of San Lorenzo, the church of San Stefano, the old church of San Martin de Corléans and the Roman Criptoporticus, the only crypt under a town in Italy, except for Monreal in Palermo.

The collegiate church of Sant'Orso is very definitely a 'must', with its magnificent capitals in the cloister and Ottonian frescoes (AD1000), now open to the public (free of charge). Before the apse was built inside it the church was originally a single rectangular space with straight sides, so the frescoes went from floor to ceiling. One side (RH when facing apse) has apostles' subjects (such as Saint James being beheaded by somebody pulling a rope with a noose round the saint's neck!), while the LH side has other New Testament subjects.

Aosta was Stage XLVII (Agusta, 47) in Sigeric's itinerary.

The Via Francigena in Italy has been waymarked in many places by walking – not pilgrim – organizations (see 'Route design and terrain', Introduction). This means that although the higher-level walk (Option A) from Aosta to Châtillon and Saint-Vincent may be a nice route in good weather, it is longer than the original AIVF itinerary, contains a lot of tiring climbs and descents, and would be unsafe in certain weather conditions. An alternative, lower-level route (Option B) to Châtillon (and, optionally, further on to Saint-Vincent) is therefore provided as well.

To leave Aosta and continue (both routes) From **Piazza Chanoux** continue along **Via Porta Praetoria** and go under its arches. *In Roman times this was the main entrance to the city (there were three other gates), which was surrounded by walls. There were two parallel rows of arches here, 12m apart, and each gate had three arches, the two outside ones for pedestrians and the central one for carriages.* Continue along **Via Sant Anselmo**, *passing the birthplace of Saint Anselm on the RH side*, to the **Arco d'Augusto**, *erected at the time of the foundation of the town in 25*BC. Go through it, cross the bridge over the **Torrente Buthier** on FP 103 (marked with VF pilgrim sign), cross the **Piazza Vuillemin** and continue along **Via Ponte Romano** over the old Roman bridge. *This was built in the first century* BC, *originally over the Torrente Buthier before this river changed its course in the 20th century due to flooding; the bridge was 6m wide and consisted of a single arch, 17m in diameter.*

Go under small stone archway ahead (**Via Monte Zerbion**), continue ahead, veering L, turn R at main road, cross over, go up steps on other side (opposite the **Via degli Abruzzi**) and then turn R onto a minor road uphill. Continue along the **Via Scuola Militare Alpina** and then **Via Lino Vaccari**, passing below the **Ospedale Beauregard** (still on an asphalt road) and KSO (still on FP 103), ignoring turns to R and L for 2km. Enter **Chaussod**. At bend, fork L up paved slope between vines to church (*seats*) of

4.5km Saint Christophe (37.5/918.5) Pop. 3000, 645m

Eglise Saint-Christophe. Statues of saints Grat, Giacomo (James) and Rocco in the presbytery (originally from the church of La Thuile). In the 12th century there was a *maladière* (*leprosarium*) in the present built-up area of Saint Christophe.

OPTION A – HIGH-LEVEL ROUTE

(For the lower-level, bad-weather option, see below.) Much of this section is shady. It follows a local walking route, the Chemin des Vignes, and has useful information boards (in four languages) at intervals along the way, explaining aspects of the history, geography, customs, vernacular architecture and so on of the area.

Pass to LH side of church then turn L up stepped street, cross minor road and KSO ahead steeply uphill on other side on tarmac lane. KSO ahead, and 300m later join road coming from back L at entrance to **Pallein**. KSO ahead. Cross road and KSO uphill on unsurfaced road. Turn R on tarmac road and at junction (**Sorrely**, 740m) either KSO for **Quart** (750m) or turn L to continue on the variant FP 103a for the Cappella della Consola (610m; marked as 2hrs 20mins walk, but not described here). At end turn hard L then hard R in **Sorrely** (740m).

KSO through walnut groves and vines, KSO(R) at fork and road becomes unsurfaced along side of hill, level. At T-junction at end of the hamlet of **Champon** turn L up road into **Sorrely** again, then 80m later turn hard R up a minor tarmac road which then becomes unsurfaced. At a branch of FPs KSO (on FP 1), KSO, then cross bridge over stream, veering R. KSO. Track becomes FP, and KSO(L) at next fork. KSO through woods, along side of hill. KSO. Cross stream, veering R on other side and KSO (similar track joins from back L). 200m later reach tarmac road, cross over and fork R onto grassy lane.

Pass above the **Monasterio Mater Misericordiae** in **Villaire de Quart**, a modern convent run by the Carmelitane Scalze (discalced; ie barefoot Carmelite nuns). KSO, go gradually downhill, then turn L on walled lane by irrigation gate. KSO on FP alongside irrigation channel (or over it when buried), fairly level, through trees. 1km later reach tarmac road coming from back L and KSO(R) along it, downhill for 300m to entrance gates to the

3km Castello de Quart (40.5/915.5) 750m

Built in 1185, this castle is much less visited than others in the area as it was used simply as a farm for a long time and is only now being restored. Quart is so named because it was the fourth Roman mile after Aosta (and the first stage of the consular road to Gaul).

Turn L through entrance gates, follow path round to LH side of castle, veering R behind it. (Do **not** turn L on FP 1.) KSO on path through woods (*good views back to castle*) and 1km later, just after a large wooden wayside cross, reach road at bend and fork R downhill. 300m later road joins from back R. KSO along it for 50m, then fork R down slope, veering L on FP alongside water channel. 250m after that reach another minor road (crossing) and turn L by **Tour/Castello di Povis**, which looks more like a farm than a castle, passing fountain on L.

Pass between houses then fork L up grassy track uphill, leading to another road 300m later. Fork R downhill. KSO on road, ignoring a turning to L uphill. KSO for 1km then, just before entrance board for the hamlet of **Chétoz**, fork L up minor road which then becomes unsurfaced, winding its way along the hillside.

800m later fork R downhill and KSO. 800m–1km later, just before 'stop' sign, turn L onto a FP between trees. Continue on small FP alongside water channel, level, winding its way along hillside. Part-way along cross large irrigation pipe and KSO ahead. Cross very minor road and KSO on other side.

When Nus comes into view and the Chiesa di Sant'Ilario down below with its tower (*like the one at the churches in Etroubles, Gignod, Fénis and Montjovet, plus others in the area but not on the Via Francigena*) look out for RH fork leading downhill on small FP, zigzagging steeply down to road above Nus. Turn L at bottom, crossing road (not foot-) bridge over the **Torrente Saint Barthélemy** in **Faberge** (a frazione of Nus).

10km Nus (50.5/905.5) 523m

Bars, shops etc, bank in the town itself, also *Hotel Florian (X Sat) with rte, Via Risorgimento 3 (0165.767968), and **Hotel Dujaney, Via Risorgimento 104 (0165.767100), but to access them you will have to continue second R ahead past the wooden footbridge, downhill, veering L, to the Via Aosta and then retrace your steps. Trenitalia.

Nus was formerly an important staging post, with a hospice for pilgrims built here in the 13th century which continued to function until the first half of the 18th. Parish accommodation available in the Parrocchia Sant'Ilario, Via Pramotton 2 (0165.767901). Castello de Nus above on the skyline – a FP leads up there from the end of the road bridge for an optional detour (after which you will have to retrace your steps).

After crossing the road bridge over the river turn L onto the **Via des Seigneurs**. At bend by farm buildings KSO(R) ahead on small lane with wall to one side,

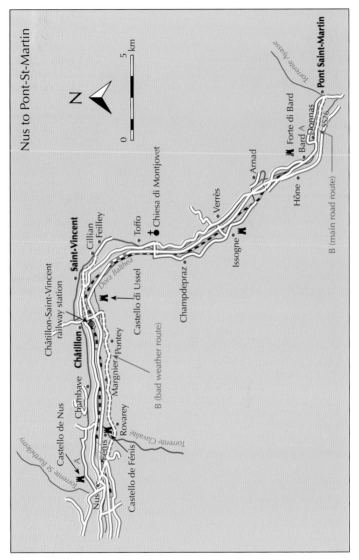

Nus to Pont-St-Martin

N

0 5 km

Castello de Nus
Torrente St Barthélemy
Castello de Fénis
Nus
Fénis
Rovarey
Torrente Clavalité
Margnier Pontey
B (bad weather route)
Chambave
Châtillon
Châtillon-Saint-Vincent railway station
Saint-Vincent
Dora Baltea
Castello di Ussel
Champdepraz
Cillian
Feilley
Toffo
Chiesa di Montjovet
Issogne
Verrès
Arnad
Hône
Forte di Bard
Bard
Donnas
Torrente Ayasse
Pont Saint-Martin
SS26
B (main road route)

Castello de Fénis

leading after 300m to the **Chiesa de Sant'Ilario** (Nus), first constructed in 1135 but completely rebuilt in 1886–7. Walk round the outside of the church (*the door opposite the river is normally open*) and reach a road coming from back R and then, 200m later, a very large sculpture with barrels, grapes, and so on at side of the road (*seat*), the **Monument au Vigneron**. Turn R here, downhill, then turn L along wide track (resembling an old railway line). Go down stepped lane and then KSO until you reach a minor road. Turn R downhill at T-junction with road coming from back R, and then turn L at 'stop' sign onto another minor road and KSO, uphill, passing wayside shrine on L. When it levels out KSO(L) on level (*Castello de Fénis visible on opposite side of the river*).

KSO, enter **Roatte** and go gradually downhill. KSO, round side of hill. KSO uphill at junction and pass church (*frescoes on front*) in **Rovary**. KSO, uphill at first, then level. Continue climbing, then watch out for RH fork downhill and track. KSO to reach the

2km Chiesa de Diémoz (52.5/903.5) 570m

The name comes from the Latin 'ad decimum' – the tenth Roman mile after Aosta. Chiesa di San Martino e Santa Lucia, 12th century, rebuilt 19th. Frescoes outside of San Martino and Saint Maurice.

If you want to break your journey (or spend the night) here you can fork R downhill (just before you reach the church) to **Champagne** *(8–10mins walk each way), on the main road (**Hotel Cristina, 0165.541237, on main road at junction), then retrace your steps the following morning.*

Continue on road past church (*a lot of the route in this section is on tarmac, but there is very little traffic*), and after a sharp bend with a wayside cross fork R up steep FP to road above, passing wayside shrine on L. *There are many such shrines along the way in the Aosta valley – edicole, orattorietti and sacelli votivi – places where pilgrims and other travellers paused to pray, ask for safe passage and so on. These were placed at crossroads, at the beginnings or ends of paths, and by dangerous places such as the edges of cliff paths, and you will see them frequently as you proceed.* Turn L, R then R again, uphill through vines to a minor tarmac road at the top, then KSO ahead, on tarmac road again.

Pass two stone barns and fork R downhill off road, down slope, zigzagging down to minor road by bridge over the torrente (*seat*).

Many hermits lived in this area (the last one died in 1864), and nearby was the hermitage of Saint Julien, a local miner who was thrown off this rock in 1777. There are also two chapels, the older one dedicated to Saint Julien, and the other (19th century) to Saint Grat, and a walking route leads up there as an optional detour (after which you have to retrace your steps).

Turn R then L along road. KSO(L) at RH turn to **Clapey**. KSO to **Granjeon** and turn R downhill between vines (opposite La Vrille, an agriturismo) to start with then steeply downhill to minor road. Turn L in hamlet of **Montcharey** (*seat*) and then continue through **Ollières**, following road down. Road joins another coming from back R; turn L along it. Continue through hamlet of **La Poya**, passing small church (*frescoes of Saint Grat and Saint Laurent outside*) and veer R.

KSO, reach bigger road (SS26) at bend with wayside cross, and KSO(R) downhill into

3.5km Chambave (56/900) Pop. 962, 508m

Two shops, bank, farmacia, bar/rte, Chiesa di San Lorenzo, AD1100, restored 18th century. The town, the site of many markets and fairs, was originally located further to the west, but was destroyed by violent floods at the end of the 11th century and then rebuilt on its present site.

Turn L along street then, opposite house No 17, turn L up stepped passage on **Chemin du Muscat**. Continue ahead uphill, cross road and KSO ahead, then veer

R between houses onto a VS ahead. At seat turn L uphill, zigzagging to minor road at bend and turn second R, uphill.

150m later turn hard L uphill, then 25m after that turn R uphill again on a VS, passing seat and wayside shrine. KSO, wending your way uphill, then turn R to wooden FB over a torrente. Then continue, level, alongside an irrigation channel, the **Ru de Chandianaz**, *one which, like many others in the area, provided power for both flour and saw mills. View of Ussel castle over on the other side of the valley, built 1341–5; it was in part a noble residence, in part used for military purposes. 14th-century Gothic, this was the first castle in the valley to be built as a single rectangular unit, unlike others in the area (Fénis, for example) which are formed from a series of interconnected buildings. Ussel castle is now owned by the regional administration and has recently been restored as a venue for temporary exhibitions.*

KSO for 1.5km, with splendid views on a clear day (*occasional seats to sit and admire them*), until you reach a junction of several footpaths (yellow signs). Here you can choose between three options.

a) Turn L uphill, up a waymarked FP, to visit the **Castello de Cly** above you (waymarks indicate that it takes 30mins) and then retrace your steps. *This was a lone castle, built 11th–12th centuries onwards, and transformed from a simple fort into a residence.*

b) KSO ahead for an optional detour to the semi-abandoned village of **Farys**, with examples of rural architecture and a 300-year-old vine. *There are a lot abandoned villages in the area. Here the farms at a higher level are devoted to cereal production, those lower down to vines.* You can then rejoin the main Via Francigena by descending along a road and then taking a VS on the L.

c) Fork R downhill, zigzagging down past house to minor road, cross over and continue downhill on other side on VS, downhill all the time. 2km later, by first (modern) building, follow deviation (*signposted as such*) – up slope and then to LH side of wooden fence, then across field, zigzagging down to tarmac lane and houses. KSO ahead here on grassy FP along side of hill.

All routes At the start of the abandoned village of **Berma** turn L uphill by first house on small FP and then veer R along side of hill. KSO until you reach a road at a bend. KSO(L) uphill, then at first bend KSO ahead uphill on tarmac lane.

KSO steeply uphill then at fork (at start of **Frayan**) KSO(R), then fork R downhill again immediately on a VS, passing below church (above L). KSO, passing the abandoned village of **Breil**, and the road becomes tarmac. KSO, descending all the time, cross bridge over very long water pipes at right angles to path (*leading down to power station below R*). KSO, then turn R to road in **Chameran**. Turn L into **Via L F Menabrea** to roundabout. Go under underpass and continue on other side (still Via L F Menabrea; *shop, bar*). At end fork L (still Via L F Menabrea)

– *Châtillon church is visible ahead*; do **not** fork R here on Via Hugonin (despite misleading waymark). At bottom turn L along bridge over a gorge and continue on **Via Chanoux**, passing the municipio. Part-way along (between houses 27 and 29) turn L up the cobbled **Via Gervasone**, and turn hard L at top up **Vicolo/Ruelle de Baqueret**, stepped, to the parish church in **Piazza Mons. Duc** in

7km Châtillon (63/893) Pop. 4814, 527m

Large town with all facilities. OP with the Franciscani Capuccini, Via E Chanoux 138 (0166.61471). *Hôtel Dufour, Via Tollen 16 (near the church; 0166.61467), Hôtel Valdostano, Via E Chanoux 178 (near bus station; 0166.62176), Hôtel Verger, Via Tour de Grange 53 (0166.62314), Hôtel Rendezvous (0166.563150). Trenitalia.

Chiesa di San Pietro, 17th-century Sanctuaire de Notre-Dame-des-Graces, Cappella di San Francesco (originally dedicated to Saint Grat) on the site of the original Châtillon hospice for pilgrims and the poor, built on land donated to the brothers of the Grand Saint-Bernard hospice in 1165. Several interesting buildings on Via Chanoux, including the Palazzo Gervasone, Palazzo Scala (a barracks today), the historic Hôtel Londres (used as a base camp for the first mountaineering expeditions to tackle the Matterhorn), and the Pantaleone Bich residence. This was the home of the last owner of Ussel castle and the person who, in 1938, purchased the patent from the impoverished Hungarian inventor of the ball-point pen, Laslo Biro; Bich then went on to mass produce the everyday article known in Britain and Italy today as a 'biro' and in France as a 'bic'. The remains of the Ponte Romano (destroyed by French troops in 1691) are visible under the replacement bridge built in 1754.

Pass between a large school (on L) and the parish house, passing the entrance to the **Château Passerin d'Entrèves** *(1242; not open to the public), surrounded by a large park (open for visits) laid out on the French model in 1706 and containing 32 historic trees.* Continue ahead, pass to RH side of cemetery on wide, level grassy track, then continue uphill on a VS, crossing bridge over torrente, and turn hard L by house uphill on tarmac lane leading to junction of paths in **Conoz**.

Turn R uphill again, veering L by fountain, then R uphill all the time. When road levels out look out for signpost leading hard R uphill, veering L to return you to minor road in **La Verdettaz**. Turn R, continue on a VS then a FP, level, alongside another ru. KSO ahead, ignoring turnings.

At the end, above a farm below R, KSO(R) ahead. *View of Ussel castle again to R as you walk.* Reach road and KSO(R) along it, and 600–700m later reach a road coming from back R. Here a signpost indicates that you can turn R here (30mins) down to Saint-Vincent, but if you want to stop there (to sleep, for example) a nicer option (and one which will enable you to either retrace your steps the following morning to continue or pick up the route further on in the town – see 'To continue (Options A and B)' below) is to continue ahead. (The waymarked Via Francigena does not enter the town on this higher-level option, but passes above it.)

Cross road and continue on track on other side, which then becomes a tarmac lane in village of **Pissin Dessus**. Pass an old wine press to L (*restored to working order in 1977*).

At end turn along 'Ru de Saint-Vincent', a local walking route, and KSO, ignoring turnings to L and R. KSO. *View of Neran tower to R. KSO. (Several seats along the way!)* Cross bridge over a torrente and KSO on other side. At the end reach junction with **Via Tromen** then KSO ahead on **Via Monte Bianco** (not marked at start) to junction with main road, the **Viale IV Novembre**. Continue up this (Viale IV Novembre) uphill then, shortly before house No 97 (on LH side) watch out for a ramp downhill on the RH side of the road. Fork R down it and at end, by garages, go R down some steps.

Here you can either turn L to continue without visiting the town or turn R to break your journey and go into the town centre. For the latter, go down steps,

Church interior, Saint-Vincent

turning L part-way down, then at the bottom turn L into **Piazza 28 Aprile** and the church in

> **5km Saint-Vincent (68/888) Pop. 4864, 575m**

To continue, follow the route after the box for Saint-Vincent below.

OPTION B – LOW-LEVEL (BAD-WEATHER) ROUTE

This alternative bad-weather route is offered as a safe means of walking from Aosta to Châtillon, and then on to Saint-Vincent, in torrential rain, snow, fog or very high winds, when the high-level route would be slippery and very dangerous (and when you would not be able to enjoy the splendid views visible in good weather). Most of the first part follows the older waymarked path of the Via Francigena, which was in use before the present energetic, higher-level option was designed by the CAI.

The low-level option is all – deliberately – on minor tarmac roads, although with little traffic. It is rarely flat, going up and down gradually most of the time, but there are no stiff climbs or descents. As far as Nus it goes along the left-hand side of the valley, but after that it crosses the Dora Balthea and continues on the right-hand side of the river, passing the Castello de Fénis and going through Ponthey before crossing back again into Châtillon by the railway station. From there it follows a road route up into the town and then on (on pavements) into the centre of Saint-Vincent. Places where this lower-level option coincides with the higher-level route are indicated so that, should the weather improve, pilgrims can revert to the more interesting higher-level option.

From Saint Christophe, just below the **Chiesa di Saint-Christophe**, do **not** fork L up the paved slope to the church, but KSO(R) ahead on the road instead. 200–300m later cross a road and KSO on other side into the hamlet of **Nicolin**. Continue ahead then veer R downhill to a bigger road by a bus stop (*bar to R*) and a lavoir opposite. Turn second R here, passing to the RH side of a small chapel with frescoes on its facade.

KSO here, through **Clapey**, and 700–800m later cross a torrente, leaving the comune of Saint Christophe and entering the comune of Quart. KSO, enter the frazione of **Olleyes**. Pass a B&B ('Chat qui dort', on L, house No 1, 349.2578401) and continue to a junction (where the RH turn leads you down to the SS26) and KSO(L) ahead, veering R, L, R and L again, gently uphill and enter the hamlet of **La Balma**.

Continue ahead at junction and, at the next one, by a chapel and a bus stop, KSO ahead. *(The turning to back L goes to the monasterio and the castillo, which you can see above you if the weather is clear enough.)*

KSO(R) ahead 20m later, gently downhill, passing to LH side of small church then, 400m after that, reach a junction by a bus stop *(seat)* with a road coming from back R. KSO(L) ahead here and enter **Moulin** (you are on the SR37), and 900m later enter **Povil**. At a junction with a road coming downhill from back R, KSO ahead. **This is where the high-level route intersects with the lower one, then crosses over and forks R down a FP.** KSO ahead here. Pass **Hotel Eidelweiss** and bar, and 100m later, at a junction after a bend, fork R downhill marked 'SS62', 'Chetoz', 'Cappella de Seran' and 'Nus'. **The high-level route re-emerges to R at next bend.**

KSO, gently downhill, and 500m after that enter **Imperiau**. The VF signs indicate a turn at the next junction, but KSO ahead on the road here, an old route, with very little traffic. Enter **Seran** 600m later and KSO (B&B 'La Casa degli Iris' signed to R at start, 333.4329053). Pass below the **Cappella de Seran** (above L) and KSO. Continue ahead, downhill, pass LH turn to **Clou de Seran** and KSO, downhill all the time (old waymarking).

Pass junction at entrance to **Chetoz** and a LH turn uphill to the Chiesa di Diémoz on the high-level route (marked 2hrs 30mins). KSO(R) on main road through Chetoz, then 200–300m later, at RH bend, turn L (signed 'Nus 2km') and enter the comune di Nus.

KSO. The Chiesa de Nus is now visible ahead, as is also the castello, above L. Go down to junction over the **Torrente Barthélemy** and turn R at a 'stop' sign. Then turn L over a sturdy wooden FB over the torrente on the outskirts of Nus. Turn second R on other side, downhill on street between houses (this is **Frazione Martinet**), veering L *(bar on L)*, then veering L and R and then R down to the **Via Aosta**, passing the municipio on R and turn L in

12km Nus

Bars, shops etc, bank, Trenitalia, *Hotel Florian (X Sat) with rte, Via Risorgimento 3 (0165.767968), **Hotel Dujaney, Via Risorgimento 104 (0165.767100).

Castello di Nus is also known as the 'Castello di Pilati', as according to legend Pontius Pilate stayed here on his way into exile in Gaul after he had condemned Christ to death. Nus ('Ad Nonum Lapidem') was the ninth Roman mile on the road from Aosta.

KSO at junction down main street (***Hôtel Dujany ahead on R*) and join SS26 at road KM89/iii coming from back R. KSO(L) ahead along it *(pavement on*

L), then 100m later cross over and turn R onto SS13 (marked 'Fénis'). KSO, pass motorway entrance/toll area on L (*Hotel Le Petit Foyer, 0165.765448, pilgrim discount*), veer R under railway line, then L on other side. *Castello de Fénis is very clear ahead now.*

Cross the **Dora Balthea**, pass cemetery (L) and entrance to a new cycle track, reach roundabout, KSO ahead past it and go up pedestrianised street veering L to main street in

2km Fénis

A very 'touristy' place, several bars, shop, bank machine. Chiesa di San Maurizio plus a smaller church. Museo dell'Artigione Valdostano di Tradizione.

Castello de Fénis, a real 'story book' castle, belongs to the local authority and can be visited daily except Tuesdays (visiting times vary according to time of year). This is one of the best-known castles in the Valle d'Aosta. Already standing in the 13th century, it was later rebuilt purely as a seat for the powerful Challant family, the numerous towers being added in the 14th century. Today it houses a furniture and interior-design museum.

Turn R to visit church, then retrace your steps. Pass the castello and KSO, pass municipio, small church, PO and KSO, gradually uphill and continuously built-up, going through various hameaux – **Etraves**, **Cors**, **Barcher** (*shop*). KSO, following road round all the time, cross the **Torrente Clavalité**, enter **Miseregne** (*bar*) and KSO, gradually uphill all the time. Pass small church (San Maurizio) and KSO. *All this section from Fénis to Ponthey is fairly shady and with little traffic.*

Continue through **Rovarey** and KSO downhill. KSO, enter the comune of Chambave and KSO. Enter **Septumian** and KSO. KSO again. Pass above small church to L with hexagonal apse and newly painted frescoes on the facade. KSO, passing fork (L to SS26 and Chambave; R to Arlier, Margnier and Ponthey) and KSO(R) ahead here.

Pass above **Arlier** (*bar/trattoria on road but not always open*) and KSO. At end of village fork R uphill, continue ahead, go through **Margnier** (*small church of Notre-Dame de Lourdes*) and KSO ahead, downhill, on road. (*FP waymarked to its RH side, 'Ponthey 40mins', but this leads uphill first.*) KSO ahead downhill here, leave the comune of Chambave and enter the comune of

9km Ponthey 523m

Look out for some of the other castles on the other side of the valley (Château de Cly, above Chambave, for example), although they are sometimes difficult to spot initially as they are built in the same stone as the hillsides in which they are situated.

KSO on SR10, passing through the hamlets of **Prelaz**, **Banchet** and then, passing a tall narrow church on R, **Lassolaz**. *Bar/Locanda Castignetti, opposite the Chiesa di San Martin, has rooms (0166.30145).*

Continue ahead on SR10 all the time past **Clapey** and to **Torin**, 4km from Châtillon *(bar/pizzeria, bar/trattoria, small chapel with fresco of San Rocco as a pilgrim on RH side of facade with stick, cape with two scallop shells, calf-length boots) but also halo, dog (but no bread), wound on his R leg; Castello di Ussel visible perched up on the hill ahead).*

Just after road KM3 turn L over road bridge over the **Dora Balthea**. Go under railway line on other side (marked 'borgo') then turn L to the **Châtillon-Saint Vincent railway station** *(snack bar next to it, useful street-plan opposite)* and turn L by **Hôtel Rouge et Noir** (looks closed) up **Via Stazione**. 150m later stay on LH side of road, and after grassed area with seats go under motorway (underpass). Turn R on other side, then almost immediately L up the continuation of Via Stazione, veer L and continue uphill. By house No 10 and a small abandoned chapel turn L up **Via**

Cappella, Torin

Barat. 100–120m later, at the top, emerge at a small roundabout, a junction of several streets, a bus stand, information office and another street plan in the centre of

5km Châtillon

See description in Option A, above.

You now have two options.

a) If the weather has improved and you would like to continue on the main, higher-level route, continue further up the **Via Chanoux** and turn R (between houses 27 and 29) up the cobbled **Via Gervasone**; turn back to the box for Châtillon in Option A for the continuing route description.

b) If you want to visit Châtillon or sleep in the OP run by the Franciscans at No 130 turn L here into the pedestrianised **Via Chanoux**, then retrace your steps to continue on Option B (low-level route).

To continue (on Option B – low-level route) Turn R opposite the bus stand in Châtillon along the busy SR10 (*pavement*), passing the **Hôtel Valdostano** and a supermarket (both on R), the **Hôtel Rendezvous** (on L) and a (large) supermarket (on R), and continue, uphill all the time, for 1.5km to the top. Cross bridge over a wide valley, after which the road divides. Stay on its LH side on a brick pavement, which then takes you (L) under the SS26 via an underpass, and continue on this when it joins from back R. Leave the comune of Châtillon and enter that of Saint-Vincent.

After crossing the **Torrente Gran valley** continue on the **Viale Piemonte**, a tree-lined esplanade as far as a mini-roundabout (on L). Fork L here, marked 'Centro storico 200m', up **Via G Marconi**, in front of a very large glass building, the **Casino de la Vallée**, and reach another roundabout. Continue ahead here on **Via Roma** (TO on L) and KSO to end. Turn R downhill to **Piazza 28 Aprile** and the **Chiesa di San Vicente** in

5km Saint-Vincent (68/888) Pop. 4864, 575m

Spa town with all facilities. Parish has accommodation for two pilgrims – ask in church. *Pensione Serena, Via Ponte Romana 54 (0166.512363, open April to end October), Albergo Leon d'Oro, Via Chanoux 26 (0168.51202), *Hotel Alba, Piazza Monte Zerbion 17–22 (0166.5126540), *Hotel Ali Baba, Viale Piemonte 11 (0166.512880), *Locanda le Terme, Viale IV Novembre 105 (0166.511520). Paradise Village Camping, Via Trieste (0166.513669; 5mins walk from town centre). TO Via Roma 62 (0166.512239).

A spa town (specialising in respiratory problems) since mid-19th century, with one of Europe's first funicular railways, built 1900. The water was discovered to be therapeutic in 1770, leading to the development of hotels and the casino (reputedly the biggest in Europe) in the town in the early 20th century. Parish church of San Vincenzo Martire is built on the site of Roman baths, which can still be seen. Hospitale di Saint-Vincent existed from the 11th century on a site near the present parish church (and outside the town walls), but there is no trace of it left today. 13 chapels in and near the town.

Panel depicting Saint Maurice, main square Saint-Vincent

To continue (Options A and B)

If you went down into the town and to the Piazza 28 Aprile, continue from there along the **Via Ponte Romana** and then, opposite the Pensione Serena, turn L up the **Via Battaglione Aosta**. Turn R 150m later by house No 24 to pick up the way-marked Via Francigena again.

If you did not go down into the town, but want to continue and pass above it, having turned L at the bottom of the steps (after the ramp down from the **Viale IV Novembre**), fork R 100m later onto a grassy track and then go through the tunnel under the funicular railway line (*bend down!*). KSO alongside water channel to road and then turn R downhill again – this is the **Via Battaglione Aosta**. Turn L part-way down (by house No 24) to pick up the waymarked Via Francigena again.

Reach road and KSO(L) along it, uphill. 800m later, by bus stop (*with seat*), fork R down slope into the village of **Cillian**. Veer R, turn L over bridge, pass small chapel on L (*with pebble tower, 1954*), then KSO to the side of house No 25. Turn L by fountain, veering R downhill, then 200m later turn L onto walled path and continue with high stone wall to L.

To see the Roman bridge over the Torrente Cillian (which empties into the Dora Balthea below, KSO here and then retrace your steps. This bridge, originally 49m long, dates from at least the second or third century BC *and was in use until 8 June 1839, when an earthquake caused the central arch to collapse. This section was part of the Roman road – the Route des Gaules – linking Eporedia (Ivrea) and Augusta Pretoria (Aosta), before continuing up to the Col du Mont Joux (Great St Bernard Pass) and Switzerland and beyond.*

Zigzag uphill (*this is marked as a geological trail*). Turn hard L onto a VS. 500m later pass near road (to L) by bend, but KSO(R) ahead on VS/FP, then KSO(R) downhill on very minor road by bus stop (seat under cover) at entrance to village of

2.5km Feilley (70.5/885.5) 621m

Small Cappella di San Rocco, built 1645, 15 years after the plague of 1630 (and dedicated to the saint, who was frequently invoked for help with infectious diseases and epidemics).

100m later go down paved ramp on R, veering R, cross and recross a small river and continue downhill on earth/stone track. When you reach railings in front of you (road ahead below you) go down grassy slope L ahead then turn hard R down FP to minor road by a garden centre. Turn L downhill then at end of village (**Lavà**) turn R down tarmac lane, downhill, which then becomes a FP leading to another part of the village. Turn L by barn onto banked-up lane up FP leading to a farm and turn L uphill (not waymarked), then L again past group of fruit trees and a large cage with turkeys in it. Then, at the start of a cased-in river, turn R up FP uphill, zigzagging up through woods. 800m later reach unsurfaced road and turn R into

2km Chenal (72.5/883.5)

The Castello di Chenal played a strategic role in the Middle Ages, but began to be dismantled in the 16th century and was then abandoned. Cappella della Madonna delle Nevi at the end of the village is mentioned as early as 1700, but then fell into decay before being restored in 1969.

KSO through village, turn R at junction and reach the chapel (*good place for a rest*). Turn L past it on FP and reach road at bend opposite a children's playground. Here you have a choice of two routes to Chiesa di San Giorgio.

OPTION A

The main waymarks direct you to turn R downhill, passing a large sports field where Tsan, a traditional Valdostano game, is played. *A pole 5m high is sunk into the ground at an angle and the tsan (a ball 4cm in diameter) is attached to the end and hit with a bat; there are two teams of 14 players, and the aim of the game is to send the tsan as far as possible – as the winner is the team totalling up the greatest distance.* You then KSO on road for 500–600m more and turn L onto a banked-up grassy lane, passing **Casa Sapé** (a small chapel) on L.

Continue, veering L (*view of Montjovet Castle and seat*). KSO on grassy paved track then, part-way down, fork L uphill alongside high wall, passing house (on R) and reach minor road. Turn R to the

2km Chiesa di San Giorgio (74.5/881.5)

Fountain. 1879. 15th-century bell tower. Church consecrated 1504. Closed for restoration at the time of writing. A path leads up to the castle but this is also closed, due to falling scree.

Pass to RH side of church and go down minor road to T-junction and turn R there, downhill all the time.

OPTION B

Alternatively you can turn L just before the sports field onto a tarred road (very little traffic), veering R downhill (this is also waymarked, with older signs) and passing through the hamlets of **Ruelle** and **Provarey**. (To visit the **Chiesa di San Giorgio** turn R at fork, uphill, but you will then have to retrace your steps afterwards – this junction is where Options A and B join up). KSO(L) ahead, downhill all the time.

Both routes

1km later road levels out a bit in **Balmas**, passing below a small chapel, above L (*dedicated to San Rocco*). *A number of hamlets in this area, like one you passed earlier, are called 'Balmas' (or 'Barmas') from the Latin balma, meaning 'shelter under the rock', describing the way many of the houses in this area are positioned. This Balmas was on the old Roman road.*

Once again you have a choice. The newer waymarks indicate that you should turn hard R here (by notice boards) to go downhill to the road below, cross over, go under motorway and then continue to **Borgo Montjovet** on the other (RH) side of the river (*note that the Chiesa di Montjovet is not in the village itself but in Berriaz, on the LH side of the valley*). *Borgo Monjovet has a Chiesa di San Rocco* and had a hospice that housed the thousands of poor pilgrims that flocked to Rome to earn indulgences between 1309 and 1614, a period during which there were numerous jubilee years.

However, a much nicer, quieter option is the older (also waymarked) route which goes straight on ahead after the **Cappella San Rocco** at the end of Balmas and along the LH side of the valley via the hamlet of Toffo. To do so, continue ahead on gravel/grassy terraced track with wall to L, mainly level along the side of the hill. *The southern exposure here gives the area a Mediterranean-type climate, and plants such as wild thyme, oregano and rosemary all thrive here, as olives do too.* Go through **Toffo** and continue ahead on a tarmac lane to a hairpin bend in minor road ahead. *(The small church on the hillside ahead is the Cappella di San Rocco in Ciseran.)* Turn (not fork) R here down a paved track, and then continue immediately below the crash barrier. Follow track down to a tarmac road in the hamlet of **Brun**, then continue to hairpin bend on bigger road.

For shop, bar and so on KSO(R) here to a roundabout 300m later on SS26 in **Berriaz** (a frazione of the comune of Montjovet). Otherwise fork L, then at the next bend KSO ahead down a slope and turn L onto a grassy path and stepped lane to the

4km Chiesa de Montjovet (78.5/877.5) 417m

Small supermarket to L on main road, PO, 2 bars, *Hotel Rte da Vicenzo (0166.579006 and 0166.79641), **Hotel Nigra, Berriaz 13 (0166.79139), *Hotel Alpi, Berriaz 80 (0166.79641).

The church, Chiesa della Natività di Maria Vergine (1830), is not in Monjovet itself but in the frazione of Berriaz.

Pass between the church and the **Maison Comunale/Municipio**, then, yet again, there are two options. *A high-level route on the LH side of the valley leads from here up through the villages of Reclou and Quignonaz, over the Col de Nâche and then straight down again steeply (on a bad surface) on the other side to the SS26 again in Torille. This option (not described here) was not well way-marked at the time this guide was prepared and the views aren't all that great either (and there is still a very long way to go until you reach Rome). Alternatively, there is the flat, not particularly interesting, but quiet and more or less level route that was originally waymarked on the RH side of the river and is described here. The waymarking is somewhat sparse, but it is easy enough to follow. The two options meet up again shortly before Issogne.*

Instead of turning L to take the high-level route over the Col de Nâche from the Chiesa de Montjovet turn R along the side of the church, turn L down some

91

steps, turn R at road then fork R down more steps to main road. Cross over and cross bridge over the **Dora Balthea** (marked 'Meran' and 'Oley'), then on other side turn L immediately onto a gravel track alongside the river. KSO, go under motorway and 100m later reach a minor road by an industrial building and turn L. *Hardly any traffic.* KSO with river to L and railway line to R above you. KSO. Go under second turning under railway line by mini-roundabout and enter comune of **Champdepraz**.

KSO through **Viéring** (*hamlet*), then at end of village, at RH fork to 'Les Sales' and 'La Fabbrique', KSO(L) ahead. 300m later veer L under railway line and then go under motorway and veer R on other side (*slightly more traffic*) on **Via Giordano Freydoz** (*not marked at start*). KSO past a lot of factories (*although the Aosta valley has a lot of castles, it is also very industrial*), then 1km later turn R under motorway again, then immediately L alongside it. 300m later enter **Mure** (*a frazione in the comune of Issogne*) and pass more factories (*that make breeze blocks, drainage channels, concrete garden furniture…*). Follow road round, go under railway again, veering L and then R on other side, with the **Dora Balthea** to your L again.

Pass the Mongas plant and two equally large businesses, after which the road veers R and crosses a tributary of the Dora Balthea. Turn L at T-junction (*despite decorative pilgrim sign indicating a RH turn to Champdepraz*) alongside the Dora Balthea to the hamlet of **Favà**. Pass the **Cappella San Solutor** on R (*probably shut, but its steps are a good shady place for a rest*). KSO, then 400–500m later pass **Hameau Fleuron** (on R) and reach a bridge over the Dora Balthea leading (L) into **Verrès**. (*This is where the option via the Col de Nâche joins up with your lower-level route, coming from the L over the bridge.*) KSO here then turn first R (marked 'Issogne 0.4'). Turn L at T-junction onto minor tarmac road, R at 'stop' sign, then L to continue, parallel to river (*dry*) again. Cross the **Torrente Beauquell** and KSO. 200–300m later, at junction, turn R uphill into **Hameau Mariette**, then turn L by house No 2 along the outside wall of the Château d'Issogne into the main square in the centre of

---

8.5km Issogne (87/869) Pop. 1370, 387m

2 shops, bank, rte, PO, café. Hotel Brenve, Via la Colombiera 20 (0125.921611), B&B Les Souvenirs (338.9012043). Chiesa di Santa Maria Assunta (1736).

15th-century Gothic/Renaissance castle (state owned; visits all year). Dubbed the 'castle of dreams' (a play on the castle's original name derived from the Italian word *sogno* – 'dream'), this sumptuous building with its collections of inlaid furniture and silver, a library, frescoes and so on is very different from the austere, strategically placed military castles in the rest of the Aosta valley. The hundreds of guests who stayed there over the years left messages praising the hospitality they received, including many pilgrims, who were accommodated in the 'cabinet des coquilles' (not open to the public) – a room, as its name suggests, whose walls were covered in scallop shells. The castle is still in good condition today, having been bought by the painter Avondo in 1872, who restored it to its original splendour. Worth a visit if your timing permits.

Turn L downhill (*bar on L*), passing a small wayside **Chapelle Saint-Suaire** (on R, with a Veronica fresco over door), then cross the bridge back over the **Dora Balthea** again and turn R immediately on other side.

If you want to visit Verrès or sleep in the youth hostel there, KSO ahead here, go under the railway line and turn L onto the **Rue des Alpes**, veering L at fork, to reach the railway station (the YH is next to it). Retrace your steps the following morning and, having gone back under the railway line, turn L (marked 'Hône 3h').

Chapelle Saint-Suaire, near Verrès

1.5km Verrès (88.5/867.5) Pop. 2585, 390m

14th-century rectangular fortress on a hilltop overlooking the town. Small town with shops, bars, rtes, etc. 2 TOs – Via Circonvallazione 119 (0125.922648 and (summer only) Via Caduti Libertà (next to municipio). Ostello Libertas Il Casello (YH), Via della Stazione 79 (0125.921652). 3 hotels (all ***) – Da Pierre, Via Martorey 76 (0125.929376), Evançon, Via Circonvallazione 33 (0125.929152), Relais Saint-Gilles, Via Circonvallazione 119/4 (0125.920148). Trenitalia.

Prevostura Saint-Gilles (collegiate church) dating from 10th century, originally also used as a hotel for pilgrims, now parish buildings. Chiesa di Sant-Egidio e Agostino (in the borgo de Verrès), Cappella di San Giorgio e Maurizio (1407), 15th-century fortified farmhouse (cascina) 'La Murasse' (now local library and town offices). Cappella San Rocco (junction of Via Duc d'Aosta and Vicolo San Rocco) with painting of San Rocco as a pilgrim over the front door (stick, and hat behind his head) and free-standing sculpture of him on the altar, also as a pilgrim, with stick and gourd. Opposite this chapel, and thus outside the town walls, was the Hospice de Verrès – the building still exists and is known locally as the 'Ospedale', although it is no longer in use and not open to the public.

However, if you do not want to go into Verrès itself, having turned R immediately on the other side of the bridge (after crossing the Dora Balthea), KSO(R) at fork, KSO(R) alongside river at next junction, then 200m later turn L towards the main road. Veer R to cross a minor road bridge over the railway line and motorway, continuing towards the SS26 at the start of

3.5km Arnad (92/864) Pop. 2710, 400m

Shops etc on main road. Romanesque Chiesa di San Martino with 13th-century bell tower. The town takes its name from the lard (pork fat) for which this area is famous.

Turn R here and then, almost immediately, turn L (marked 'Clos de Barme'), and 100m after that turn R onto a cobbled street with large restored wine press (dating from 1838). KSO (*do not turn L, waymarked uphill – this is another walking route*) and continue ahead, entering the hamlet of **Barme**. Cross bridge over (dried-up) river by junction with fountain, and then fork R to 'stop' sign. Turn L

Rebuilt Romanesque bridge over Dora Balthea, Echallod

here on minor road. KSO, passing above church (below to R) and then in front of the **municipio** to a junction. KSO(L) ahead here. KSO again, then fork L at entrance to hamlet of **Prouve**, uphill.

If you want to make the (waymarked) detour to visit the Santuario de Machaby, turn L just after crossing the river. Originally founded in the 13th century, then rebuilt in 1687, this is situated in a gorge and dedicated to the Madonna delle Nevi (Our Lady of the Snows), although it is rarely open.

Cross the **River Prouve** and enter the village of **Ville** (a borgo; shop on R, M–S, X Thurs pm). KSO through village, pass small 15th-century chapel (on R) and reach a crossing (*where the detour, above, to the Santuario de Machaby rejoins the main route*).

KSO ahead here, passing the exit boards for the hamlets of **Ville**, **Pied de Ville** and **Costa**. Cross the bridge over the (dry) torrente and turn R downhill on other side. Turn L at the end, then R downhill past a sports complex, veering L then R to go under the motorway. Continue downhill, either veering R to go under the SS26 or, if the path under the road is badly flooded, veering L onto a grassy track and crossing the road itself. KSO (staggered) on other side, go under railway and cross the **Dora Balthea** by the Romanesque-style Echallod bridge (*rebuilt 1770–76, with an oratory on the L as you cross for the safeguarding and protection of wayfarers; seats at start*).

Turn L on other side and KSO on minor road. 1km later, after a factory, turn R onto gravel track to RH side of motorway (*Bard fort, 19th century, visible ahead*).

95

KSO. 1.5km later pass **Cappella di San Grat** (*rarely open*). *The chapel was erected following a bequest in 1722, but construction work was difficult, and by 1765 the chapel was not yet consecrated and open for worship. In 1864 the building was badly damaged due to recurring flooding of the Dora Balthea, and was then elongated and raised. More floods in 1908 resulted in further reconstruction, and the building has recently undergone structural restoration. There are other chapels of this type and size in the area, with a protruding pitched roof at the front (like the peak on a baseball cap).* KSO. 600–700m later reach crossing (with level crossing through tunnel to L) and KSO ahead on **Via Verifie** up to church in

7km Hône (99/857) 372m

Small town situated at the junction of the rivers Ayasse and Dora Balthea. Shop, bakery, **Hotel/bar/rte del Mulino. Via E Chanoux 123 (0152.803334), Hotel Bordet, Via E Chanoux 54 (015.803116). Chiesa di San Giorgio (1776), frescoes; currently being restored. Trenitalia.

Go under archway, then there are two alternatives.

OPTION A

The waymarked route takes you on a 1.5km horseshoe-shaped detour above the town (and then back down again) to visit the Cappella di San Rocco (*built 1665, rebuilt 1901, statue of San Rocco over altar*) and the Ospedale Santa Lucia (*19th century, rebuilt a century later*). On a clear day there are good views of the town, the Forte de Bard ahead and the surrounding area, but the two churches it passes are unlikely to be open. To take this option turn R on **Via Vareyna** in front of the church, then turn R uphill behind it, going steeply uphill on a rocky stepped path.

OPTION B

The alternative (level) option is, after going through the archway, to KSO for 300m on **Via M Collard** right to the very end, then turn L down **Via E Chanoux** (*where the 'loop' detour joins you from the R*).

Both routes

The two routes join here and go under the motorway ahead. KSO(R) at bend by petrol station and hotel, still on **Via E Chanoux**, and cross the **Ponte Antico** (pedestrians and cycles only) over the Dora Balthea into

1.5km Bard (100.5/855.5) Pop. 130, 400m

A very 'touristy' place with bars, rtes, but no proper shop. B&B at 39 Via Vitt. Emmanuele II. Hôtel Stendhal, Via Vitt. Emmanuele II 12 (0125.809873).

Medieval village set in a deep gorge, with many extant 16th-century buildings. Forte de Bard is up on the hill above. The first fortress dated from the 11th century, but was razed to the ground by Napoleon's troops in 1800. The present castle (X Mon) dates from 1838 and is accessible either by funicular railway from the bottom or on foot by a path which continues from the parish church at the top of the town near the municipio. The original building on the site of the present Hôtel Stendhal (at the top of the hill) was the Ospizio De Jordanis, founded in 1425 by two brothers of that name. It was destroyed by fire and then rebuilt in 1830, serving as the town hall until 2002, when it became a hotel. Bard also had a second hospice to assist poor travellers, now in ruins, next to the 11th-century Chiesa di San Giovanni Battista; this was run by the Knights of the Order of Saint John of Jerusalem (Knights of Malta).

After crossing the bridge over the Dora Balthea cross the SS26 and fork R immediately up **Via Umberto I**, which then becomes **Via Vitt. Emmanuele II** (*bar part-way up*). *Pilgrims interested in architecture will find several old houses of interest (with information boards outside them) to either side of the street, including the Casa Merediana at No 73, the 'sundial house', with a dial on both sides and*

Roman road near Donnas

the end of the building. Reach the **mairie/municipio** and church at top then KSO ahead, downhill on former Roman road.

At bottom KSO(L) on raised walkway with railings alongside main road, continue on the Roman road (when repaired!) then, just before a church, go up steps and KSO on street behind it on **Via Principe Tommaso** in

---

2km Donnas (102.5/853.5) Pop. 2631, 336m

Market town with shops, bars, etc. OP in Parrochia San Pietro in Vincoli, Via Roma 81 (0125.80703), Albergo Sant'Orso, Via Principe Tommaso 74 (0125.344527).

Donnas was the 36th Roman mile on the consular route from Aosta. The town originally had walls, but only the eastern gate is left. Donnas also had a leper hospital and three hospices, but the only trace left today is in a street name – Ruelle de l'Hôpital des Pèlerins. It had a mint as well, set up in 1341 in the Hôtel des Monnaies. The parish church of San Pietro in Vincoli (Saint Peter in Chains) is one of the oldest in the Aosta diocese. It was destroyed by floods in the 12th century and rebuilt in the 13th, while the present building, with scenes from the life of Saint Peter on the pulpit, dates from 1829–30. Cappella de Sant-Orso, at western end of the built-up part of town, was built in 1176 to invoke divine protection against the frequent floods of the Dora Balthea. (The original village, where Treby is now, was completely destroyed by floods.) Museo della Viticultura.

At the top of **Via Principi Tommaso** go under arch where (once again) you have two options for the route to Pont Saint-Martin. *The longer, more recently waymarked route (Option A) leads high up along the hillside above the towns to Pont Saint-Martin, with good views, but if it is foggy pilgrims can use the old (still waymarked) VF route (Option B) along the main road, with quite a lot of traffic but a proper pavement all the way.*

OPTION A – HIGH-LEVEL ROUTE TO PONT SAINT-MARTIN

After going under the arch turn L uphill. Turn R 400m later (marked 'Les Pians') on another minor road through vines, then 200m later fork R at junction, downhill ('Rovarey, 0.5'), veering R downhill to junction. Turn L opposite house No 1 onto another tarmac road (pick up 'F' waymarks and old arrows here) – this is **Via Barmes**.

Turn L uphill again by house No 124 on **Via Ronc-de-Vaccaz**, veering L and then R, and KSO, continuously uphill for 1km, zigzagging up to a very large cross

Bridge over the Lys, Pont Saint-Martin

on rocks directly above road (*marked 'Souvenir de Mission Pont Saint-Martin Donnas et vert 14–19 mars 1995'*). KSO ahead here (*exit boards for Donnas*), go through **Ronc** (*a hamlet*) and KSO for 1km. At T-junction by bus stop turn R downhill (on SR1), and 600–700m later, by bend, fork L through the neo-Gothic **Castello di Baraing**. Continue down on FP, then a staircase (**Salita Jacoma**), and turn onto pedestrianised street leading through archway and over the single-arch Roman bridge over the **River Lys**.

OPTION B – MAIN ROAD ROUTE TO PONT SAINT-MARTIN

From the **Via Principi Tommaso** go under arch then KSO ahead to **Piazza XXV Aprile** and then return to SS26. (*To visit church of **San Pietro in Vincoli** turn L up steps after house No 79; church porch open; glass doors prevent entry, but allow visit visually instead.*) KSO, pass small roadside chapel (on L), continue ahead to a big roundabout at entrance to town (TO after 250m on R, on main road). KSO(L) ahead up **Via Nazionale per Donnas** passing **Cappella San Rocco** part-way up on L. *Faded frescoes outside and inside, and free-standing wooden statue of Saint Roch to R of apse – cape (with shells?), stick, dog.*

Continue ahead (**Via Emile Chanoux**) then, just as the Ponte Romano becomes visible ahead, fork L up **Via Roma**. Part-way up on L is the **Piazza San Giacomo**, where the Chiesa di San Giacomo (Saint James) was destroyed by Allied bombing

99

on 28 Aug 1944. Go under archway at top and cross Roman bridge over the **River Lys** in

---

3.5km Pont Saint-Martin (106/850) Pop. 3842, 345m

Town with shops, banks, bars, rtes, etc. Trenitalia. Ostello-type accommodation in the Foresteria Saint Martin, Via Schigliatta 1, 56 beds (0125.804433/830619/830611). ***Hôtel Ponte Romano, Piazza IV Novembre 14 (0125.804329), ***Hôtel Crabun, Strada Nazionale per Donnas 3 (0125.806069), ***Hôtel Carla, Strada Nazionale per Carema 104–106 (0125.807281). TO on ring road on edge of town (Via Circonvallazione 30, 0125.804843, pontsaintmartin@turismo.vda.it).

Roman bridge (36m long and 23m high) over the River Lys, built in the first century BC and a rare example, still intact, of a single-arch bridge from that period. It was known as the Ponte del Diavolo ('devil's bridge') as it was believed to have been built by Satan. However, another legend relates that Saint Martin, Bishop of Tours, stayed a few days in the town on his way to Rome, during which time the bridge was washed away by floodwaters. The devil is said to have suggested to Saint Martin that he would repair the bridge in a single night in exchange for the soul of the first person to cross the newly repaired bridge at daybreak, an arrangement to which the bishop agreed. But the following morning Saint Martin put a piece of bread at the end of the bridge, so that the first to cross was a hungry dog. The devil, reportedly exasperated by being so easily taken in, disappeared into the waters of the River Lys and never caused any more trouble to the inhabitants of Pont Saint-Martin.

Two castles – the neo-Gothic Castello de Baraing, built in 1883 on a rock overlooking the ruins of the town, and the ruined 13th-century feudal Castello di Suze. Casaforte dei Signori di Pont Saint-Martin (16th-century mansion) in the centre of the town.

Stage XLVI (Publei, 46) in Sigeric's itinerary.

For some reason the waymarking now leads pilgrims backwards over the modern bridge and down to the tourist office on the ring road at the entrance to the town – where the waymarking stops completely with no indication of where to go next. So there is again a choice here.

If, having taken the high-level route into Pont Saint-Martin and just crossed the Roman bridge, you do want to go to the tourist office (to get a stamp in your pilgrim passport, for example) turn hard R back over the river on the modern bridge and go part-way down the street ahead (**Via Emile Chanoux**). Then turn

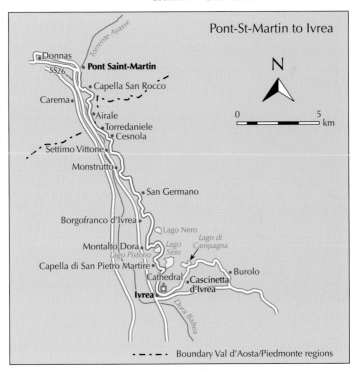

Pont-St-Martin to Ivrea

Otherwise, continue from the Roman bridge. Go down the steps at the end of the Roman bridge, rejoin **Via Chanoux**, turning L along it, and shortly afterwards KSO(L) ahead on **Via Boschetto**, picking up the newer waymarking system at street level, with white arrows, a white stencilled pilgrim figure or a black pilgrim logo on a red and white background. KSO. Path becomes paved, then a grassy lane, passing behind houses then continuing as a FP downhill to the SS26. Turn L here onto **Via**

L onto the street before the municipio, cross an area with a modern building in the middle and KSO past side of a shop onto **Via Repubblica**. At end turn R then almost immediately L onto **Via Brigata Lys** to main road (**Via Circonvallazione**) and turn R to tourist office at No 30 (on other side; large supermarket nearby). Then retrace your steps back to the Roman bridge.

Both routes
Otherwise, continue from the Roman bridge. Go down the steps at the end of the Roman bridge, rejoin **Via Chanoux**, turning L along it, and shortly afterwards KSO(L) ahead on **Via Boschetto**, picking up the newer waymarking system at street level, with white arrows, a white stencilled pilgrim figure or a black pilgrim logo on a red and white background. KSO. Path becomes paved, then a grassy lane, passing behind houses then continuing as a FP downhill to the SS26. Turn L here onto **Via**

S Erasmo. KSO to the very end, return to the SS26 again, and then decide whether you want to go to Carema via the Cappella San Rocco or keep to the road.

The path up to the Cappella San Rocco is well waymarked, with both white pilgrim logos and the brown VF signs, but parts of it are very narrow and uneven and could be difficult in poor visibility or very slippery in bad weather. You do not need a good head for heights, but you do need to be fairly agile, especially if you have a heavy rucksack, as parts of it are 'mountain goat' style.

If it is very misty you may prefer not to take this higher route, in which case continue on the SS26 until the road turning for Carema, turn L and pick up the waymarks again in the **Piazza della Chiesa** and the **Via San Matteo**, where the two routes join up again.

To go via the Cappella di San Rocco continue for a few metres more along the SS26 then turn L onto **Via Schigliatta** (the foresteria is at No 1 if you want to sleep there), passing sawmill (on L). At LH bend KSO ahead down grassy slope then KSO on FP, gradually uphill more steeply, on rocky FP (slippery in wet weather) leading, 1km later, to the

2km Cappella San Rocco (108/848)

17th-century votive chapel, built by the inhabitants of Carema to thank San Rocco for protecting them against the plague when it struck in that area; painting of San Rocco over altar. Picnic area and good place for a rest.

Pass to LH side of chapel and turn L on FP. Follow it round, downhill, steps, then along level through vines along hillside. KSO on **Via Roma** and then KSO(R) ahead, passing **Casa della Musica** (on L). KSO(R) at junction, and at the very end of Via Roma reach junction with **Via Basilia** and the **Fontana di Via Basilia** (1571). Turn L here uphill to church (**San Martino**) and municipio, and then turn R into **Piazza della Chiesa**, which then becomes **Via San Matteo** (note Fontana di San Matteo, 1460) in

1km Carema (109/847) 350m

Chiesa di San Martino, originally built in 1261, rebuilt 1749. Torre degli Ugoni, remains of Castello di Constructione.

After Carema pilgrims leave the Val d'Aosta and enter the regione of Piemonte ('foot of the mountains') where, in general, the route is a great deal flatter. The

route now leads through an area characterised by vine groves clinging to man-made terraces on the mountain slopes.

KSO on Via San Matteo to **Grand Maison** *(Gran Mason; an early medieval fortified house)*. Turn R downhill then L (**Via Antonio Vairos**), cross road and KSO ahead down lane, veering L to join VS at the bottom. Turn L. At junction turn R, veering L, then at next junction turn L onto level grassy lane, parallel to the road below, veering L to SS26. Turn L and KSO on road for 1km.

Turn L onto a minor road, turning R into

2km Airale (111/845)

Chiesa di San Defendente.

Pass remains of a very small chapel (now restored) and KSO ahead at bend on **Via Giasso** (grassy FP) parallel to SS26. *(500m after the turn-off to Airale, on the SS26, is the **Hotel Tripoli (0125.7577100) and rte on the LH side, opposite the turning to Quincinetto, and the **campsite is on L next to it.)*

KSO, cross track (by wayside shrine) and KSO ahead through caravan and camp site (entrance on SS26), cross bridge over torrente and reach a minor road. Turn R (**Via Chioso**) and reach church in

1.5km Torredaniele (112.5/843.5) Pop. 152, 278m

Chiesa di San Pietro.

Turn L up ramp to church tower, turn R behind it, veering L under arch (**Via San Luca**), then turn R, veering L onto a tarmac lane. Turn R ahead towards road (near KM45) but then turn L, parallel to it, on gravel track. KSO.

Just before returning to the road fork L up slope then turn L alongside walled lane, veering L up side of (dry) torrente. Turn R to cross it, then L on other side, going uphill to **Cappella Sant'Agata** *(sundial – there are many in the area)* in

1km Cesnola (113.5/842.5)

Continue veering L ahead on **Via Municipale** to fountain. Turn R downhill then turn next L, veering round side of hill to continue parallel to and above road below, passing tall chapel on L, the **Cappella San Rocco**. KSO to junction with redundant **Chiesa di San Sebastiano** in

---

1.5km Settimo Vittone (115/841) Pop. 1579, 282m

Shops, several bars, bank, Hotel Gambino, Via Nazionale 48 (0125.658508). B&B Figlei (0125.658340), Ospitalità del Castello, Piazza Conte Rinaldo 7 (0125.659083 and 348.45452701).

'Settimo' refers to the town's position on the seventh Roman mile from Ivrea. Castello (7th–12th centuries), Chiesa di San Lorenzo (8th–11th centuries), octagonal Battistero di San Giovanni Battista (eighth century), one of the most important High Medieval monuments in the area.

Turn L uphill (**Via Pettiti Giuseppe**), veering R, then fork L at 'stop' sign by bend in road. *(To go into the town KSO(R) here, downhill, and retrace your steps to continue.)* Turn L immediately, marked 'Battistero San Lorenzo', continuing uphill on grassy walled lane to road. KSO(L) up it for 100m then KSO(L) up cobbled lane, with Stations of the Cross, to **Chiesa di San Andrea** (*large square porch, useful for shelter in bad weather*).

Turn R in front of it, cross road and go towards archway – but then turn L round the remains of the **Battistero San Lorenzo**, ninth century (*now a B&B*). Go down steps on L, veering round field, then on path under vines to minor road. Turn L uphill. When road bends R, KSO(L) ahead towards vines. Go down narrow walled lane (*walk on grass to L if very wet*) then zigzag down rocky 'staircase', after which path veers L then goes along side of hill, descending gradually. Turn R down flight of stone steps, then continue on grassy path to L of vines with wall to LH side. Cross torrente, continue past vines, enter woods, go under arch, then turn L up rough tarmac road uphill, passing small chapel on R (1704).

At top, by house (*view of neo-Gothic Castello di Monstrutto to R*), the road becomes a track then rocky FP, gradually downhill. At junction of FPs turn R down old paved road, downhill to **Via Nomaglio** and a small square in

---

2.5km Monstrutto (117.5/838.5)

B&B **La Rondina, Via Vittorio Emanuele 28 (348.2927982), B&B Il Pellegrino, Via Nomaglio 6 (348.2725840).

Turn L and continue on **Via Vittorio Emanuele**. At end of public park fork L down side of first house onto grassy FP. Reach minor road and turn L along it, veering R along base of hill. Go through **Ivozio** (*Hotel La Gria, Via Aosta 240, 0125.751009, on main road at end of Via Ivozio, on R*), passing small church on L, on **Via Palma**, and **La Cascinassa** (an 18th-century self-sufficient farm), and KSO to the **Chiesa di San Germano**.

Turn L just before the church to end of street, then turn R into **Balmetti** onto **Via del Buonumore**, veering R at end. Turn L 100m later onto track between fields parallel to road (to R) and hills (to L), which then becomes **Via Falcone**. 700m after that reach bigger road (opposite **Piazza del Mercato**) and turn R, past bar and petrol station, to crossroads. Turn L onto **Via Marini** to reach the bell tower at the entrance to

4.5km Borgofranco d'Ivrea (122/834) Pop. 3667, 253m

Shops, bank, supermarket. Trenitalia. B&B Verde Musica, Via Cavour 10 (349.0835837). Note that the Via Francigena does not go into the town itself.

Torre Porta (13th–18th centuries) was originally a defensive tower on the town gate, but it became a bell tower when the church was built next to it.

Turn L onto **Via Mombarone** (*shop on L*), veering R, then turn L onto **Via Andrate**. Turn R down **Via Mulini** (by house No 40), then 200m later, before you reach a bridge ahead, turn R onto an unsurfaced lane into woods. KSO on track, ignoring turnings, then for a while continue to RH side of small river, crossing its bed when it turns R. KSO on track, ignoring turns. Pass large abandoned house (*former mill?*) and KSO. Reach industrial buildings and KSO. Reach junction (road has become **Via Aldo Balla**) and KSO(L) ahead to square with the municipio, **Piazza IV Novembre** (*seats*), in

3km Montalto Dora (125/831) 248m

Shops etc on main road.

Turn L onto **Via Casana**, passing **Villa dei Baroni Casana** on L. *This was built in 1732 as a modest residence with a small garden, but was enlarged in 1818 by the architect Talucchi to become a sumptuous palace with a very large garden, whose centuries-old cedar trees can be seen from the picnic area further up the cammino (look through the grille in the gate to L). The building was remodelled in 1890 by Andrade, and since 1939 it has been the Benedictine Monasterio di San Michele, occupied by Cistercian nuns in semi-enclosure.*

Continue uphill, passing picnic area on R. Continue uphill again veering R. Pass the **Chiesa di San Rocco** (*probably originally 13th century; frescoes inside, including San Rocco*). Reach junction of several paths and KSO(L) ahead (*picnic area to L*).

Reach the **Castello di Montalto Dora** (*originally 9th–14th centuries, but restored 1965–85*). Pass below it and KSO downhill. By wayside shrine (on R) turn R (signed to 'La Locanda della Vigne, Cucina'). Pass to LH side of lake, pass bar/rte (on R), veering R to cross its parking area, then fork L uphill ahead into woods, along LH side of **Lago Pistono**. KSO. Track joins from back L. KSO and reach the

2.5km Cappella di Santa Croce (127.5/828.5)

Probably originally a private chapel belonging to the cascina opposite. Supposedly built on the site of the martyrdom of San Tegolo, a Christian soldier in the Theban legion. The present chapel dates from 1642 (the original monument was just a cross). Restored 1982 onwards, with the help of the local population. Seat, fountain.

Pass to LH side of chapel and KSO. Some 300m later turn hard L (marked 'Cappella di San Pietro Martire') then turn R (uphill again) by entrance gate to a large property. Track levels out and goes downhill on walled lane/road to small chapel on L, the

1km Cappella di San Pietro Martire (128.5/827.5)

Continue ahead to junction with bigger road, then turn first L at junction (*rte to L*) down shady, small, rocky FP, which gradually becomes wider. Continue ahead on road (*car park below L*) uphill to junction (*view of Lago Sirio ahead L*) and KSO ahead. Turn next R (**Via S Ulderico**) and KSO. Road becomes unsurfaced for a while – KSO. Start descending and KSO to end (still Via di San Ulderico), veering L (*large supermarket on L*). Cross the *circonvallazione* (ring road) and KSO(L) along it (*walk on FP to R of pavement until it finishes*) round to the **Piazza Aldo Balla** in

3.5km Ivrea (132/824) Pop. 24,280, 250m

Medium-sized town with all facilities. Trenitalia to Aosta and Turin. Ostello Francigena/Ostello Ivrea, Canoa Club, Via Dora Balthea 1/d (near railway station; 347.9092391 and 328.0999579; 15€, kitchen, April–end Oct, but all year for groups of more than 8), Ostello Salesiano Eporediese, Via San Giovanni Bosco 58 (on way into town on old VF route; 0125.627268; 151 beds). **Albergo Aquila Nera, Corso Nigra 56 (0125.64146; reduction for pilgrims walking the Via Francigena), **Albergo Motel Luca, Corso Garibaldi 58 (0125.48697). TO Corso Vercelli 1 (0125.618131, X Sun, but open 8am Mon–Sat).

The Roman colony of Eporedia was founded here in 100BC on the Dora Balthea. Castello d'Ivrea is the fort-like, red-towered castle built in 1328 high up overlooking the town, although most of the tower was destroyed by lightning in the 17th century. Used as a prison from 1750 to 1970, it is now open for visits. Roman amphitheatre, remains of Roman theatre, and 11th-century Torre di Santo Stefano – the only surviving part of a Benedictine abbey founded

Detail of fresco in Ivrea cathedral

1044 and demolished mid-16th century. 10th-century Cattedrale di Santa Maria, built on the remains of a Roman temple.

However, Ivrea is probably best known today for the Olivetti industrial complex, both factories and workers' housing, set up by Camillo Olivetti in 1908 for the manufacture of typewriters and calculating machines and now an international IT giant. Today the buildings also form part of the MAAM, an open-air museum of modern architecture. If you have time the best way to explore Ivrea is to obtain the TO leaflet (in the 'Trekking in Città' series) with a 7km walking tour of the town.

Stage XLV (Everi, 45) in Sigeric's itinerary.

There is a choice of two routes from Ivrea to Santhià. *Option A passes to the north of the Lago di Viverone via the medieval villages of Bollengo, Palazzo Canavese, Roppolo and Cavaglià, while Option B takes the south side of the lake*

Municipio (town hall), Ivrea

via Azeglio and Alice Castello. The northern route is hillier, but with more facilities and places to stay, and became the main route in the 12th and 13th centuries. Sigeric, however, took the southern or 'Roman' option when he made his journey to Rome in AD990. This is 5–6km shorter and more or less flat, but with few places to sleep or buy food. Both routes are waymarked – the northern one with the usual VF signs; the southern one with AIVF signage. Note that after Ivrea (and for most of the way to Rome) there are hardly any public fountains along the route.

To continue (both routes) Turn L onto **Corso Massimo d 'Azeglio** and KSO, passing the **Chiesa di San Lorenzo e San Stefano**, then head along **Corso Vercelli** to the tourist office (in a modern, bright blue building at a junction), which is where the two options split, although there is nothing here to indicate this in the waymarking at present.

OPTION A – NORTHERN ROUTE: IVREA TO SANTHIÀ VIA CAVAGLIÀ

Fork L at the tourist office into **Via Cascinette**. KSO for 500–600m to a roundabout with wayside shrine, then fork L (still Via Cascinette). 400m later fork L onto a minor road (**Via Monte della Guardia**).

109

At junction turn R into woods (*white pilgrim signs start again here*), then turn L shortly afterwards, veering R. The road becomes unsurfaced. Turn next L down side of field. At bend KSO ahead on grass towards **Lago Sirio** (*picnic tables*) and then turn R onto small FP through woods, up and down along RH side of lake. Cross field (*with more picnic tables*), veering R to road on outskirts of

4km Cascinette d'Ivrea (136/820) 241m

Turn L (**Via Lago di Campagna**) to bigger road. Turn L, then R 50m later, to **Via Gorrere**. Turn L at small crossroads onto track into woods, then R on a similar track. KSO. Cross small river and KSO. 1km later turn L. 300m after that reach crossing by bridge, and turn R to minor road (**Via Maresco**) 500–600m later. At T-junction turn L, then 250m later turn R (**Via Vivier**), veering L uphill at fork (still on Via Vivier) leading to main road on outskirts of **Burolo** (260m). *OP in Associazione 'Mondo di Comunità e Famiglia', Via Parrochia 15 (0125.676448).*

KSO(R) ahead, downhill, passing on R small **Chiesa di San Rocco e Sebastiano** (*18th century; 'per voto durante la pestilenza' – it was built to fulfil a vow made during the plague*). Fork L (**Via Bollengo**), passing cemetery (*on R, with sosta di pellegrino (pilgrim resting place) – seat and water*), then turn L at junction (still Via Bollengo) and enter

5km Bollengo (141/815) 250m
Shops, bars, rtes.

Road becomes **Via Burolo**, passing behind **Cappella San Rocco** (*seat in small public garden at sides*) at junction. KSO(L) ahead on **Via Roma** then **Via Cossavella** (*fountain at start*), then KSO(L) ahead at fork (*seats to L*) on **Via delle Scuole**. KSO(R) at fork by wayside shrine, then KSO ahead at crossing (marked 'Palazzo, Piverone') on **Strada da Palazzo**. KSO! Watch out carefully for first turning to the Romanesque **Chiesa San Pietro e Paolo** in **Pessana** (*picnic tables and good place for a rest*).

Turn R by church onto minor road to continue. KSO on **Strada Pianne Inf.**, gradually uphill along side of hill, with splendid views on a clear day. 1km later turn hard R at hairpin bend, then L, then R to the junction with the **Strada da Palazzo** again and turn L along it. KSO.

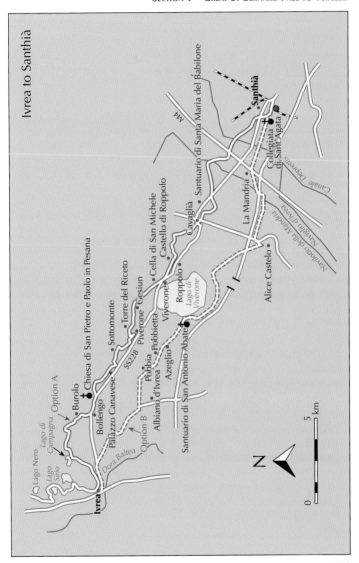

Ivrea to Santhià

2.5km from Bollengo reach outskirts of Palazzo Canavese and turn R (**Via Garibaldi**), veering R to **Piazza Adriano Olivetti** in

4km Palazzo Canavese (145/811) 240m
Rte, PO, shop.

KSO(L) ahead (**Via Vittorio Emmanuele**), veering L to square with municipio, church, the Torre Campanario, chapel and Palatium Acqua, a chilled water dispenser (*5 centimos per litre of either acqua gassata or naturale – take your own bottle*).

Turn L at tower, turn R at end, then turn L down steps 50m later, R down **Via XX Settembre**, then L then R onto **Viale degli Studi**. KSO. Turn L over bridge, veering R through **Sottomonte** and the road becomes unsurfaced. Continue to farm, then turn hard R along grassy track. Reach second field (large) and turn L along RH side of line of trees. 600m later watch out for LH turn in clearing between lines of trees. 120m later turn R onto unsurfaced road, leading to T-junction on outskirts of Piverone.

Turn L, then fork L up **Via della Guietta**, uphill very steeply, veering R. Near top turn L opposite house No 3 onto **Via Disesa**, then turn L again (**Via Roma**), then R (**Via Torrione**), then R along **Via Giovanni Flecchia** (*No 99 has 'Casa per ferie' notice and VF sticker on the door – these facilities are run by the comune of Piverone, see below*), passing church, and reach the clock tower in

4km Piverone (149/807) Pop. 1272
Shops, café, OP in Casa per Ferie La Steiva, Via Giovanni Flecchia 99 (0125.72154 and 328.7077186). Chiesa dei Santi Pietro e Lorenzo.

Continue past arch to **Piazza Marconi** and pass to RH side of church on **Via Castellazzo** (*level!*) then, at bend 600–700m later, KSO(L) ahead downhill. KSO, as the route becomes an unsurfaced road, uphill again. KSO, veering L and then L by farm up onto track along a ridge (*views out to Lago Viverone to R*), passing above/between vines. KSO to

2km Gesiun (151/805)
Ruins of 11th-century Romanesque Chiesa di San Pietro.

Reach road, turn L then immediately R, passing to LH side of farm on a VS, veering R to a walled lane, fairly level. 800m later reach unsurfaced road coming from above L, and turn R then turn L onto tarmac road. This shortly becomes unsurfaced, then tarred at the **Via Cascina di Ponente Beato Federico Albert 1820–1876**. KSO (a very long road) passing **Casale della Via Francigena** (*B&B, 0161.987171 and 339.80355701*) on L.

It is very often misty in this area in the mornings.

KSO, gradually downhill all the time. Pass **Cella di San Michele** over to R (*a 12th-century Benedictine abbey in private hands since 1798*).

At entrance to town, at junction with road coming from back L, KSO ahead on **Via Umberto I**, passing **Oratorio di San Defendante** in

3km Viverone (154/802) 311m

Small town with bars, bakers, shop, PO, farmacia on main road (turn R through public park to access these). **Camping La Rocca, Via Lungo Lago 35 (0161.98416). You are now in the province of Vercelli.

Oratorio di San Defendante – this church was originally dedicated to San Stefano, but its dedication was changed to San Defendante, the patron saint of *contadini* (farm workers), when it was rebuilt in 1600. Oratorio di San Rocco at end of town – 16th century, rebuilt 17th, relief carving of San Rocco on tabernacle door (the 'cupboard' where the reserved sacrament is kept). 18th-century Chiesa dell'Assunta. 14th-century Gothic Chiesa di Santa Maria on site of previous church – this was previously the parish church (until 1778), was restored in 1926, 1966 and 1977, and is now a national monument.

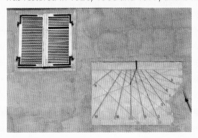

Sundial on house wall, Viverone

Continue past municipio on **Via Umberto I**, passing slightly bigger chapel on L, and KSO ahead (*bar part-way up on L*), uphill all the time. At end pass large brick **Oratorio di San Rocco**. (*There are many brick churches in this area, often with stuccoed facades, and this one, like most of the others, is rarely open to visit.*)

113

At end of street KSO ahead on SP419 (*pavement to start with*), passing **Chiesa di Santa Maria** and cemetery on **Via Viverone** (*Tenuta della Cura, B&B, on opposite side of the road, 345.3530779*) into **Roppolo**. Pass **Villa Rampone** (*on L, Villa delle Rose and small church, formerly part of the monastery of Santa Margherita*). *There are many sundials in the area.* Continue ahead on **Via G Massa** and KSO (*seats at junction*) to **Chiesa di Santa Maria dei Rosario e San Michele** and the municipio in the centre of

2km Roppolo (156/800) 350m

Bakery, bar? **B&B Casa del Movimento Lento, Via Al Castello 8 (0161.987866 and 349.2356561; at end of village, prior telephoning essential), **B&B Villa Emilia 1899, Piazza Rampone 1 (next door to Villa delle Rose, 347.5879408), B&B Le Lune, Via Cavaglià 2 (0161.980938 and 346.2109706). Chiesa delle Vergine del Rosario, Chiesetta di San Rocco (with fountain), several interesting old houses on main street.

Turn L up **Via Al Castello**, gradually uphill, below castle, then at junction by small church turn R along **Via Petiva** (*restaurant on R*). KSO and pass another cemetery (*seats*). 300–400m later look out for RH turn at bend – ie KSO(R) – onto shady track, veering R, gradually downhill between fields, then woods, emerging on minor road 1.5km later. Turn L, then immediately R by sign pointing (back uphill) to **Cascina Moncavallino**, going gently downhill, then KSO(R) 200m later on track alongside wall (on R). Turn L at end past sports ground onto minor road, then KSO(L) at bend on **Via Moriondo**. Reach main road (large church with octagonal dome ahead) and turn R (*shop on R*).

To visit the circular Oratorio di San Rocco, KSO here along Via Roma then retrace your steps to continue.

Turn L here, passing the **Chiesa di San Michele Arcangelo** (the large church) into **Piazza Parrochiale** in

3.5km Cavaglià (159.5/796.5) 271m

Shops etc, bank, farmacia. Ostello comunale, Via General Salino (0161.96038 and 0161.967016), donation. You are now in the province of Biella.

18th-century Chiesa di San Michele Arcangelo. Circular Oratorio di San Rocco – the church was rebuilt in its present form in 1744, enlarged in 1836, and has a depiction of San Rocco in the niche over the door.

KSO ahead on **Via Maria Mainella**, passing **municipio**, then at end turn L towards junction with large red-brick castle ahead, the **Castello Rondino**, then turn R immediately afterwards. 100m later fork R up **Strada Vicinale della Crocetta**, which becomes a lane, veering R then L. Continue ahead on **Via Don Alberto Virgilio** and at end (*very large church and cemetery over to L on main road, the Santuario di Santa Maria del Babilone, built about 1600 on the site of a previous church*) turn R, passing farm. Turn L at T-junction onto minor road, wending its way between fields.

Turn L at junction 500m later (*seat to R*), veering R, then KSO(R) ahead at bend, veering L to SP143. (*Here you are only 250m away from the cemetery and the very large church.*) Cross over by factory and KSO on second road (ie R of two), veering R. KSO, passing entrance drive/road to several cascine. 1.5–2km later the road becomes unsurfaced. KSO. Cross two bridges (over two rivers) and KSO, veering R then L. KSO, ignoring turnings, until you reach a crossing of tarmac roads, with farm (*road stops being unsurfaced here*) 100m to R and motorway bridge over to the L.

Turn L towards motorway, veering L then R to cross bridge over it. Turn hard L at end of crash barrier (waymarking not clear here) along side of field, then R 100m later on unsurfaced road to pass under railway line. *In this area red painted pilgrim signs have replaced the white ones.*

KSO. 500m later cross bridge over a canal. Continue ahead, then 200m later turn R on grassy track along side of dyke, pass farm and KSO ahead along side of dyke again. Veer L, R and KSO for 1.5km or more on **Strada Barletta** (a grassy track) until reaching a minor road by a farm (*seat at end*). Turn L (**Via Monginevro**) then turn R (by wayside shrine). Cross ring road and continue on other side on **Strada Vecchia di Biella** (not marked at start).

At crossroads with **Via Gramisci** KSO ahead on **Via Svizzera**, turn L onto **Via E De Amicis**, and turn R onto **Via Jacopo Durando** into **Piazza Roma**, with **municipio** and **Antico Pieve di San Stefano** (12th century, now the Collegiata Sant'Agatha) in

10.5km Santhià (170/786) Pop. 10,000, 183m

See box at end of Option B.

For the continuing route, see after Santhià box, below.

OPTION B – SOUTHERN ROUTE: IVREA TO SANTHIÀ VIA AZEGLIO AND THE SANTUARIO DI SAN ANTONIO ABATE

Buy food and take water with you before leaving Ivrea. Most of the route is on quiet tarmac roads and is flat, and there is quite a lot of shade. It has recently been waymarked throughout with the AIVF's own signage, adequately, but with few 'reassurance' markings in sections where you simply keep straight on ahead all the time.

From the tourist office in **Ivrea** (a bright blue building at the junction of the **Via Cascinetti** and the **Corso Vercelli**) continue R ahead (along **Corso Vercelli**), despite waymarks for the northern option indicating that you fork L here, and reach a big roundabout with two petrol stations. KSO ahead here for 200m, then at road KM2 fork R along **Via Casale** (*the AIVF waymarking starts here*). 200m after that turn first L, opposite a bus stop, down **Via Bollengo** (signposted to 'Via Fornace') and KSO to reach an empty wayside shrine. Here KSO(R) ahead on the **Via della Fornace**, a very long road.

As you leave Ivrea the countryside and scenery change rapidly, and the hills and mountains visibly shrink on the horizon to L and R. There are flat maize fields to either side, and fields, houses or farms every few hundred metres. Few places to sit down and hardly any fountains.

KSO. 1km later pass a gypsy encampment and KSO ahead. KSO(R) at fork then 500m later, at next fork, by a house (**Cascina La Rossa**) KSO(L) ahead, still on the **Via della Fornace**. Cross over a stream (road bridge) and pass a group of large houses, the **Case degli Fornese** (5km from Ivrea).

KSO(R) at fork ahead to **Sant'Anna**, another group of houses. Pass them, then at a junction with a bus stop/terminus of suburban bus No 1 from Ivrea 1km later, KSO(R) ahead to a junction with a bigger provincial road coming from back L, with a house (**Cascina Sant'Anna**) and a small chapel ('per Maria ad Jesum') on the RH side. KSO(R) along the road for nearly 1km, leaving the comune of Bollengo and entering that of Albiano d'Ivrea. Then, just before the town entrance boards for **Albiano**, turn L onto a minor tarmac road signposted 'Pobbia'. KSO along this (fairly shady) ignoring any turns to L or R for 2km to

9.5km Pobbia 239m

Trattoria Angela opposite church (X Mon). Chiesa della Madonna della Neve.

Continue through village past church (*seats*) and KSO on road. 1.5km later pass through **Pobbietta** (a hamlet), then nearly 1km after that, at junction (with 'stop' sign at end of lane coming from back L), fork R steeply uphill on smaller

Ivrea, 'replacement window'

tarmac road to a bigger one. Cross over and continue along street ahead (**Via Luigi Rolla**, but not marked at start) to a T-junction. Turn L here along **Via Roma** to **Piazza Massimo d'Azeglio** and the **municipio** in the centre of

3km Azeglio Pop. 1303, 254m

Shop, farmacia, bar (with limited food), rte. B&B Giardini Semplice, Via Roma (0125.687549). Pilgrims should make sure they have enough to eat and drink with them, as – except for Alice Castello (off route) – there are no facilities of any kind until Santhià, 21km further on.

Originally a Roman penal colony, Azeglio became a fortified town in the 11th century. Castello/palazzio (remodelled in the 19th century), Baroque Rococo Chiesa di San Martino Vescovo (1790). Once famous for the manufacture of chairs, Azeglio is now an agricultural town.

From the square in Azeglio KSO ahead on **Via Roma**, passing second church (on L). KSO at crossing (still Via Roma) marked 'Boscarina' and 'Santuario de S Antonio Abade', passing a round chapel, and then KSO(R) at fork on **Via Boscarina**. Fork L by children's playground, then turn L opposite tall wayside shrine (on R). KSO. *(Note wayside shrine with Black Madonna and child partway along, the Vergine d'Oropa. Monte Oropa is one of the nine sacred mountains of Piemonte and Lombardia, where Saint Eusebius of Vercelli founded a sanctuary and brought the original statue of the Black Madonna from the Middle East in the early fourth century AD.)* Go through **Boscarina** (a hamlet) and reach (on R) the

2km Santuario di San Antonio Abate 275m

Large white church, 11th–12th centuries, with covered porch, seats and fountain. Notice says that this was the hermitage of San Antonio and a hospice for pilgrims on the road to Rome via Ivrea and Vercelli – there was a pilgrim hospice here by the 12th century. Nice place for a short rest.

Santuario di S.Antonio Abate
Antico Eremo ed Ospizio per i pellegrini posto sulla strada Romana Ivrea-Vercelli
anteriore al XII sec.

Notice outside the Santuario di San Antonio Abate

KSO ahead on the road, which then becomes unsurfaced, ignoring turnings to R and L (*shady*). 2km later the route opens out with a view over the Lago di Viverone to LH side. Shortly afterwards leave the comune of Azeglio by a large farmhouse at the side of the road. KSO ahead all the time, passing **Cascina Baserna** (on R), after which the route does a series of bends, gradually uphill, and at the top reaches a minor tarmac road. KSO(R) ahead along it for 400m to a

5km T-junction with the SP41 290m

Road also known locally as the Strada della Polveriera.

Turn R here and KSO in the direction of *Alice Castello*. *Here pilgrims leave the province of Biella and enter that of Vercelli.*

KSO, ignoring turnings, for 4km, cross the motorway and go gently downhill to the town entry boards. KSO ahead here for another 500–600m, then turn L into the **Via San Sebastiano**. Continue for 200m to a crossroads with the **Via Cavaglià** and the **Chiesa di San Sebastiano** on the outskirts of

5km Alice Castello Pop 2603, 253m

Shops, banks etc, but note that the waymarked route does not go into the centre of the town. To get there, turn R long the Via Cavaglià at the junction with the Chiesa di San Sebastiano and then retrace your steps to continue. B&B Garden, Via Giardino 34 (0161.90859 and 347.5100510). The Salussolia family, Via Circonvallazione 22b (0161.90142 and 338.9404282), offers simple accommodation to pilgrims with a credenziale and a sleeping bag, on a donation basis.

Medieval castle, substantially rebuilt in the 18th and 19th centuries. 18th-century Chiesa di San Nicola and 16th-century Chiesa dei Santi Fabiano e Sebastiano, built with funds from the local population in thanksgiving for being freed of the plague, and containing frescoes depicting Saint Roch.

Turn L along the **Via Cavaglià** and then KSO(L) ahead on the SP593 when it joins from back R. Pass a petrol station, and just before the motorway turn R onto a strada bianca (unsurfaced road) marked 'Agriturismo Il Ciliego' and KSO.

KSO ahead at first junction 700m later, then at next, 1.5km after that, turn L onto a tarmac road, passing **Cascina Stella** (on R, a large modern farm), and 300m later reach another T-junction. Turn R here onto **Strada Ciorlucca**. 600m later cross 'Il Naviglio', a canal, turn L on other side, then at LH bank take the right hand of two LH turns, leading 400m later to the motorway in front of you. Turn R alongside it on a small tarmac road, below it to its RH side.

500m after that, turn R away from the motorway, between fields, and 400m later, by two houses on the R, turn R alongside a second motorway. At the end KSO(L), veering R then L down a slope to go underneath it. On the other side KSO ahead alongside a field, then between them towards a large railway embankment ahead. Turn L here and KSO ahead along its LH side. On reaching a bridge (above you on your R) at the end, turn L to go under a motorway slip road, then go under another motorway bridge 100m later.

Continue ahead on the other side, past a farm and then the **Cascina Mandria** (on R). Turn L, R and L again to go under a railway line. KSO for 1km on the other side (this is the **Strada Mandria**, but is not marked at the start) until you reach the main road from Alice Castello coming from back R – this is the **Via Valdora**, which then becomes the **Strada per Alice Castello** and then the **Corso Santo Ignazio de Santhià**. Follow this right to the very end (with a large public garden to R), then KSO ahead again at a junction along the **Corso Nuova Italia**. Turn third L into **Via Roma** and then the **Piazza Roma**, with the Chiesa Sant'Agata, the municipio and the pilgrim refuge in the centre of Santhià.

10.5km Santhià (170/786) Pop. 10,000, 183m

Shops, bars, banks, etc. Trenitalia to Milan/Turin. TO in municipio. OP run by the Amici della Via Francigena di Santhià in Via Madonnetta 4, just off the Piazza Roma by the church; 8pl., key from Caffé della Piazza (333.6162086) or other addresses posted on the refuge door. The only hotel in the town itself is the ***Hotel Nuovo Victoria, Piazza Verdi 1 (0161.94702), by the railway station; Hotel Residencia ***San Massimo, Corso XXV Aprile 18, (0161.94617) is outside the town on the ring road on the eastern side of Santhià.

The town's name comes from Sanctae Agathae, a fourth-century saint for whom the parish church, Collegiata Sant'Agatha, is named; this formerly had a hospice for pilgrims and other travellers. Cripta Santo Stefano. Chiesa della Santi Trinità.

Stage XLIV (Sca Agatha, 44) in Sigeric's itinerary.

Both routes

With your back to the municipio KSO ahead on **Via Roma** then turn L on to **Corso Nuova Italia** and continue right to the very end. Here veer L to cross several railway lines by lengthy FB with a ramp as well as steps. (If you come down the ramp, as opposed to the steps, KSO at end on street with canal to your RH side.) 350m

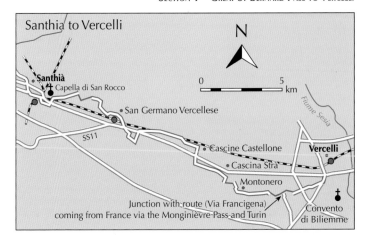

Santhià to Vercelli

N

later, by the town exit board and at junction with this street and the SP143, reach the **Cappella San Rocco**. *Fresco over main door (inside porch) of three figures has San Rocco on L, a saint with a halo and sore, no dog, but also a pilgrim with stick, gourd and scallop shell on (his) LH lapel of cape.*

Turn L here along the SP134, then at road KM4 turn L onto a minor road. Cross railway line, veering R to continue past farms, parallel to SP134.

KSO. 2km later, by brick electricity tower, turn R onto an earth track. 500m later turn L on similar track. 1km after that cross dyke to R and turn L towards farm buildings ahead. At the buildings veer R and then L to cross bridge over **Canale Cavour**, turn R on other side alongside canal then veer L. 700–800m later reach a railway line at a bend and KSO on its LH side until you reach a radio mast. Turn L, 250m later turn R, veering L then R 400m later to road. Cross over, then 100m after that turn R onto a more minor road. KSO, and 400m later reach the railway station in

8.5km San Germano Vercellese (178.5/777.5) Pop. 1790, 159m

Two shops, bank (+CD), bakery, PO, farmacia, bar/rte **Albergo delle Minere, Corso Matteotti 89 (0161.933866), and two other bars.

18th-century Chiesa di San Germano, the fifth-century Bishop of Auxerre who died in Ravenna in AD484. According to tradition his body was taken back to France following the route he had taken on his outward journey, causing miracles and prodigies to happen at every stopping place.

The section from here to Vercelli does a lot of zig-zags to avoid the extremely dangerous SS11. The road has constant very fast traffic, no proper hard shoulder on the RH side and only raised flagstones on the left, which are very nerve-wracking to walk on as there are high-speed heavy vehicles whizzing past all the time. There have been (and still are) a lot of fatal accidents, as the bouquets of flowers by the roadside attest. As a result the AIVF and the local VF association have waymarked a quiet, safe alternative, described here, although it is considerably longer than the 15km route from Santhià to Vercelli via the SS11.

Turn R to go down a ramp, pass under the railway tracks and up ramp/steps on other side to exit and reach **Piazza Pietro Perazzo**. Turn L (**Via Modesto Cugnolo**), then at junction at end turn L (**Via Cavour**). *If you want to go to the shops and other facilities, KSO ahead here and then retrace your steps to continue.*

Continue down **Via Cavour** to **Piazza Guiseppe Mazzini**, passing **Chiesa di San Germano** (*brick with stone facade*) and **Chiesa del Corpus Domini** (*18th century*) adjoining it, and continue ahead on **Via Jacopi Suigo** to the **Piazza Garibaldi** and the **Palazzo del Comune** (town hall). Turn R.

Cross the SP11, turn L along the side of a public garden then R down the side of the **Carabinieri** building. Cross the canal, and then turn L immediately along the side of the **Canali d'Ivrea** on **Viale Augusto Franzoi**. Reach SP11 again, then turn R immediately on **Via per Salasco**, passing behind a petrol station to open country with cereal fields to either side. 150m after a sharp RH bend turn L onto a gravel track with electricity cables. 300–400m later fork L onto a similar track, then turn L 100m later onto a dirt road coming from **Cascina Pettiva** and turn L back to the SP11 again. Cross over (very carefully), turn left, and 70–80m later turn R over bridge over canal, veering R on other side on earth track. *Here, frustratingly, you are barely 200m from the petrol station passed some 15–20mins ago...*

KSO. 1km later cross dirt road coming from bridge over railway line (to L) and KSO ahead again on other side. *No shade at all in this area.*

Track veers R to go alongside railway line for a while. Go under a road bridge and KSO ahead again.

After passing another farm (over to L) track veers R away from railway, crosses canal and passes large pond on L. KSO ahead for 1km, veering R and then L to reach **Cascina Castellone** (a very large farm) 1km later. Turn R here onto farm entrance road and reach SP11 again, 7km after San Germano.

Cross over, turn L on other side, then turn R by electric pylons onto a VS between more cereal fields. Cross dyke; then, at crossing of similar tracks 400m after SP11 and before a line of trees and a very large farm ahead, turn L on track parallel to SP11. KSO for 500–600m, then cross dyke and turn L, veering R. Reach minor road, turn L, then just before SP11 turn R on grassy path to a small (pale yellow) building that looks more like an ordinary house than a chapel, the **Cappella di Maria Madre del Cammino sulla Via Francigena** (*small plank bridge over dyke to access it – seats*).

Continue on path (after stopping at chapel), and 300–400m later reach minor road on the outskirts of

8km Cascina di Strà (186.5/769.5)

The Via Francigena does not go into the village, but there is a bar/rte on the RH side of the main road at the entrance at road KM67 (X Thurs, with a menu fisso). To go there turn L here, then R (or turn R along hard shoulder from chapel), then retrace your steps to continue. The village takes its name from *strata*, referring to the road that the Via Francigena formerly passed along.

If you are not going to the village, turn R here along a minor road, then 500m later turn L over bridge onto grassy track through fields, parallel to the SP11 to start with, then veering R, L and R again (alongside canal/dyke to R), turning L by bridge to enter village, passing church on L (*seat and fountain*) in

2km Montonero (188.5/767.5)

Pilgrim cyclists before Vercelli

Continue to junction with tarmac road (to L) and KSO ahead on grassy track alongside a dyke for nearly 2km. Reach a bridge crossing a canal at right angles to you and turn R along it. 150m later turn L over two bridges, and KSO on FP with canal to R (*Vercelli visible ahead*). At end (*waymarking very poor*) cross another small bridge by a sluice gate and KSO ahead, veering R and then L alongside bigger canal to next sluice gate, then veer L towards farm ahead. KSO past it alongside canal (to R). KSO, following canal round to R, then at T-junction by bridge (to R) shortly before a farm, turn L towards busy road ahead. (*When passing the farm, a RH turn leads to Santiago(!), but straight ahead to Rome – this is where the pilgrim route coming from France and crossing the Alps over the Montgenèvre Pass and then continuing via Turin joins up with this one.*)

Cross ring road and KSO ahead on grassy track to LH side of dyke. Pass between buildings, turn R opposite sports field (**Via Cascina Martorelli**) then L (**Via Giovanni Paisello**). KSO at first roundabout, then after a second one fork (not turn) R down **Via Puccini**, then turn R into **Via L Einaudi**.

If you want to sleep in the pilgrim-only accommodation in the Convento di Billiemme, turn R here onto Via Trino and then turn L along Corso Avogadro di Quaregna, going up over the railway line and then continuing ahead for 1km until reaching the Piazza Sardegna. Turn R here up Corso Salamano, and the Convento is on the L, next to the church and just before the cemetery.

To continue the following morning you do not need to go into the centre of Vercelli, but can go directly to the bridge over the Fiume Sesia, where you will pick up the waymarks again. Retrace your steps to the Piazza Sardegna, then fork

Vercelli, main square

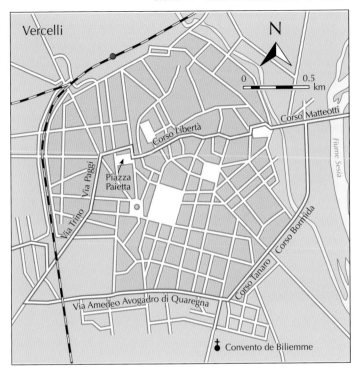

R along the Corso Tanaro. Continue along Corso Bormida and then Via Viviani to the junction with Corso Matteotti, where you turn R onto Corso Novara to cross the river.

From Via Enaudi turn left into **Via Trino** and cross railway line (Strada Trino). KSO(L) ahead on **Via Giuseppe Paggi**. Turn R, cross **Piazza Baldo Mazzucchelli**, then KSO ahead on **Via Goito** to **Piazza Pietro Paietta Nero** in the centre of

8.5km Vercelli (197/759) Pop. 47,837, 131m

OPs: Convento di Billiemme, Corso Salamano 139, has a pilgrim dormitory (6pl.), 10€. Hotels: *Croce de Malta, Corso Prestinari 2 (0161.124432), *Albergo Valsesia, Via G Ferraris 104 (0161.250842 and 349.3942427), HR Giardinetto,

Vercelli cathedral, interior

Via L Sereno 3 (0161.257230), **Albergo Cerruti, Corso Novara 71 (on other side of the river) (0161.213567). Trenitalia to Milan, Turin; TGV to Paris.

Large town with all facilities, also known as the Capitale Europea del Riso ('European rice capital'). Vercelli is a town of probably Celtic origin, and has been important since Roman times both as a staging post on the pilgrim route to Rome and for merchants travelling all over Europe. As a result it always had a significant hospitality structure, and 16 ospedale for all types of traveller are documented from the 12th century, both within and without the city walls. From 1115 a Hospitale Sancti Eusebio is recorded – connected, in all probability, to the cathedral presbytery. From 1162 a Hospitale Scotorum dedicated to Saint Bridget is also recorded, an establishment set up to provide accommodation for pilgrims coming from the British Isles. The Sala Dugentesco, still standing, near the Basilica Sant'Andrea, was built in 1223 as an ospitale for pilgrims. Today Vercelli is the headquarters of the Associazione 'Amici della Via Francigena'.

The town's sights include the Basilica di Sant'Andrea, the Duomo di Sant'Eusebio (first Bishop of Vercelli and Piemonte) and the Palazzo Arcivescovile (Archbishop's Palace), which houses the new Museo del Tesoro del Duomo (Cathedral Treasury museum), containing, among other rare works of art, the Vercelli Book, the first known book in existence to be written in Anglo-Saxon.

Stage XLIII (Vercel, 43) in Sigeric's itinerary.

VERCELLI TO THE PASSO DELLA CISA

Footbridge at entrance to old part of Fidenza

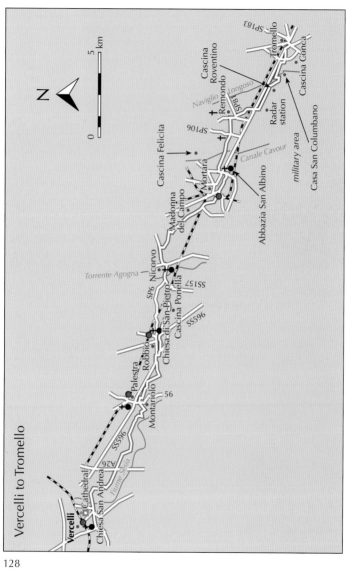

Vercelli to Tromello

SECTION 2
Vercelli to the Passo della Cisa (244km)

Rice fields after Vercelli

To leave Vercelli, cross the square and continue R ahead along the **Corso Libertà** (*a very long street*), cross **Piazza Cugnolo**, continue along **Corso Matteotti** and then **Corso Novara** to cross the **Fiume Sesia**. On other side, some 300m later, by bend, turn R down **Strada Boarone**, a minor road. 300m later fork R before farm and KSO between fields. KSO at first turning, then turn L at second, just before another farm, veering R. At crossing with embankment/banked-up farm road, turn L along it and KSO. 1.5km later go under motorway. *Many farms and semi-deserted farms in this area.*

3–4km after going under motorway you pass a VF notice announcing that there are now 720km to Rome!

5km after joining this road (just after No 43 on the 'Magistro' boards) watch out for RH turn down slope, then veer L alongside the **Fiume Sesia**. 400–500m later (not waymarked) turn L away from river at right angles, in the direction of Palestra, crossing a wooden bridge over a tributary of the Sesia, and then turn R by a small farm. Veer L, then turn L towards Palestra, emerging on **Via Porto**. Turn R into **Via Garibaldi** near the end of

11.5km Palestra (208.5/747.5) Pop. 2000, 120m

Shops etc (turn L along road at entrance, and then retrace your steps to continue). Trenitalia.

Site of a fortified *castrum* in medieval times as well as a *domus infirmorum* (shelter for the infirm) run by the Hospitalers of Sant'Antonio di Vienne. Romanesque Chiesa di San Martino.

Turn L (*waymarking in both directions*). *You are now in Lombardy.*

Continue ahead then continue on **Via Giovanni Cappo**. There are now two options for Robbio.

OPTION A

The waymarked route to Robbio takes a lengthy detour to keep off the road, which is not, in fact, all that busy. So if you are short of time or in bad weather you can use this option (1.5km shorter), which simply continues on the road as far as the roundabout at the entrance to Robbio. KSO ahead there, towards the centre, then turn R by a petrol station onto **Via Giacomo Matteotti**. After that turn second L into **Via Rosasco** (5km).

Chiesa di San Pietro, Robbio

Otherwise, from the Via Giovanni Cappo in Palestra turn R into **Via Rosasco** and leave the **Città di Palestro** on minor road. Veer L, then 150m after bend watch out for track to L, by back of 'bend' sign, veering R to continue above dyke to L below. Follow it round for 600–700m, then turn L over river by a canal in a concrete trough (ruined house to L), then turn R onto clear track, passing to side of large factory. KSO.

1km later reach a gravel road coming from back L. Turn R here, veering L, then 100m later turn L, veering L and R, L several times by farm and continue until you reach a minor road 1km later. Turn L then R over bridge, KSO to the SS596, cross it and enter Robbio on **Via Giacomo Matteotti** then turn R onto **Via Rosasco** (6.5km).

Both routes

Pass the brick **Abbadia di San Valeriano** (*part of a former monastery; the present building dates from 1081*) and continue on **Via Cernavia** (*turn L part-way along to the main street if you want to visit the town centre, then continue ahead, forking first R to the church*) to the junction (by public garden) with the (also brick) **Chiesa di San Pietro** in

6km Robbio (214.5/741.5) Pop. 6145, 122m

Shops, banks etc. OP in Oratorio Parrochiale, Piazza San Stefano 2 (donation). **Albergo Moderno, Via Mazzini 1–5 (0384.670367), Hotel Rte La Mondina, SS596 dei Cairoli (0384.679611 and 339.1951317). Trenitalia.

Former Abbadia di San Valeriano, Chiesa di San Pietro, with hospicium for pilgrims here in 1236. 14th-century castello built on site of another dating from the 11th century.

Fork R to side of church to continue on **Via Mortara**. 300m later fork L up **Via Rogetta**. Cross road ahead at end and continue on other side on gravel/earth road leading past sports stadium (on R) into open country. Pass sewage works/water treatment plant, cross bridge over canal/dyke (the Roggia), fork L and pass entrance to **Cascina Ponella** (a farm) on L and a big hangar on R. KSO ahead. *The area around here continues to be completely flat, with dykes between the rice fields.*

KSO, ignoring turnings for 1.5km, and then go over a level crossing. KSO, then 300m later tarmac road joins from R. KSO ahead for 400m, cross large dyke and reach SP157. Turn R, cross **Torrente Agogna**, pass cemetery (*seats outside*) and continue for 1km, arriving in **Via Robbio** at T-junction in the centre of

6km Nicorvo (220.5/735.5) 114m

Bar/Tabac, bakery. OP available in Casa Parrochiale, Piazza Libertà 2 (0384.524042), or ask in bar.

Turn L (**Via IV Novembre**) then R at church on **Via Albonese**, marked 'Mortara'. 1km later, just before a long line of trees on L and before a 'bend' sign and an isolated tree on R, turn R over dyke onto grassy farm track. 200m later, at T-junction of similar tracks, turn L towards **Cascina Afficiati**. Cross farm road, pass to LH side of building and KSO ahead through fields.

400–500m later turn R to cross bridge over dyke, veering L towards **Madonna del Campo** (village) ahead of you to R. KSO, ignoring turns, until track becomes **Via Maestra** and reach the church in

5.5km Madonna del Campo (226/730) 112m

Church known from 12th century as Santa Maria de Pertica, rebuilt 15th century; open 8.30am–4.30/5pm and worth a visit for its splendid frescoes, including one of Saint James as a pilgrim.

Continue ahead on **Via Maestra**. Go over level crossing, KSO on other side, then at junction 1km later fork L (*but turn R here if you want to go shopping for food, then retrace your steps*) and continue ahead to station entrance on other side in

3km Mortara (229/727) Pop. 14,464 108m

Shops etc. **Albergo/Rte Bottala, Corso Garibaldi 1 (opposite station entrance; 0384.99021 and 0384.915930), ***Albergo San Michele, Corso Garibaldi 20 (0384.98614 and 0384.99106), Albergo della Torre, Contrada della Torre 7 (near Basilica di San Lorenzo; 0384.90775). Supermarket on Corso Torino (behind railway station). OP 2km further on – see Abbazia di San Alcuino, below. Trenitalia.

Town of Gallic origin, then a fortified city in Roman times, Mortara was an important road junction to the main towns along the River Pô in the Middle Ages. Abbazia di Santa Croce dates from 1080, rebuilt 16th century. Gothic Basilica di San Lorenzo.

Turn R at station along **Corso Garibaldi**, passing **Chiesa di Santa Croce** (on L) and **municipio** (on L) to **Piazza Martiri della Libertà**. KSO(L) ahead on **Corso Cavour**, passing to R of municipio, then follow **Via Parini** to a roundabout (**Rondò Carlo Magno**). KSO ahead here along **Via S Albino Alcuino** (not marked at start), then just before junction turn R and cross road via underpass. KSO on other side, then turn L along RH side of SS596.

2km Abbazia di San Alcuino (231/725) 106m

OP available in abbey (0384.298609 and 348.4283403).
 Abbey founded in the fifth century; reconstructed in 774 by Charlemagne and then again in the 16th century. Visits by prior appointment.

You are now, it seems, 1233km from Canterbury, with 754km left to go to Rome…
 Turn L along SS596, go over crossing with traffic lights (*large supermarket on L*), then turn R on earth road/track, signposted 'Cascina Felicita'. At fork at end of woods, fork R and KSO. 1km later cross brick bridge over canal at R angles to the path you are on, cross over and KSO on similar track on other side. Cross a canal/dyke and small tarmac road (*village of Casoni di San Albini over to R*), KSO ahead, cross two more canals and reach a tarmac road at a T-junction opposite a large, ornate cemetery (*seats*) on the outskirts of

5km Remondo (236/730) 98m

Bar, shop.

Turn R here, then turn L (marked 'Gamolo') by small square (*bar, shop*) and continue past church, then at junction by war memorial turn R into **Via Arturo Ferrabin**, passing sports field (on L). At next junction (still the Via Arturo Ferrabin) KSO(L) at fork by caravan site. The track becomes earth/gravel, and just after crossing the railway line reach the SS596 (main road) again. Cross over to a similar track on the other side, then 300m later turn L onto another similar track, passing to the LH side of radar masts. KSO.
 3km later pass to LH side of **Cascina Roventino**, a large farm. Cross its entrance road, then continue ahead on path to LH side of dyke, veering R and then L behind buildings. KSO, then 400m later track turns L by small concrete building (electric post). Turn L 150m later, and then R 150m after that, alongside

133

a short section of canal at first (which you can hear but not see), then KSO with small river to L after crossing it, when it does a bend to R. KSO at crossing, then pass entrance road to **Casa San Columbano**, then veer R when you see the slip road to the flyover above you to L. Turn L at T-junction 100m later. KSO(L) ahead at next junction and reach main road.

Cross over and continue on track that becomes **Via Roncti dei Legionarei**. Turn R at end (big VF sign) into **Via Cavour**, then **Via Trenti** and then **Via Danti**, passing 17th-century **Chiesa di San Rocco** (on L), and reach **Piazza Campeggi** and bell tower in centre of

---

7km Tromello (243/713) 96m

Shops etc. OP in Ospedale San Martino, Via Branca 1, donation (0382.86020, 335.6609347, 349.3325080). **Hotel le Duca de Tromello, Via Marconi 4 (0382.86494 and 347.6944734). Chiesa di San Martino, just off piazza, 17th–19th centuries. 17th-century Chiesa di San Rocco.

Stage XII (Tremel, 42) in Sigeric's itinerary.

Turn L here into **Dr G Mussoni** and then at end turn R into **Via G Marconi**, the main road, and continue along it (*supermarket on L, with water dispenser – own bottle needed*). Cross the **Torrente Terdoppio** and turn L on **Via Borgo S Siro**. Go over level crossing, then turn R immediately onto **Via Cascinino** (marked 'Cascina Pavese'). 300m later fork R by an enclosure with an *oleodotto* (oil pipline) inside it onto grassy track. Pass large farm complex (**Cascina Pavese**) over to your L and KSO at crossing.

Reach a wide canal and turn R alongside it (don't cross over it). When it does a sharp LH bend 200m later you have a choice – turn L to visit the Santuario Basilica Madonna delle Bozzole or KSO(R) ahead to go into Garlasco. The two options join up again after shortly after that.

OPTION A – VIA THE SANTUARIO BASILICA MADONNA DELLE BOZZOLE

(1km longer) turn L along the RH bank of the canal, then pass to its LH side after crossing a track. Reach the SP206, where the canal does a sharp bend to the L, cross over, turn L on other side, then veer R on track through fields. Pass two junctions of tracks then veer L to the SP176 and the

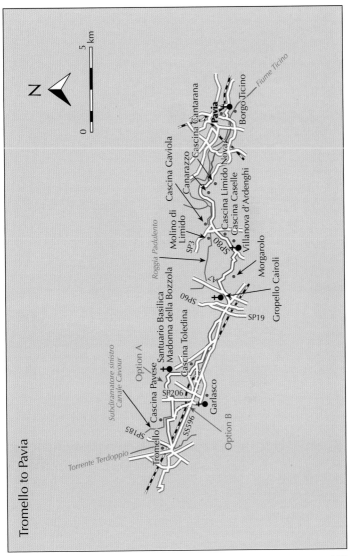

Tromello to Pavia

7km Santuario Basilica Madonna delle Bozzole

OP available (0382.822117).

On the first Sunday in September 1465 Maria, a 13-year-old deaf and dumb girl from Garlasco, was leading her flock to pasture when suddenly the sky turned black, with a storm approaching. She tried to take cover in the roof of a niche with a fresco depicting the Virgin Mary when, equally suddenly, the Virgin Mary herself appeared to Maria surrounded by a great light and asking her to tell all the people of Garlasco to build a sanctuary there, as protection for the whole of the Lomellina area. Maria did as she was bidden, and – since a miracle had obviously occurred, as she could now both speak and hear – a small church was built on the site shortly afterwards. This was enlarged in 1600, renovated many times since, and granted basilica status in 1927. The name 'Bozzola' derives from *buslà*, the local dialect term for a bush, as there was a lot of hawthorn in the area where the apparition was seen.

To continue cross the SP176 on the LH side of a canal, veering R. Reach the SP185, cross over, continue ahead on other side veering L, pass the **Cascina Toledina**, and reach a track coming from back R (*the option coming from Garlasco joins up with you here*).

OPTION B – VIA GARLASCO

Fork R (ie KSO(R) ahead) and KSO, ignoring turns, gradually veering R (after you can see the big industrial estate ahead of you) until route becomes **Via Grassano**. Go over level crossing and reach main road just before a junction with traffic lights at entrance to

6km Garlasco (249/707) 91m

Shops etc. Castello from different periods with Renaissance tower. 18th-century parish church of Vergine dell'Assunzione e San Francesco.

Turn L on **Via Cavour**, pass roundabout with large supermarket on L and continue ahead right through the town. The road becomes **Via Pavia**. From **Piazza della Repubblica** (on main road – still SS596) KSO ahead, with the **municipio** to L and the **Chiesa dell'Assunta** (*18th century, but on site of Romanesque Santa*

Chiesa di San Rocco, Gropello Cairoli

Maria; frescoes from fourth century). After crossing a dyke/channel reach mini-roundabout with supermarket to R and turn L down **Via Dante Alighieri** (not marked at start but signposted 'Vetrero Melotti'). Turn R at end on tarmac lane leading to open country and go over a level crossing. 400m later reach junction with bridge over Canale Cavour (*this is where the route from the detour to the Madonna delle Bozzole joins from back L*).

137

Both routes

Turn R here along RH side of canal and KSO. 1km later reach SP206. Cross over and KSO ahead again. 250m later cross minor road, then 150m after that fork R away from canal on earth road. KSO, passing cemetery (on R) and small way-side chapel on L (*seat*). Continue ahead, ignoring turns, and veering R as the road becomes the **Via Chiesulo**, to SS596 again at entrance to town. 200m after chapel fork L onto grassy lane. Cross FB over wide canal and turn R along it, then turn L onto main road to Gropello Cairoli. Turn L (**Via Marconi**) to brick **Chiesa di San Giorgio Martire** in

5.5km Gropello Cairoli (254.5/701.5) Pop. 4213, 90m

All facilities. OP in parish centre in Piazza San Giorgio (behind church), donation (0382.815049 – note that it is essential to phone ahead). **Hotel/ rte Italia, Corso della Libertà 160–214 (0382.815082).

Chiesa di San Giorgio Martire (14th–19th centuries, parish church). Chiesa di San Rocco, 18th century; medallion of San Rocco above front

door outside, with saint as pilgrim (stick, gourd, scallop shell on shoulder), but also with halo and dog – portrayal from the knees up only. Inside, to LH side of altar rail, in a large glass cubicle, is a life-size, free-standing sculpture with a worried-looking younger saint (the outside one looks older) in brown Franciscan-type robes, with a short, light greenish shoulder cape with red cross (square) and two scallop shells, staff, gourd, halo, dog (and bread), barefoot. 14th–15th century castello.

Medallion of San Rocco, Chiesa di San Rocco

Continue ahead on **Via della Libertà** to junction by **Chiesa di San Rocco**. Pass to its LH side and fork L to **Viale CB Zanotti**. KSO, cross motorway, veering L on other side, after which road becomes **Strada del Morgarolo**. 700m later reach canal, turn R (signposted 'Cascina Morgarolo' – the farm to R), turn L in front of buildings, then R at crossing shortly afterwards, veering R to continue on LH bank of canal. KSO. At second bridge track moves to RH bank, then at third (brick) bridge turn R, cross another (smaller) canal then veer L, gradually uphill (which becomes **Via Pollini**), veering R up into the village. Pass **Chiesa di San Cristoforo** (*18th century*) on L and continue to junction with **Via Roma** in

5km Villanuova d'Ardenghi (259.5/696.5) 87m

Bar/Trattoria (X Mon) and another bar (X Thurs), small shop.

Turn L (on **Via Roma**) and KSO. *This is the SP80, which goes all the way to Pavia.* Continue on this (*an embankment above the fields to either side*) for 7km, passing the **Cascina Caselle** and the **Cascina Limodo Nova**. *Both are examples of typical Lombardian farmhouses – a series of buildings round a central, usually rectangular courtyard, with a threshing floor for drying rice, a well, cowsheds, barns, equipment and other storage buildings. The owner's house was on a grand scale, whereas those for wage earners and seasonal workers were a lot smaller. The landscape of this area – the Lomellina – altered when Cistercian monks from France reclaimed the land in the Middle Ages and established a dense network of irrigation canals, making the large-scale production of rice (the region's main crop) possible, as well as the plantation of poplar trees.*

Reach a road crossing, and just after a sharp 'kink' to the R in the road fork L off it downhill, to continue beside it on the E/1, a local FP that becomes a wide track alongside the **Fiume Ticino**, passing behind a beach bar (on L). Continue ahead on wide track then KSO(L) at fork to a more grassy track. *Mainly shady, with one or two places to access the (sandy) beach alongside the Ticino, Italy's seventh largest river (248km) and the main tributary of the Pô. Pavia was known as Ticinum in Roman times.*

1.7km after the RH fork up the bank to **Canarazzo** (*trattoria, but not always open*) reach a T-junction of similar paths (*Pavia is 6.7km from here*) and turn L towards the river, veering R. Shortly afterwards reach another junction (*bar/rte to L*) and turn R. 200m later turn L on shady FP with woods to L. 300–400m later pass another bar/café (*food available*) and KSO. *All this section is very well waymarked.*

At next T-junction the Via Francigena turns R (Pavia 4km; other route turns L), veering along side of field with woods to L. Reach metal gates. Turn L (twice), then 400m later turn R to parking area and at end reach a small tarmac road. Turn R on FP to LH side of road and KSO. 300m later reach another small tarmac road, turn R and then L along it, and go under the motorway. The road turns R on the other side, but you KSO ahead, on FP to the LH side of a plantation of trees. *Mainly shady walk.*

KSO, go under railway bridge then under the road bridge, and 3km after the motorway reach the **Ponte Coperta** (covered bridge) over the **Ticino**. This is a reconstruction of the original 13th-century bridge destroyed by bombardment during the Second World War. A few metres before you reach it turn R up a flight of stone steps, then turn L to cross bridge and enter

11.5km Pavia (271/685) Pop. 71,660, 77m

All facilities. OP in Ostello Santa Maria Santa in Betlem, Via G Pasino 7 (331.3046459; turn R before crossing the Ponte Coperta into the town, go down Via dei Mille and then turn L into Via Pasino). ** Albergo Aurora, Viale Vittorio Emmanuele 11, 25 (0382.23664), Albergo Rosengarten Dipendenza, Via Lombroso 21–23 (0382.526312), ***Hotel Excelsior, Piazzale Stazione (0382.28596). Ask in TO for affittacamere (rented rooms) as well (such as Melisende Carlos, Via Indipendenza 70, 0382.468777 and 339.8896466). **Camping Ticino, Via Mascherpa 10–16 (0382.527094). Trenitalia.

To explore town (note street plan by bus stop opposite bridge), go to TO in Palazzo del Brocetto in Piazza della Vittoria nearby (0382.079943 and 0382.597001) for street plan giving tour of town's monuments.

University of Pavia students, then...

...and now

Pavia (called Ticinum) was already in existence in Roman times, when it was laid out on a grid plan, which can still be seen in the old part of the city. There is a lot to see here, but the main sights include the Romanesque

Basilica di San Michele (where Frederick Barbarossa was crowned), the Chiesa di San Pietro in Ciel d'Oro (dating from 1132 and housing the tomb of Saint Augustine), the Chiesa di San Teodoro (late 12th century), the Duomo (dating from 1488) and the Chiesa di San Giovanni Dominarum (11th–12th centuries). These, and the numerous other churches in the city, not only fulfilled a religious function but were also hospices for pilgrims and other poor travellers. Prominent civic buildings include the Palazzo Broletto in the Piazza dell Vittoria (originating in the eighth century), today housing the tourist office but originally the Bishop's Palace, the Ponte Coperta (see above) and the Castello Visconteo (founded 1360 and now housing the Museo Civici). The University of Pavia was founded in 1361.

Stage XLI (Pamplica, 41) in Sigeric's itinerary.

Go up **Corso Strada Nuova** ahead then turn third R into **Via Severino Capsoni**. Turn L at end into **Via S Michele** in front of **Chiesa dei Santi Michele, Enodio ed Elencadio** (*12th century, then 1861–76*), then turn R into **Corso Garibaldi** and KSO. Pass **Chiesa dei Santi Primo e Feliciano** (*12th–14th centuries*) part-way along. KSO. At the **Porta Garibaldi** cross the **Viale Gorizia**, then the canal, after which the road becomes, successively, **Viale Partigiani**, **Viale Montegrappa** and then the **Via San Pietro in Verzolo**, passing a large **Chiesa de Santa Maria della Gracia** and then **Chiesa di San Pietro in Verzoli** (*remains of Romanesque cloisters*), both of them on the R.

Cross the **Roggia Vernaola** (a small canal) shortly after the Chiesa di San Pietro, after which the road becomes **Via Cremona**, and then turn R, veering L, into **Via Francana**, passing the **Chiesa di San Lazzaro** on R. Continue to the end (*small supermarket on R*), then KSO on an unsurfaced road between fields. At end go uphill on a short street, then turn R onto **Via Montebolone**. At the end, by a 'stop' sign, fork R and continue ahead on FP/cycle track past a park with seats to L. Follow it round, passing **Cascina Scaglona**, to reach the SS617 by a road bridge and turn R along it (*bar/trattoria on L*). KSO for 800m to junction with SP13 by a factory, and continue L ahead along it on **Viale F.lli Cervi**. KSO for 800m (*pavement, seats on R after cemetery*), passing Pavia town exit boards, to junction at start of village and continue ahead on **Via Nobili** to the church in

7km San Leonardo (278/678) 62m

Bar/Trattoria, shop, farmacia.

141

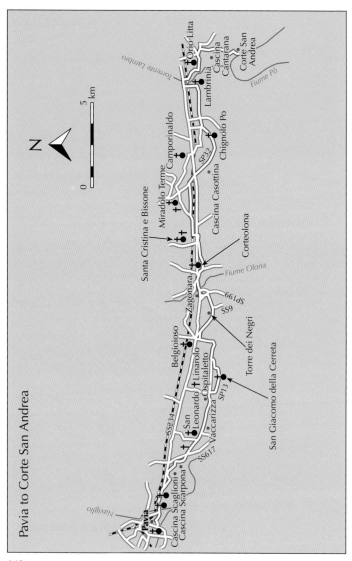

Pavia to Corte San Andrea

Continue through village (ignoring any waymarking directing you to the R) and KSO on the road (SP13; not much traffic) through **Ospitaletto** (*its name recalls existence of a former templar hospital there; bar*), after which, at the turning to **Linarolo**, the SP13 bends L. Turn R here instead, on a minor road, following it round to the L to take you to

6km San Giacomo della Cerretta (284/672) 71m

Bar. 15th-century Chiesa di San Giacomo has a magnificent series of frescoes of life of Saint James the Pilgrim (San Giacomo Pellegrino) – key available nearby.

After that continue on the same minor road, which veers L, R and L again, and then turn R to go through **Santa Margherita** 2.5km later. KSO, following road round, to enter **Belgioioso** on the **Via Molini** then the **Via F Cavalotti**.

The waymarked route does not lead into the town centre, so if you want to go there turn L in front of house No 21 into Via Dante Alighieri and then L onto Via Garibaldi to the SP234 and shops and the square. Afterwards you can either retrace your steps and then turn L up Via P Nenni or continue on the SP234 (turn R onto it), fork R onto the Via XXV Aprile, then turn L onto Via Gerolamo Criminali, which then becomes the Via Belgioioso (see continuation of route below).

4km Belgioioso (288/668) 75m

Shops etc. ** Hotel Rte Cavaliere, Via F Cavalotti 50–51 (0382.969666), **Albergo Rte della Pesa, Via Settembre 111 (0382.969073). OP in Associazione Saman – comunità terapeutica, Via Cantone 42, donation (0382.960268). Trenitalia.

Chiesa di San Michele Arcangeli. 14th-century castello, originally built for defensive purposes but later converted into a residence.

To continue without going into the town, just after passing the Hotel Cavaliere (on L) turn R down **Via P Nenni**. At the end of Via P Nenni veer R, and then turn R onto **Via Belgioioso** near the edge of the town. KSO, go through **Torre dei Negri** (*bar to L at junction at end of village; seats to R behind water tower*) and then continue ahead on road until it bends sharp R. KSO(L) ahead here, on gravel track, turn L at bend (no waymark) and reach the SP199 at road KM7. Cross over, continue on similar track, and 150m later reach the SP234 and turn R along it. *There*

143

Chiesa di San Giacomo della Cerreta, interior

is a lot of traffic on the road, but there is no choice about using it, as you need to cross the bridge over the Fiume Olona 1km later.

Pass entrance boards for Corteolona, and 200m later fork R into **Via Cavalotti**. KSO and reach square and church in the centre of

5km Corteolona (293/663) Pop. 1977, 66m

Shops etc. Chiesa di San Stefano. Site of a large monastery dedicated to Sant'Anastasio (martyred in Persia) during the Middle Ages.

Pass church, reach **Piazza Matteotti**, and then turn R into **Via Mons. Faustino Giovanni**. Veer L into **Via Castellaro**, veering R and then L, and then turn L into **Via Vigna Vecchia**. KSO and near the end, just past **Via Martiri della Foibe** (on R), turn L onto gravel track, veering R. KSO ahead.

1km later a track joins from R; KSO again. Road becomes paved when houses start and becomes **Via Pila Vecchia**. Further along the waymarks indicate that you should turn R along **Via Zara**, ▼ L along **Via Trieste** and then R along **Via Dante** into the centre of Santa Cristina. *(This route follows three sides of a square, the object of which is to pass a former hospitium – for wayfarers, pilgrims and other travellers – belonging to a Benedictine abbey; the building was still in use as an osteria until the late 20th century.)*

Alternatively you can KSO ahead here to the public garden and church in Santa Cristina.

3km Santa Cristina e Bissone (296/660) 71m

Shops etc. OP in the parish hall, Via Vittorio Veneto 118 (0382.70106), behind the building next to the church. No charge, but you should leave a donation.

Site of a formerly very important abbey, where Sigeric is reported to have stayed on his return journey. Museo Contadine (local history) in Via Fiume.

Stage XL (Sce Cristine, 40) in Sigeric's itinerary.

Note *At Corte San Andrea (see below) there is the option to cross the River Pô by boat (the* **taxi fluviale***). If you intend to do that, it is* **essential to** *telephone ahead to the ferryman (Danilo Parisi, 0523.771607 – at meal times, for example) to say what time you want to cross. (Do not wait until you get to Corte San Andrea as there is no public phone there, and the ferryman needs advance warning as he other things to do – the 'taxi' service is only part of his activity.) If your Italian is not up to using the telephone go into a café, buy yourself a drink, and then ask the person behind the bar if they can ring up for you (local calls in Italy are very cheap).*

The 4km journey takes 15–25mins, according to the weather (wear warm clothes, even in summer) and how full the boat is. It can also take (one or two) bikes. 10€ for pilgrims with credenziale.

Note *At the time this guide was prepared the shorter, alternative route to Chinolo Pô via Bissone was waymarked only at the start (turn R after the church into Via Giberti) and so is not described here.*

Go past the church in Santa Cristina and then turn L (marked 'stazione') on **Viale Rimembranze**. Cross the SS234 (pedestrian crossing) then continue ahead to the station. Go over level crossing and turn R on FB over dyke. Continue, parallel to railway line, on an embankment with a (probably dry) canal between them. The track is very clear in many places, but more difficult in others.

KSO for nearly 4km. On reaching the first house on the L you may find it easier to cross to the other side of the canal via a sturdy, covered water channel and reach a local road and the railway station. Alternatively, if it is very overgrown, turn L along the side of the field here and go up the bank to a road coming from your L, and turn R to the railway station in

4.5km Miradolo Terme (300.5/665.5) 67m

Bar by station (the village itself is 400m away to L). Trenitalia.

Turn R over railway line, reach SS234, cross over and KSO ahead on more minor road (marked 'Chinolo Pô 2'. KSO for 1.5km then fork L opposite house No 28 and enter

4km Chignolo Pô (304.5/651.5) Pop. 3411, 65m

Shops etc. Small wayside chapel on L at entrance has shady porch for rest. Neomedieval Castello Cusani Visconti (much photographed, worth a visit), one of the most sumptuous residences in the area, is set back from the road at the end of the town.

Continue through village (very long) on **Via Casottina** past chapel and cemetery, and then on **Via XXV Aprile** (*supermarket on R at end*). Pass church (on R) and KSO. Pass second church (on L) and KSO (**Via Garibaldi**). At end, 1.5km from start, reach impressive castello ahead L and small **Chiesa di San Rocco**, then turn R on **Via Lambrinia**. 600m later reach SP193, cross over and KSO on other side until you reach

4km Lambrinia (308.5/647.5) 65m

Neomedieval Castello Cusani Visconti, Chinolo Pô, viewed through gates

Pass cemetery (R) and fork L at church onto **Via Mameli**. At next junction turn L into **Via Mariotto** and KSO. Cross railway line then turn R (*bar*) onto the SP234 and cross the bridge over the **River Lambro**. On the other side turn R immediately onto small tarmac road, which becomes unsurfaced, go under big brick bridge and KSO.

KSO at first crossing; then at second crossing VF signs point L to take you to **Orio Litto**. *To sleep in the OP in the Hospitium Pellegrini nel grangio medievale di Cascina San Pietro, Piazza dei Bendettini (0377.944436, donation), in Orio Litto turn L here.* If you don't want to go to the OP KSO here, and after passing three brick pump houses turn R onto an embankment. Continue along it then fork R down slope to the landing stage for the ferry by the **Fiume Pô** on the outskirts of

6.5km Corte San Andrea (315/641) 49m

Osteria.

Here you have two options. *You can cross the Pô by boat (provided you have telephoned ahead) and continue for 15km to Piacenza on the RH side of the river, via Calendasco, with facilities along the way (Option A). Alternatively, for Option B turn L here along the LH bank of the Pô and cross over via the road bridge at the entrance to Piacenza (21km, but with only one bar en route – about half-way along, in the sailing club by the river near the turning to Somaglia).*

Stage XXXIX (Sce Andrea, 39) in Sigeric's itinerary.

OPTION A – PIACENZA VIA RIVER CROSSING AND CALENDASCO

After crossing the river, reach the other side and the small hamlet of

4km Soprarivo (319/637) 53m

This consists of just a few houses, one of which belongs to the boatman Danilo Parisi, who also has a very large pilgrim register and a timbro (pilgrim stamp).

After getting off the boat (and having your pilgrim passport stamped in the boatman's house, if you came on his ferry) turn L on embankment above river. 1km later fork R downhill, veering R between fields. Reach tarmac road and then

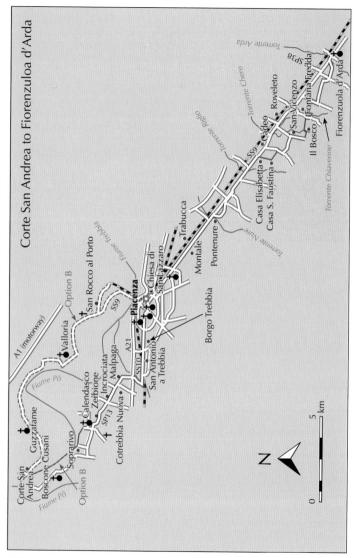

Corte San Andrea to Fiorenzuola d'Arda

Landing stage at Corte San Andrea

turn R along it, entering the village via **Via Pô** (*Locanda Masero on R has rooms, 0523.772787; discount for pilgrims with credenziale*). Turn L in front of the **municipio** on **Via Mazzini** in

2km Calendasco (321/635) 53m

Shops etc. Ostello Le Tre Corone, Via Mazzini 59 (0523.772894 and 334.1866556) has dormitory-type accommodation with pilgrim rate and menu, bar and meals (the owners lived in England for a long time and so are completely bilingual).

Continue to church, veering R on **Via Roma**, and KSO on road (SP13) to Piacenza, passing **Incrociata** (2km), then turn L by bar at bend. 1km later reach **Contrebbia Nouva** (*2 bar/shops, Chiesa dei Santi Pietro e Paolo*). KSO, and 500m later enter **Malpaga**, then turn R at junction and continue on cycle track to LH side of road. Follow it round when it veers L to go under the motorway to L of where the road does this, then the cycle track continues again on the other side.

Enter **Ponte Trebbia**, passing large picnic area on L when cycle track ends. Go under railway bridge and then turn R (do not go under road bridge) and then hard L to cross the road bridge over the **Fiume Trebbia** (a very long bridge with a small pavement on LH side). Enter the province of Piacenza on the other side and continue on the **Via Emilia Pavese**, entering the city of Piacenza after the first roundabout.

KSO for 5km. *There are plenty of bars, shops and so on along the way, but although there is a fairly wide hard shoulder there is hardly any pavement – and nowhere at all to sit down!*

At the very end of the **Via Emilia Pavese** (by a small roundabout) KSO ahead on **Via Guiseppe Taverna**. At end fork R into **Via Garibaldi**, and at the end of that cross the **Corso Vittorio Emmanuel II** and continue ahead on **Via San Antonino**. Continue on **Via GB Scalabrini** at the end and then, at the very end of this, reach **Piazzale Roma** in

15km Piacenza (336/620)

The route continues after the box for Piacenza below.

OPTION B – PIACENZA VIA THE BANK OF THE PÒ

There is very little shade or shelter on this route. Turn L by the entrance to the landing stage in **Corte San Andrea** and continue along the embankment. KSO.

After 4km pass the turning to the **Cascina Case Nuove Guzzafame** then KSO again, to the second turning to **Senna Lodigiana** *(to L, where there is a wayside shrine with shady seats). (Turn L here for OP in Ostello Transitum Padi, Via Dante 1 (0377.802155, 0377.802191, 339.1268946), then retrace your steps the following morning.)*

KSO ahead again. 3km later, when you reach the (smooth tarmac) road from **Somaglia** (on the L, by the Protezione Civile building below you), if you want something to eat and/or drink you can turn R off the track down to the **Centro Nautico Somaglia**, a boat club by the river, which has a bar/rte open to the public (then retrace your steps.) Otherwise KSO ahead all the time.

300m before reaching Valloria (the church is visible, outlined against the sky-line ahead) turn R to continue on an embankment at a sharp RH bend. 200m later turn hard L downhill, then turn R onto **Via Dante** (not marked at start) and continue to the church in

11.5km Valloria 42m

KSO on the main street, out of the village, and 1km later turn L at a T-junction onto an unsurfaced road along an embankment between fields. KSO for 3km then veer L, going down to the SS9 below. Turn R along it for 1km, then after the cemetery (and 100m before road KM266) fork L along **Via Manzoni**. Turn second L by a mini-roundabout into **Via Roma** in

5.5km San Rocco al Porto 46m

Shops etc. Chiesa di San Rocco with large sculpted statue of the saint at the top of its freshly painted facade. Shady park opposite, with seats.

The route from here into Piacenza is somewhat tedious, but it is safe and keeps pilgrims off the dangerous SS9.

Continue along **Via Roma**, veering L, then by house No 131 turn L into **Via Don Minzoni** and then continue ahead on **Via G Matteotti**. At the end turn R into **Via A Gramsci** (where the waymarks are picked up again, which are then very obvious all the way into the province of Piacenza). 400m later reach a roundabout and go straight over it, passing the sports ground of the Biffi factory (*coffee, cake, fruit juice and sauce…*) (on L), then the factory itself and the **Lago Biffi** (a lake), both on the RH side, then veer R and L past a recycling plant. Cross over to the RH side of the road to continue on another cycle track.

Veer R again to pass behind a large industrial estate and then a sports stadium (this is the **Via Guigno**). At a small roundabout turn L (*pavement*) along the side of the Auchan superstore, veering R past the front (and a 'Flunch' – a French self-service restaurant chain), and reach another roundabout. Take the first exit (on your L) – this is the **Via Ottobre 2000** (named for an 'evento alluvione', recalling some very bad floods at that time) – but then turn R immediately over a pedestrian crossing towards the **San Sisto Parco Commerciale**, where the cycle track begins (ahead) that will lead all the way to the Piazzale Milano in Piacenza.

KSO ahead along the cycle track and cross the **Fiume Pio**, passing from the province of Lodi to that of Piacenza and from the regione of Lombardia into that of Emilia Romagna. KSO to reach the **Piazzale Milano**, a junction with a large roundabout in the middle, where the cycle track comes to an end.

Here you can either: turn L into the **Via Roma** and continue to the **Piazzale Roma**, if you want to continue on straight away (see continuation at 'Both routes' below); or, to visit Piacenza, continue straight ahead up the **Viale Risorgimento** and then the **Via Cavour** to the **Piazza Cavalli** (with TO) in the centre of the town.

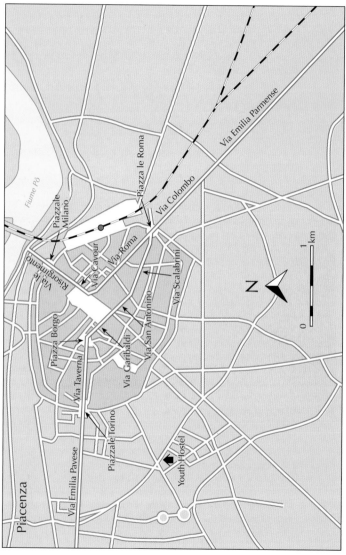

Piacenza

15km Piacenza (336/620) Pop. 98,583, 57m

Large town with all facilities and, like all towns of similar size, the outskirts are very industrial. TO (IAT) Piazza Cavalli 7 (0523.329324). YH Ostello Don Zermani, Via Zoni 38–40 (0523.712319) on outskirts of town to southwest. Hotels mainly expensive, apart from Hotel VIP, Via Frasi 20 (0523.712420). OP – see in box for Montale, below. Trenitalia.

Piacenza, dating from AD218 and probably built on Celtic and Etruscan foundations, is a river port on the Pô and situated on the Via Emilia. It is known to have had at least 30 hospices in the late Middle Ages, including the San Sepolcro, annexed to a Benedictine monastery, the Santa Brigida, which accommodated pilgrims from the British Isles, and the San Lazzaro, a hospice-leprosarium. Piacenza has a great many sights worth visiting, both religious and civil – Duomo (12th–13th centuries), fourth-century paleo-Christian

Piacenza cathedral

Detail from column in Piacenza cathedral – wheelwright at work

Basilica di San'Antonio (the city's first cathedral), Romanesque Basilica di San Savino, 16th-century Santuario di Santa Maria di Campagna, 12th-century Chiesa di Santa Anna and Chiesa di San Giovanni in Canale, Renaissance Chiesa di San Sepolcro and Chiesa di San Sisto, and many more. Chiesa di Santa Maria has free-standing statue of San Rocco in nave.

Among the town's notable civic buildings are the Gothic town hall (Palazzo Gotico), the Palazzo Farnese (now housing a museum) and the Palazzo del Colegio dei Gesuiti (1593), which houses the Biblioteca Comunale Passerini Landi, a library in existence since 1774 and containing, among the many rare books in its collections, the oldest edition of Dante's *Divina Commedia* (1336).

Piacenza was Stage XXLVIII (Placentia, 38) in Sigeric's itinerary.

Both routes

From the **Piazzale Roma** continue ahead on **Via Cristoforo Colombo** (this is still the SS9), which then continues as **Via Emilia Parmense**. Pass the **Chiesa di San Lazzaro** on R, *(rebuilt 1720; with very large statue of San Rocco as pilgrim on facade)*. KSO. 1.5km later reach a junction with large roundabout; go under ring road and continue to church in

5km Montale (341/615) 57m

OP next to the church, Via Emilia Parmense 189 (but key from the parish of San Lazzaro at No 71, 0523.614256 and 333.1493595).

Chiesa di San Pietro Apostolo – this had a hospice in the 11th century, run by the Templars and then the Knights of Malta, whose duty it was also to maintain the Roman bridge over the River Nure (its base can still be seen upstream from the modern one).

KSO, and 1.5km later finally leave Piacenza. KSO again.

An alternative route via San Giorgio Piancentino is planned just before the bridge over the Torrente Nura, to the left of the SS9, that avoids the Via Emilia until Fiorenzuola d'Arda (although it would add 8km to the journey). It is not described here, as it is not yet waymarked.

Cross bridge over the **Torrente Nura** (probably dry), then turn second R onto a FP, veering L to run parallel to the **Via Emilia** (SS9), which becomes a tarmac road at entrance to the town. Continue ahead and then, on leaving the built-up area, the road becomes a track again and does a quick 'dogleg' to the R before turning L to return to the SS9 again. Turn R along it, and 1km later reach

3.5km Pontenure (344.5/611.5) Pop. 5440, 66m

Shops etc. Albergo/Rte Savi (near church), Piazza Tre Martin 9–10 (0523.510743). Chiesa di San Pietro Apostolo (shady seats outside).

5.5km after Pontenure, just before road KM147/vii and shortly before an enormous factory on the outskirts of **Cadeo** (*whose name comes from 'Casa Dei' and which had a large ospitale in the 11th century*), turn R onto a strada privata by a large isolated tree, the **Casa Elisabetta** and a memorial, by the side of the road, to a young man shot dead by the Nazis in 1944. *From here, in a series of zigzags, the route sidesteps Cadeo, Roveto and Fontana Fredda, returning to the SS9 shortly by the road bridge over the Torrente Arda at the entrance to Fiorenzuola d'Arda.*

Having turned R by the Casa Elisabetta, continue ahead, and 1km later turn L, passing **Casa Liberata** (on L). 800m later reach junction with SP29 (coming from Cadeo, over to your L) and turn R along it. Turn L (tarmac, 'Chero 5') on **Via Fornace**, cross small river/canal, and at a junction KSO ahead. Turn R on asphalt road coming from **Roveleto** (which is now over to the L), then third L onto a track. Ford a shallow river, the **Torrente Chero**, go slightly uphill, then turn L on other side, parallel to river. Continue along edge of woods, veering R, then across fields ahead and reach a tarred road coming from **Fontana Fredda** (over to the L). Turn R along it, and then turn L shortly before **Colombaia** (a farm) ahead. Ford the **Torrente Chiavenna**, go slightly uphill, turn L and then R, and continue to a road coming from the SP9 (on L).

Turn R then second L (*note large sundial on side of building*) – this junction is **Ballabene**. KSO. Some 300-400m before the SP38 watch out for a RH turn onto a track, turn L at bend, and go under the road (SP38). KSO ahead at crossing. KSO, veer L, R and L again at very end along the **Via S Protasio**. 100m before the end turn R onto a walkway, cross metal pedestrian/cycle bridge over the **Torrente Arda**, and turn L on other side to reach the SP9 again by the end of the road bridge. Cross main road and turn R and then L down **Corso Guiseppe Garibaldi** in

10.5km Fiorenzuola d'Arda (355/601) Pop. 13,746, 86m

All facilities, OP in Caritas house (ask in Duomo di San Fiorenzo, Piazza Molinari 15, 0523.982247). ***Hotel Arda, Via Luigi Scapuzzi 35 (0523.943072).

Saint Peter with book, keys and fishing net, pointing the way up to heaven, in nave of Collegiata di San Fiorenzo

The town takes its name from Saint Florent de Tours, a disciple of Saint Martin who, on stopping in Fiorenzuola on his pilgrimage to Rome, is said to have performed miracles there. The 14th-century collegiate church of San Fiorenzo contains many 15th- and 16th-century frescoes from the Lombard school. Fiorenzuola also had a hospice, said to have been built in the eighth century by the Danish king Erik Svendsson, known as 'the Good', to accommodate pilgrims coming from northern lands. This facility was recorded by the Icelandic bishop Nikulas de Munkathvera in his account of his pilgrimage to Rome and the Holy Land in the 12th century.

Stage XXXVII (Floricum, 37) in Sigeric's itinerary.

After crossing the bridge over the **Torrente Arda** KSO on **Corso Garibaldi** (*turn R to visit Duomo*), which then becomes **Via Luigi Scapuzzi**, leading to the SS9 again. KSO for 1.6km then, just after road KM238, by petrol station, turn R on new road between crash barriers that goes over a fast main road. *(Note small oratory on R – good place for a short shady rest.)* KSO on other side, veering L, R and R again, and 2.2km later (after leaving the SS9) watch out for turning to L (very well waymarked) 150m after a drive leading to a farm (on L, set back from the road).

Turn L through yellow metal barrier onto track leading to woods ahead. Cross bridge over stream, and in top LH corner of large field see the **Santuario della Madonna di Moronasco** (a church). *All this area is devoted to the large-scale production of tomatoes.*

KSO at crossing by farm and KSO ahead, follow track round past farm to reach a minor road (to **Alseno**, 1km to L), the **Strada dell'Agola**, at a staggered junction.

Pilgrims can make a short detour from here to visit the Abbazia di Chiaravalle della Colomba, one of the oldest Cistercian abbeys in the Pô valley. It was founded in 1135 by the monks of the Abbey of Saint Bernard of Clairvaux in France,

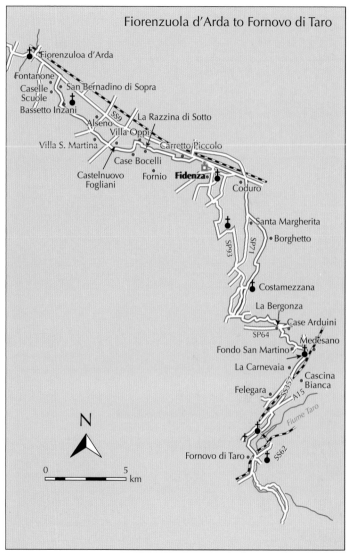

Fiorenzuola d'Arda to Fornovo di Taro

which pilgrims who have walked from Canterbury will have seen along their way. Pilgrims with credenziale can sleep there (0523.94013).

At the junction turn R, then immediately L (marked 'Val Ongina'), and continue on SP13 (busy). 1.6km later reach another staggered junction – turn R then immediately L on **Strada Salsedian Est** (*bar X Mon*) into

9km Castelnovo Fogliani (364/592) 111m

Two shops, rte, bar.

Fidenza cathedral

After this the countryside starts to change and becomes hillier. Go uphill and turn L at top towards castle on **Via Rimbranza** (*seats*), then turn R on **Strada Caminna**, passing **Chiesa di San Biagio** and cemetery. KSO, then at T-junction 1km later turn L onto **Strada S Francisco**. Turn L.

From here you can see the traffic whizzing back and forth on the Via Emilia and an impressive house (the Villa Oppi) set among trees to R in front. 400–500m later go under HT cables, and by very tall isolated tree with a single tall, circular brick pillar/gate post next to it turn R on gravel track towards the **Villa Oppi**.

Turn R before its entrance on grassy track, then R again at T-junction, veering L. KSO to **La Razzina di Sotto** (on R, a farm) and here pick up a gravel track, veering L. Then immediately before first tree turn R onto grassy track towards woods ahead. KSO (route does a brief 'kink' to R) and reach minor tarmac road. KSO ahead on other side.

Reach tarmac road by industrial buildings then turn R, then L 150m later on slightly bigger road (marked 'Fidenza'). KSO. Reach SS9, turn R along its cycle track, cross the **Torrente Stirone** (probably dry) at the entrance to the town, go under railway line and KSO in **Via Abati Zani** (*church to R is the Orthodox Santissima Trinità*).

KSO. Reach a square, cross diagonally to R through archway to cathedral, then retrace your steps to continue.

8km Fidenza (372/584) Pop. 23,675, 79m

All facilities. TO in Casa Cremonini in Piazza Duomo 16 (0524.83377). OP in Chiesa di San Pietro, Via Goito (0524.522620), and also in Convento dei Padri Cappuccini, Via Francesco 7 (0524.5220118 and 0524.520118). Albergo San Donnino, Via G Beremi 134A. Hotel Ugolini, Via Malpeli 90 (0524.83264). Trenitalia.

Duomo di San Donnino, built over the tomb of this saint, a Roman soldier persecuted for his Christian faith and then martyred in this area in AD299; decapitated, he is represented in art carrying his own head. Note the relief sculptures of a line of pilgrims on the exterior of the cathedral. The town was known as Borgo San Donnino in the Middle Ages and reclaimed its Roman name – Fidenza – only in 1928.

Stage XXXVI (Sce Domnine, 36) in Sigeric's itinerary.

Detail from facade of the cathedral – Gaspar, Balthasar and Melchior (Three Kings) on horseback

Continue ahead on **Via Cavour**, **Via Berenini** and **Via Martiri della Libertà** (*a very long street with plenty of seats*) and continue on main road as far as **Coduro** (church at corner, 2.5km from the centre of Fidenza; *hospice of San Leonardo here in the past*), then turn R onto SP71. (*Here the first road sign says it is 4km to Santa Margherita, the next one that it is 5km…although in fact it is only 2.5km!*) KSO on road to reach

5km Santa Margherita (377/579) 87m

Former hospice of San Giacomo (Saint James).

Fork L (marked 'Borgetto') towards church (*shady seats*). KSO. Quite a lot of traffic.

2km Borghetto (379/577) 106m

Bar/Rte, shop next to it.

KSO, passing to L of church and KSO. At KM6 on SP93, turn R towards 'Costamezzano' (*bakery on L*) and KSO for 1.5km to

3.5km Costamezzano (382.5/573.5) 172m

Trattoria, Ostello Comunale in former school, 10€ (key from house opposite) – trattoria, no kitchen, gets full at weekends (0521.622137).

Here there is a choice of routes.

OPTION A

Continue on road (SP93, very little traffic), passing to R of church (**Strada Costa Pavese**) and KSO, passing small chapel on R, uphill all the time (*no waymarks after Costamezzano until after Casa Barratta*). *Castello di Costamezzano visible to R.* Reach a T-junction at the top, and 2.5km later (*splendid views if no haze*) turn L (marked 'Medesano').

OPTION B

Retrace your steps on the SP93 for 250m, then turn L towards the **Castello di Costamezzano**. KSO(L) at fork towards the castle, pass to its l, then continue ahead on a track for 2.5km to reach a junction with a tarmac road coming from the R. 100m later reach a junction with another tarmac road and turn L.

Both routes
Follow road round, ignoring two LH turns, and reach a T-junction nearly 2km later. Turn L. 900m later take third gravel/farm road on R, which has a 'stop' sign at the end. 200m after that, by bend to R, turn L onto clear, wide grassy track, veering R then L, doing a 'kink' to L then R, and reach **La Bergonza** (a house). Pass to L of it, veering L then R downhill. Turn R at T-junction of similar grassy tracks, then turn L by woods, veering R 100m before another house, downhill. Veer L along side of road, then turn hard R along it (the SP64) and reach a farm by a wayside shrine by road KM8. *(All this is a very fiddly section, and there were no longer any waymarks when this guide was being prepared.)*

Turn L here, on earth track, veering L past large rectangular concrete structure. Veer R along side of woods and then turn hard R to cross/ford the **Torrente Recchio**. KSO on track on other side between fields, KSO to LH side of woods and reach T-junction with tree-lined gravel track. Turn L along it. Pass **Casa Baratta** and KSO on road, downhill, and then reach bigger tarmac road at top. Cross over and enter town on **Via Giuseppe Verdi** (*bar on R*).

10.5km Medesano (393/563) 135m

Small town with shops etc, bank, OP in Oratorio Don Bosco, Via Concilliazione 2 (0525.420447). Hotel-Rte Primo Piano, Piazza Italia 1 (0525.420789).

13th-century Chiesa di San Pantaleone. Two *spedale* ('hospitals') in the past – one dedicated to San Lorenzo, the other to San Giacomo. Waymarks reappear.

Stage XXXV (Metane, 35) in Sigeric's itinerary.

Reach roundabout and KSO on other side (still on **Via Giuseppe Verdi**). Continue to church (*seats*), where waymarks lead R via its grounds, turning L down a flight of steps opposite its main door. After this turn R onto the SS375 (busy, but with pavement on RH side far as the railway station). Cross over to LH side here and continue on cycle track (*ignore old waymarks, pre-cycle track, leading uphill off the road to its RH side*). Continue on SS375 for 2km (from church), then at roundabout ('Felegara Zona Industriale') with bar, large supermarket etc to

161

R, fork L and go under a railway line on **Via Marchi**. KSO and ahead, and some 2km later pass the entrance board for

4km Felegara (397/559) 127m

Small town with shops etc that route skirts but does not enter. 13th-century hospice dedicated to San Ginesio.

Some sources equate Felegara with Stage XXXIV (Philemangenur, 34) in Sigeric's itinerary, rather than Fornovo di Taro.

Pass cemetery to R with three lines of trees in front and very large factory on L (*bar/rte opposite, X Sun*) and reach junction with roundabout (*you are on Via Marchi up to here*) and public garden with a lot of seats (*church to R*). KSO ahead here on **Via Dordone**. 700m later, at RH bend with factory ahead, turn L and go under the motorway. (*On the other side you are in the Parco Fluvial del Fiume Taro, although there isn't much water in the river.*) Do not turn R here, but continue ahead and then turn second R onto earth track and KSO.

KSO through scrubby woods with the (partly dried-up) **Fiume Taro** to L below, ignoring turns to L and R. *Often shady*. After nearly 2km cross FB over tributary of the Fiume Taro and then go under railway bridge high above you. On the other side turn R and then veer L, to continue between motorway (now closed, on R) and large gravel works to L. At end reach gates (closed, but you can pass to the side of them) and then turn L immediately, veering R along side of gravel yards. Turn R, then L and turn L onto road bridge (on SS357) into

Taro valley, entering Fornovo

5km Fornovo di Taro (402/554) Pop. 6100, 151m

Shops etc. TO Via del Colegiati 19. Via Nazionale 74. OP in Parrochia Santa Maria Asunta, Via Cesare Battisti 11 (0525.2218). Trenitalia.

The town was founded in Roman times – its name derives from 'Forum Novum' (market place) – at the junction of three valleys (the Taro, Ceno and Sporzana) and (hence) three roads coming over the bridge over the Taro. Fornovo was also the place where the alternative route from Fidenza, via Parma, rejoined the Via Francigena. Romanesque Duomo di Santa Maria Assunta – this originally had a porch outside where pilgrims were accommodated, but this was later incorporated into the main body of the building. Former pilgrim hospital of San Nicolo.

Stage XXXIV (Philemangenur, 34) in Sigeric's itinerary.

At end of bridge a staircase leads down to RH side of **Piazza del Mercato** (the square is in two parts), but this is damaged at present so continue further on, cross to LH side of bridge, and then turn hard L and then L under the bridge to reach the piazza. At this point there is a choice of a low-level route on quiet roads (described below) or a high-level route which goes straight up above the town (not described here).

To visit the town turn L, after which either retrace your steps or pick up the **Via Nazionale** in the town centre and KSO along it.

To continue (on low-level route) KSO ahead, joining **Via Nazionale** (SS62), and continue with railway line to RH side all the time. 1km later fork L by offices of Carbinieri and Polizia Stradale (signposted 'Respiccio' and 'Sivizzano') and KSO for 1km to entrance to

4km Respiccio (406/550)

Osteria on road. Pilgrim hospital here from 1250, but closed in the 16th century.

Note Here pilgrims can follow either the waymarked route (uncomfortable underfoot) or the alternative suggested below.

Following the waymarks, fork R after village name board to church, veer R, then cross bridge over **Torrente Sponzano** and turn L onto a gravel road. After second entrance to a large house (**La Cà**) continue ahead on a track that follows – and uses – the dried-up river bed of the Torrente Sporzana all the way to the road

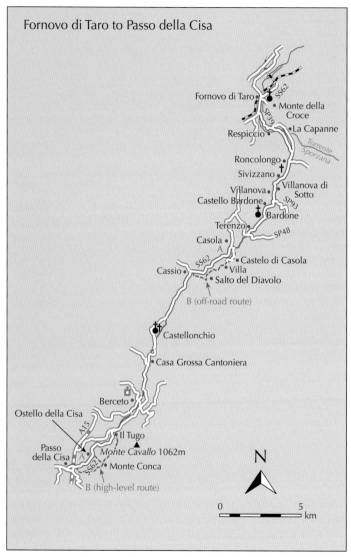

Fornovo di Taro to Passo della Cisa

bridge before Sivizzano, 2km later. It is easy enough to follow, but is extremely uncomfortable to walk on, especially with a heavy rucksack.

It is therefore suggested that at the entrance to Respiccio pilgrims continue on the SP39 (very little traffic) all the way to

4km Sivizzano (410/546) 248m

OP with 2 beds but a lot of mattresses (and shower) in hall next to church – ring bell at priest's house next door, but if no answer ring the other bell as the people who live upstairs look after the pilgrim accommodation. 10€ plus 2.50€ per person to use kitchen. Shop (in middle of village), bar/trattoria by church.

A very long, straggling village, nearly 2km from end to end. Excavations of Roman farm (first century BC to first century AD) at entrance on R, opposite Cappella Madre dei Cristiani (fountain, seats). Chiesa di Santa Margherita. Sivizzano originally had a hospice adjoining the Benedictine monastery of San Roberto ultra Montes, of which only the cloister remains in the centre of the village. Sivizzano is one of the places where the Angelus is to be heard ringing loud and clear – the church bells tolls over 40 times each and every evening at 8pm, and 40 or more times again each and every morning at 6am. This was originally to wake people up and summon them to work, and then, at the end of the day, to tell them when it was time to stop work and return home to rest.

The next stage, from Sivizzano to Berceto, is only 23km, but is very hilly and probably one of the most strenuous and tiring stretches of the whole Via Francigena in Italy – so allow a lot more time than you think you'll need.

KSO through village, passing shop (on R). Near the end fork R to church and trattoria, then return to the SP39 again (the **Strada Val Sporzana**) and KSO. Pass road KM6 and then fork R at junction up **Strada Terenzo-Bardone** (marked 'Bardone, Terenzo'), going steeply uphill, and 1km later reach

3km Bardone (413/543) 390m

Three fountains, one with modern (2000) pilgrim plaque. Small village on a Roman road. Very ancient church, possibly dating from the sixth century, altered in ninth, 11th and 13th centuries, and extensively in the 17th to suit the needs of the Counter-Reformation.

Bardone church

Turn R to visit church, then retrace your steps and turn R to continue on road, veering L, L and R in

2km Terenzo (415/541) Pop. 1274, 540m

Chiesa di San Stefano, whose tower is all that remains of a former ospitale.

KSO(L) at entrance on **Strada delle Poste**, passing through village. Follow it round past church (*tap, seats*) to a T-junction with tarmac road at end of village and turn L uphill (marked 'Municipio'). Turn hard R at bend, then hard L onto a bigger road (SP48, **Strada Terenzo-Calestano**), then 50m later turn hard R uphill on clear stony track, going steeply uphill through woods. *This is an old mule track, which cuts off a big loop in the SS62. Track marked with the red and white flashes of the CAI. Very steep, but nearly all in the shade.*

After 1.5km reach junction with a formerly tarmacked road coming from back L (*information board with maps and picnic tables behind it*). KSO(R) ahead on gravel track, then turn R on minor tarmac road. *(Bar at junction 250m further along road.)* 100m later (here you are at 788m) there are two options. *Option A (3km shorter) is a more level road route, while Option B is off road on the hillside. Option A should be taken in bad weather or very poor visibility, and anyone with bad knees and a very heavy rucksack might also like to consider it.*

OPTION A

KSO on road for 400m more to junction (this is **Casola**; *bar/rte, also advertises rooms*). Turn L here and KSO for 3.5km on SP62 (not a lot of traffic), up and then down for the last part, to **Cassio** (7km). Enter the village on the road, going downhill past the shop and bar, and join Option B (which goes via the Castello di Casola) by the bar/rte **Da Veronica** (on LH side of main road). See 'Both routes' below to continue.

OPTION B

This longer, off-road route wends its way along the hillside, up and down, to Cassio; it loses a lot of height as it goes, which then has to be made up. It is mainly shady, but there aren't as many good views as you would expect.

Turn L down steep grassy track to RH side of house. Continue steeply downhill, then track levels out to continue. 1km later reach crossing by the **Castello di Casola** (749m, *visible below*). Turn R by house No 16, steeply at first then levelling out along side of hill. KSO at crossing 300m later, on clear FP, going very steeply downhill (*be careful if you have a heavy rucksack*). At T-junction by small wooden hut KSO(R) ahead, passing behind houses, then KSO(R) at next (*seat over to L*). Then reach tarmac road in hamlet of **Villa**.

At bend KSO(L) ahead on **Strada Cá Chioldi**, cross minor road at end (*seat*) and KSO up **Strada della Fontana**, steeply uphill, then continue (uphill again) on a VS by last house. 200m later turn L at T-junction, then KSO(L) ahead 20m later on fairly level grassy track (to start with). Continue uphill before levelling out again. KSO uphill, reach the entrance drive and gates (on L) to a large property, then KSO uphill again on the other side before levelling out again. KSO.

Reach T-junction of similar tracks and turn L. *It is possible to join Option A here (if so, KSO ahead here) if you don't want to go through the* **Salto del Diavolo** *('Devil's leap', of interest to geologists) which goes repeatedly up and down.* 60–70m after T-junction turn L on FP through trees. Go downhill then up again (*by now the road is only 20m in front of you, if you want to take it*). KSO downhill, and 300m later reach a junction with a clear forest track and turn L onto a very steep track with a very bad surface (*difficult for anyone with bad knees*). KSO, then 400–500m later turn R at junction with a path coming up from the L.

Uphill slog...

167

KSO uphill, and the path becomes a walled lane. Continue uphill, ignoring turns, then emerge from the woods into a clearing, with a view of Cassio ahead. KSO on walled lane, uphill all the time. Go under an arch, veering L on **Strada degli Scalpellini** ('stone-cutters' road' – a common occupation in the area in the past), passing the church, then veer L on **Strada Romea**, veering R at the end to the main road (**Strada della Cisa**) by the bar/rte **Da Veronica** in

7.5km Cassio (422.5/533.5) 813m

Bar (X Mon, does food), farmacia, shop, PO, Da Veronica bar/rte has rooms (0525.526002). Ostello Via Francigena opposite, at 100 Strada della Cisa (SS62), in former casa cantoniera at road KM76 (0525.526110 and 339.7577670). Former Ospitale di Sant'Ilario. Chiesa dell' Assunta.

Turn R up the main road for bar, shop, post office, then retrace your steps to continue.

Both routes
Leave Cassio on the SS62. Shortly afterwards VF signs lead off to R as a deviation from SS62, but this road isn't very busy and has good views. KSO for 4km to

4km Cavazzola di Sopra (426.5/529.5) 750m

Chiesa dell' Assunta, Cassio

There are two options here. *The next (waymarked) section (Option B) is very hilly, and it would be difficult to see the waymarks in bad visibility. Option B is also mainly on bad surfaces, whereas Option A is on the road, which is not very busy.*

OPTION A

Stay on road for 2.5km and watch out for second LH turn into **Castellonchio** at the end of the village, just before road KM70/ii. Turn hard L (*seat*), then hard R and continue to last house, where tarmac stops. Route continues at 'Both routes' below.

OPTION B

Fork L off road at entrance to village, by house No 67, up tarmac lane that veers round to become a shady earth track on the level. 300–400m later turn hard R up rough track, steeply uphill, veering L through woods, going uphill all the time. Veer R, then L then R again, steadily uphill. Continue to veer L and R and continue uphill until, at a junction with a similar track coming from back R, it levels out a little. KSO.

Continue through woods and KSO(L) at fork, slightly uphill. Track joins from back R. KSO slightly downhill and reach first house in

1.5km Castellonchio (428/528) 910m

Turn R on street, paved at first (turn R by house No 4 to visit church, then retrace your steps), then tarmac, passing fountain and seats. Follow road round, veering L, to end of village (main road now below to R). By notice board for *trattoria rurale* take middle of three options ahead, continuing ahead to last house, where tarmac stops.

Both routes

Continue on unsurfaced road, and shortly afterwards, at fork, KSO(R) (road now near again to R). Go steeply uphill, and 50m later fork R again to continue along LH side of field to 'U' bend in road, then KSO ahead up stony track uphill. KSO(L) at fork, mainly level, and 500m later rejoin SS62 and turn R. Pass the **Casa Grossa Cantoniera**, a big square house with a red tiled roof, and KSO for nearly 1km to a junction with a wayside shrine and a house marked **Monte Marino**. ▼

KSO(L) on road here (although VF signs fork R, leading you off the road for a while, parallel to it). 1.3km later watch out for a path that forks R down LH side of

169

field just before road KM66/iv. Go through woods ahead on FP along side of hill back to the road at a 'stop' sign, then turn R by a wooden gateway (with no gate) and go down (and then up) clear grassy/gravel track to a viewpoint (879m, *seat*) with a plunging view over the whole area.

Alternatively, by the house marked Monte Marino, stay on the road for 700m further, until you see the 'stop' sign by the gateway, and join the route there. The waymarked path described above seems designed to take pilgrims off the road just for the sake of it.

Continue downhill then up, and 500m after gate by road pass a very small chapel (*large representation of San Moderanno, picnic tables, with good views of the area on a clear day*). KSO, entering town on **Salita Ripasanta**. At very end continue ahead on **Via Pier Maria Rosa**, a small cobbled street veering L to **Piazza San Moderanno** and the cathedral in

5km Berceto (433/523) Pop. 2389, 806m

All facilities. Buses to Parma (X Sun), but note that Berceto railway station is 15km from the town itself. TO Via Romea 5 (0525.629027). OP in the Casa della gioventù parrochiale (the priest lives at Via Roma 1, next to main door of cathedral, 0525.60087). OP in former seminary, Via E Colli 8, on way out of town has accommodation for large pre-booked groups. Albergo da Rino, Piazza Micheli 12 (0525.64306).

Cathedral of San Moderanno, Bishop of Rennes in northwestern France and patron saint of the Duomo in Berceto, who retired to a Benedictine monastery there in the eighth century on his return from a pilgrimage to Rome. Originally built in the 11th and 12th centuries, the cathedral has been altered several times and contains an important treasury and the relics of San Remiglio (Saint Remy) and San Broccardo.

Stage XXXIII (Sce Moderanne, 33) in Sigeric's itinerary.

Saint Peter (with only one key), Berceto cathedral

Berceto, Cathedral Treasury

To leave Berceto continue ahead past the main door of the cathedral on **Via Roma**, turn R into **Piazzale Barbuli**, L into **Via Seminario**, and then continue ahead on **Via E Colli**, passing a former seminary (on R). At end turn R onto the S62 (**Via Voluntari di Sangre**, signposted 'Valbona'), then 100m later fork L uphill on wide stony track through woods, mainly uphill. *This whole section is only very sparsely waymarked.* At T-junction turn R onto better path and KSO. At division of paths take either option, as they join up again shortly afterwards. At clearing (*good views if no haze, rocks to R*) another track joins from back L. KSO.

KSO. On reaching the first houses at road KM61/ix (on the SS62) the asphalt starts, veering R past disused factory building up to the SS62, just before road KM61/viii. This is

2.5km Il Tugo (435.5/520.5) 875m

To sleep in the Ostello de la Casa Grossa, in the former casa cantoniera at road KM58/vi (0525.629072 and 328.8741814, closed in winter), continue ahead here for 3km on the SS62 (and from there on the road up to the Passo della Cisa). There is not too much traffic, as all the heavy-goods vehicles and most

171

cars go on the motorway and through the road tunnel under the Passo della Cisa. The following morning either continue for 2.5km on the road or, 100m above the ostello, fork L to join the higher-level route Sentiero 00 (see Option B below).

Cross over the SS62 then turn L uphill on old tarmac lane. KSO. *This section is not very steep, but further on the surface is often very uneven underfoot.* 1km later, just before a farm 200m ahead on L, fork R up gravel lane. Shortly afterwards reach an open area that looks like a former quarry; do not turn L here, steeply uphill, but KSO(R) ahead up a shady lane. Fork L 100m later, uphill again, veering L, on old VS. *The waymarking is adequate, but there are few 'reassurance' markers to let you know that you are still on the right track.*

When the track appears to divide (with no waymarks), don't worry, as the two join up again shortly afterwards. KSO, levelling out a bit, until you reach a fork, some 2km after the quarry, where there are two options (both the same length) to the Passo della Cisa. *Option A, the lower-level route, is recommended in bad weather and poor visibility, but Option B is very nice, with splendid views, on a clear, bright day – and when you have plenty of time.*

OPTION A

Turn R, marked 'Ostello' (this route leads back down to the SS62, 100m above the former casa cantoniera). Follow a wide grassy track downhill, very steep in places and often slippery, through woods for nearly 2km, turning hard R at a T-junction near the end to emerge at road KM58/v on the SS62 – only 4km above Il Tugo! Turn hard L here and KSO on the road (not very steep now), going uphill to cross the Apennines by the Passo della Cisa (road KM56/iii) – see below.

OPTION B

KSO(L) ahead at fork, on Sentiero 00. This is a higher-level option waymarked by the CAI and has superb views on a clear day. However, it involves an extra 200m of climbing and descent via the Monte Valloria (1226m) before it descends to the Passo della Cisa at 1041m, which is therefore approached from above. Note that there is nowhere to sleep en route until Pontremoli (241m; see Section 3), another 20km at least from the pass, according to which option is taken after the pass. There are no facilities at all before Pontremoli, apart from two small bars by the junction in Molinelli (see Section 3), halfway down on the LH route, and one bar in Arzengio (see Section 3), barely 3.5km before Pontremoli on the RH option. So pilgrims should make their decision here based on the weather, how fit they are, and what time of day it is when they reach this junction (ensuring that they will have enough daylight to walk in).

Ostello (formerly a casa cantoniera) before Cisa Pass (Section 2)

For the Sentiero 00, proceed as follows. KSO(L) ahead at fork on a similar type of track, but with fewer trees – so less shade but more views. 500m later KSO(R) at fork and KSO, gradually uphill. On reaching an open plateau (*covered with alpine flowers in springtime*) turn R uphill towards the back of a wayside shrine. Turn L there, downhill, on small FP, then at a junction with a similar path turn R along the side of the hill (*view of entrance/exit to motorway tunnel ahead, below L*).

Veer L down through woods and continue downhill. Go over stile in clearing and KSO downhill, with woods to L then both sides. Go over another stile, KSO downhill, then track becomes wider and more level, veering L to bring you out on the main road at the

5.5km Passo della Cisa (441/515) 1041m

Napoleon was responsible for building a road over this pass in 1808, connecting Pavia and Sarzana. There was formerly a hospice at the pass. There is a chapel (91 steps up to it) on a hill to RH side of the road. Bar/Rte (X Wed; open all year, but only at weekends in winter), souvenir shop.

In medieval times the route, following the valley of the Torrente Magriola, went further to the west. The first overnight stop after the pass was a *xenodochio* (hospice for travellers), already in existence in the eighth century, situated between Montelungo (833m) and Succisa (585m) and belonging to the Monastero dei Santi Salvatore e Benedetto di Leno.

This was a very dangerous area for pilgrims, though, as the route was far from habitation of any size and so was beset by robbers, who lay in wait to ambush pilgrims and other wayfarers. The problem reached such proportions that the medieval statutes of Pontremoli decreed that the trees along the road should be cut down to a distance of a crossbow on either side.

This was Stage XXXII (Sancte Benedicte, 32) in Sigeric's itinerary.

You are now in the regione of Toscana (Tuscany).

PASSO DELLA CISA TO LUCCA

Mountains near Passo della Cisa

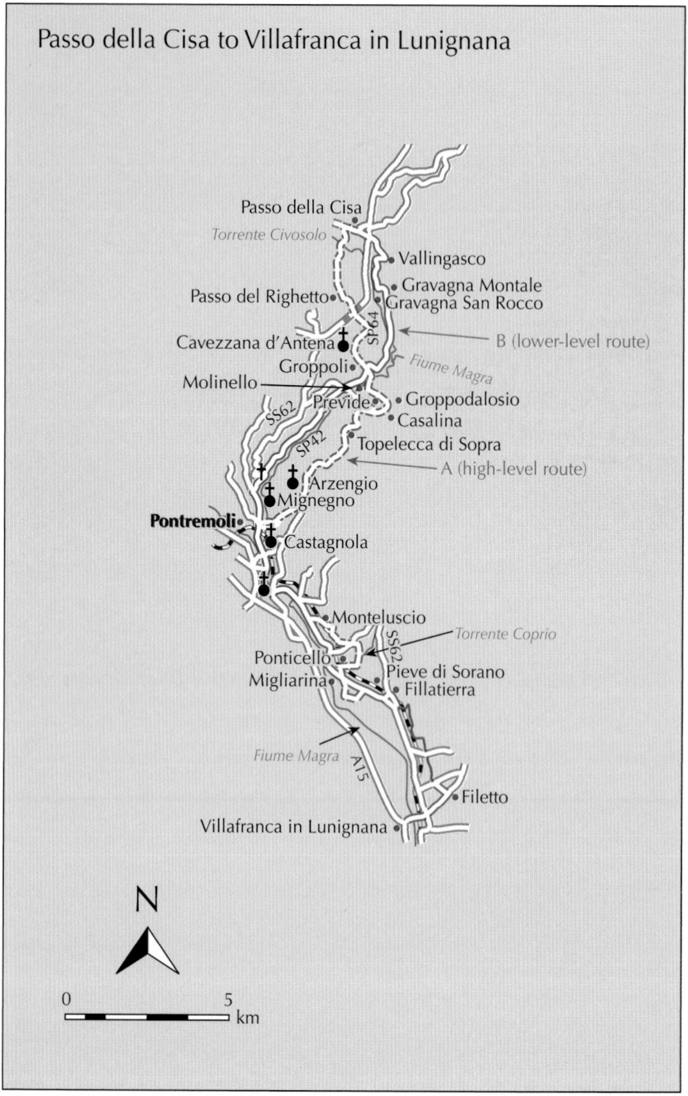
Passo della Cisa to Villafranca in Lunignana
Passo della Cisa
Torrente Civosolo
Vallingasco
Gravagna Montale
Passo del Righetto
Gravagna San Rocco
SP64
Cavezzana d'Antena
B (lower-level route)
Fiume Magra
Groppoli
Molinello
Previde
Groppodalosio
SS62
Casalina
SP42
Topelecca di Sopra
A (high-level route)
Arzengio
Mignegno
Pontremoli
Castagnola
Monteluscio
Torrente Coprio
SS62
Ponticello
Pieve di Sorano
Migliarina
Fillatierra
Fiume Magra
A15
Filetto
Villafranca in Lunignana
N
0
5
km

SECTION 3

Passo della Cisa to Lucca (140km)

Pontremoli

At the Passo della Cisa there is a choice of routes to Pontremoli, where the two routes reunite. *Option A is a high-level route that runs to the right-hand side of the SS62. It is 2.5km longer than the lower route, Option B, which goes to the left-hand side of the road.*

Option A, *the high-level route (designed by the CAI), is 22km long and leads down to Pontremoli (at 240m) via Monte Cuchero (1000m) Groppoli, Groppadolosio Inferiore, Arzengio and several other villages. This is a very nice route in good weather, but it will take a lot longer than expected for the distance involved. It goes up and down constantly, taking in 527m of ascent and 1327m of descent, going over the Monte Cucchero (1000m) and two passes – the Passo del Righetto (960m) and the Passo della Crocetta (699m) – before finally reaching the last downhill section only 5.5km before Pontremoli.*

This option is almost all on paths and tracks, but many of them have bad walking surfaces – cobbles, loose stones, gravel, shale or rocks – so it is extremely difficult to build up any sort of walking rhythm, especially on the steep downhill sections. As a result, while a fit walker might elsewhere proceed at a steady 4–5km per hour, walkers on this route will find themselves reduced to only 2–3km an hour, especially with a heavy rucksack. This is in no way intended to deter the user of this guide from taking the high-level option, but to alert him/her to the need to allow far more time than might be expected and to go equipped with enough to eat and drink (especially water in hot weather) for the whole day. You should not attempt this route in bad visibility or without enough time to reach Pontremoli in daylight.

Option B, *the lower-level route via Gravagna, is 19.5km long – an easy walk, all on tarmac, but there is very little traffic. It goes steadily and continuously downhill all the way down to Pontremoli, passing two bars (one with food) along the way.*

Note *Walkers can change routes where the high-level route crosses the SP64 just outside Groppoli (about 1km before Molinello). This gives pilgrims on Option B the chance to take the higher route if they have more time left than expected; and it provides an 'escape route' for pilgrims on the higher route if the weather turns bad or if they are running out of daylight.*

OPTION A – HIGH-LEVEL ROUTE

At the **Passo della Cisa** either go up the steps to visit the church and then pass to the side of it or go up the slope to L of steps and go through the wooden archway marked 'Porta Toscana della Francigena' (*seats to R*). Enter woods and path levels out, clear and fairly wide. KSO.

600m after the church fork L downhill onto a small FP (clearly marked). The path winds its way up and down the hillside, shady and clearly marked, but be attentive. KSO ahead all the time, and after a while the path becomes wider again.

600m later cross a wooden FB over stream (dry in summer) and KSO ahead in dappled sunshine on a clear day. 300m further on watch out for a fork to L, a small FP downhill. KSO. Cross/ford a stream as necessary, reach picnic tables some 50–60m later, and turn L over another stream. Emerge very briefly from the woods, go back into them, and 200m from picnic tables reach a forest road/track and turn R along it, forking L 60–70m later over another stream.

KSO(L) at next fork shortly afterwards, going gradually downhill most of the time then up and down along the hillside. Continue downhill and reach a junction with a FP to L to the SS62 (KM53/ii), 10m to L. Either continue on the road for the next 200m or KSO(R) here across a small field, then head back into the woods again before you arrive back at the SS62 200m later at road KM53.

Turn L here onto the other side, but be careful. Do not continue ahead on the more obvious, fairly wide path in front of you, but fork R onto a small rough FP, uphill at first, then level, then downhill below a line of fencing to the LH side. Reach a bend in the old SS62 (KM52/viii of the new one), with seats and splendid views on a clear day.

Turn hard L here past an electricity transformer, go through a gate onto a clear gravel track leading steeply uphill to start with then levelling out. Reach three radio transmitters then KSO steeply downhill. Track becomes a path on ridge with splendid views. This is the **Passo Righetto** (960m).

KSO on a ridge. *Two hamlets, both with churches, are visible in the valley below. If you look back behind you here you will see, on the skyline, the buildings and the church at the Passo della Cisa.*

Continue on a ridge, then downhill, after which the FP becomes wider, but with very rough rocky/stony surface (and therefore difficult to walk on). KSO, downhill all the time, often steeply. Reach clear fork in path, KSO(R) ahead, and 700–800m later emerge by a house on the edge of the hamlet of

7km Cavezzana d'Antena (448/508) 608m

Seat at junction. To visit church turn R then retrace your steps to continue.

Turn L here on grassy track at first, then rocky lane. KSO. 1km later veer R down side of barn to main street in

1km Groppoli (449/507) 514m

Cross street and go down cobbled lane. 500m later watch out for a LH turn down narrow lane with wall to L, and 100m later reach the SP64 and the junction with Option B. *(To change to Option B at this point continue on the SP64, having turned R, and proceed below.>)*

Turn R here, then only a few metres later turn L down steep walled lane all the way down to the **Torrente Civasola** (412m) and cross it by a new suspension bridge. A few metres after that watch out for a steep LH fork uphill, and 700m later reach a road. Turn R, then immediately L down a similar path to the one you have just come up on, and 200m later reach a road again. Turn L, and then KSO(L) at fork between houses in the hamlet of **Previdè** (455m).

At last house, at fork, KSO(L) up walled lane, uphill. KSO ahead along it, either uphill or on the level all the time. 600m later, at fork, KSO(R) ahead and 700m after that enter

2.5km Groppadalosio (451.5/504.5) 510m

Go along its only street, turn R just before house No 11 and opposite an empty wayside shrine, and then turn R down unevenly stepped lane leading down to a very fine example of a hump-backed bridge (16th century) over the **Fiume Magra**.

Continue ahead on small cobbled path on other side. KSO uphill on it for 800m to level tarmac road and turn R to the entrance to **Casalina** (488m), 1km later. 100m after that fork L up along a grassy embankment, then veer L up and behind the village. At junction (*fountain*) KSO(L) ahead uphill, veering L up tarmac lane, R over bridge over stream and past a small chapel (on L). KSO. 400m later a road joins from back R – KSO ahead along it. Pass cemetery (*tap*), and 100m after that fork L up cobbled path uphill into woods, veering R. It then levels out and goes just gently uphill until 1km later it reaches a clearing with large HT pylons.

KSO ahead L on wide stony lane, then 150m later, at junction, KSO straight ahead, downhill slightly, on small FP which gradually becomes wider and cobbled. KSO. Pass **Fosso del Pratello** (a wide ditch) and a stone bridge over a river and KSO, the ground continuously cobbled and continuously uphill. Eventually it levels out a bit. Pass **Fosso della Spergiura** and another stone bridge over a river and KSO again, still uphill, to reach a tarmac road in

3.5km Topelecca di Sopra (455/501) 584m

Turn R, and 70m later turn L up cobbled lane by a garage, veering R up to a T-junction. Turn L (still cobbled) veering R uphill yet again. Reach a roundabout by a stone wayside shrine, cross over and go downhill to its RH side, still cobbled. Route levels out, turns R over ford and then starts uphill again, albeit less steeply. KSO. KSO. KSO to reach the chapel at the

2.5km Passo della Crocetta (457.5/498.5) 699m

The path now becomes a wide gravel track, but a few metres after the second building fork L and KSO downhill. Pass several identical wayside crosses (part of a series of Stations of the Cross) and continue downhill all the time. Reach the first house in the village by a wayside shrine, pass to L of house and KSO ahead (on tarmac) into

2km Arzengio (459.5/496.5) 481m

Bar.

Follow the road down then turn L, passing bar, turn R under arch at end and continue on raised walkway. KSO(L) ahead on concrete path, then at a division of paths turn R, marked 'Via F'. (The LH turn is also marked in red and white but goes to Ceretoli). 100m later reach a road by the place-name board for Arzengio and turn second L here (ie the RH of two LH options) towards the cemetery (*tap*) on a tarmac lane. KSO downhill here, steeply, on stony track. KSO, pass house on L and KSO, downhill all the time. Road becomes tarmac. KSO(R) at fork past an agriturismo and veer L, R, L and R downhill to a T-junction. Turn R (by house No 8) alongside a parking area, turn L over a bridge back over the **Fiume Magra** again, go under the building ahead and emerge on the SP42 to the LH side of the **Vecchio Ospedale** at the entrance to **Pontremoli** (3.5km). Turn L, and the route description continues after the box about Pontremoli.

OPTION B – LOWER-LEVEL ROUTE

A few metres past the bar (on L) at the **Passo della Cisa** fork L behind the crash barrier onto a FP that becomes wider and clearer, leading down to the SP64 500m later, by two houses. Turn L, and shortly afterwards pass a memorial plaque (on R) to two British servicemen (Dudgeon and Blunt) who were shot here in 1943 by a firing squad.

KSO – literally! *Very little traffic on this road; it is wooded and so mainly shady. On this section of the route there are so many woods and so few villages that there are hardly any views, and there is almost nowhere to sit down either.* Continue downhill steeply to start with, zigzagging past the villages of **Vallingoso** and then **Gravagna San Rocco** (*with modern stucco church of San Rocco and completely free-standing bell tower*). Follow the road round to L, then R, then reach a junction with the road (on L) to **Gravagna Montale** in Gravagna. KSO ahead.

Just after the turning on the R to Groppoli there is one on the L, waymarked for the Via Francigena. ❮ This is where Option A from the Passo della Cisa crosses the SP64, *after which you can either continue following Option B to Pontremoli or, if you have enough time, turn L downhill to follow Option A and continue to Pontremoli via Arzengio (follow route description from* Groppoli, *above).*

To continue on Option B go downhill to the junction with the turning (on L) to

11km Molinello 455m

Bar, and another bar/trattoria (does meals).

Pilgrim route through Pontremoli

At next junction 200m later the road becomes the SP42. KSO, mainly down-hill on level, and 4.5km later reach junction with SP62 (16km from Cisa Pass by road), and continue on this (ie KSO(L) downhill). *Pontremoli visible ahead below.*

1km later cross the **Torrente Magriola** and, veering L, enter **Mignegno** (294m; 2 bars) on the outskirts of Pontremoli. 1km after that pass the mod-ern hospital (on L). Then pass the old hospital as well (also on L, **《** where Option A rejoins Option B), then the remains of the 11th-century **Chiesa di San Giorgio**. *This was originally a three-nave building annexed to the hospi-tal (where pilgrims were accommodated), but only one apse is left.* At fork by bridge KSO(R) ahead, then either turn L at end under railway bridge then continue on metal walkway to **Ponte Pompeo Spagnoli**, turning hard R then L to go under archway into the old part of Pontremoli (8.5km); or fork R at end uphill to the **castello**, then come down again and go through the archway to continue as above.

8.5km Pontremoli (463/493) Pop. 8153, 241m

All facilities. OP in Convento dei Capuccini, Via Capouccini 2 (up on hill across from railway station; 0187.830395). Ostello Castello del Piagnaro Porta di Parma (0187.4601211 and 0187.831439; need to pre-book, X Mon). B&B Francesca, Via Piagnaro 3 (339.5970871). ***Hotel Napoleon, Piazza Italia 2 (0187.830544). TO Piazza Repubblica 33. Trenitalia.

In medieval times there were many inns for travellers and many pilgrim hospices here, as the town is situated at the junc-tion of the rivers Verde and Magra and on the main thoroughfare from Parma to Sarzana – some-thing reflected in its elongated layout. The hospices included one dedicated to Santi Giacomo e Leonardo set up by the Knights of Saint John of Jerusalem, one run by the Knights of the Tau de Altopascio (an important hospice order on the Via Francigena) next

Pilgrim badges for sale

183

to the church of San Giacomo, and one attached to the ninth-century Chiesa di San Giorgio. In the Chiesa di San Pietro there is a sandstone sculpture depicting a labyrinth, symbolising the pilgrim's journey, beset with difficulties.

There are also many other churches worth visiting in Pontremoli, including the Duomo di Santa Maria Assunta, the Chiesa di San Nicolò and the Chiesa di San Lazzaro. The Chiesa di San Francesco is said to have been founded after the saint himself passed by in 1219. Castello del Piagnaro (9th–10th centuries), converted into a fortress during the 14th–16th centuries, now houses the Museo delle Statua-Stele and an ostello (see above).

Stage XXXI (Puntremel, 31) in Sigeric's itinerary.

Both routes

Continue down street to end, go through two squares and, from **Piazza Centrale**, continue ahead on **Via Armand Ricci Armani** (*but turn L here on Via Cairoli, over the river, to sleep in the Convento dei Capuccini*) and then along **Via Cavour**. Turn L into **Via Ponte Cesare Battisti** and go over the bridge. Go through arch and turn R into **Via Mazzini** then continue on **Via Petro Cocchi**, passing the Chiesa di San Giacomo di Altopascio. This became a closed convent (nuns) in 1508, and was rebuilt with a church in 1641.

Reach a road with a three-sided 'square' in front of you (*shop ahead on L*), and at the end of this join the SS62 (*pavement on RH side*) coming from back L (**Viale dei Mille**). KSO then, opposite house No 14, note remains of the **Chiesa di San Lazzaro**. *This church was built at the junction of the Via Francigena and one of the fords (guado) over the River Magra, connecting it to the Via di Saliceto (an alternative route). The church was remodelled in 1878 for road widening. Originally dedicated to San Martino, it changed to San Lazzaro, as it was near a lazaretto (an isolation hospital for people with infectious diseases, especially leprosy and the plague), maintained by the comune di Pontremoli.*

KSO again, then opposite house No 50 fork L onto paved street towards the church of the **Santissima Annunziata** (*fountain*).

Part-way along, before reaching the church of the Santissima Annunziata, a VF sign indicates a L turn under an archway (with '1776' above it) after house No 63; but there are no more waymarks there at present, so continue to the church and rejoin the SS2 further on.

Return to the SS62 and continue along it (carefully). At road KM34/iii watch out for VF sign turning L off road to the side of a furniture store (*fountain and seats on L*), veering R, and then KSO(R) ahead on unsurfaced road leading to main street in the lower part of **Moneluscio**.

Turn L at end on street under the railway line, veering R, then KSO(R) at fork. Veer R, cross bridge over river at parking area with seats, veering R, reach crossing and KSO ahead on unsurfaced road. Turn L at end, veering R to church in

6km Ponticello (469/487)

Chiesa dei Santi Rocco e Bernado

Pass to LH side of church (marked 'Borgo Ponticello'), go under arch to R ahead (*seat*), then turn L along the main street in the old part of the village (*cobbles and tarmac*). Continue ahead to a T-junction 300–400m further on, then turn L, taking RH of two options almost immediately afterwards, veering R.

Tarmac stops. Cross a brick three-arched bridge over the wide (but very likely completely dried-up) **Torrente Coprio**. KSO on wide shady, stony track on other side, gently uphill all the time, then about 1km later watch out for a hard RH turn uphill, levelling out. KSO, ignoring turns, for 400–500m, then go downhill, steeply at first, then more gently, and then KSO on the level.

Go down at end to some houses, KSO ahead on walled lane, turn R at end, veering L, and then go under the railway line. Turn L on other side, but then turn R immediately through a tunnel under the buildings to the SS62 by a war memorial in

2km Migliarina (471/485)

Cross over to the other side, go down the street ahead, veering L, and KSO ahead when the tarmac stops, through several fields. At the end the track turns R towards some houses. Turn L in front of them, and 150m later reach a minor road and turn R. Follow the road round for 500m, then turn L at a junction, veering R and then L onto a minor road with fenced-in horse enclosures to either side. Continue to the end, turn L and reach the SS62 again at KM31 (*supermarket on R*) opposite the

2.5km Pieve di Sorano (473.5/482.5) 157m

Parish church (*pieve*) of Santo Stefano, dating from 5th–12th centuries and built of river stones on the base of a large Roman farm dating from the first century BC. Normally open. TO up lane behind church. Picnic tables.

Pieve di Sorano, Santo Stefano

Pass church, then fork L here off the SS62 (*bars, shop, bakery, bank, PO*), and then turn L under railway line. Veer L uphill, then L, then turn R shortly afterwards up a very long flight of (93) steps into

1km Filattiera (474.5/481.5) Pop. 2453, 203m

Castello, built on the ruins of a Byzantine defensive structure, with its small 12th-century Chiesa di San Giorgio, in which an eighth-century stone plaque mentions Bishop Leogar's duties with regard to providing an ospedale for pilgrims.

Turn L in parking area at the top, then R into **Via Giacomo Matteotti** past castle, and then R into **Borgo S Maria**, passing church on R. (Alternatively, turn second R into **Via Volperone** (*bar in square*) and then R into **Borgo S Maria**.)

Veer L at end to **Piazzetta San Giorgio** (*go uphill R to visit church, shady seats, then retrace your steps*). Continue downhill, through arch, and turn R to continue. Go downhill to railway line, but instead of turning R under tunnel, turn L then immediately L over bridge over stream. KSO(R) ahead uphill on grassy/cobbled lane into woods, veering L to pass small church. KSO. KSO(R) at fork, and track becomes grassy. KSO. At fork KSO(L) ahead, up and down on a rocky FP, its surface gradually improving. At junction of tracks KSO(R) ahead towards HT pylon, uphill to start with, but then going gradually downhill as gravel/earth track. *This is another section of the route where pilgrims were likely to be ambushed by robbers, as well as being harassed by small landowners who demanded payment of a toll from travellers.*

KSO at next junction, descending all the time. On reaching a T-junction above a river bed in front of you, turn R past isolated house. Continue on unsurfaced road, KSO(L) ahead at fork, cross bridge over small river and reach minor tarred road. Turn L along it, then 300m later turn R onto gravel road into woods, which gradually becomes a grassy track. Follow it round, ignoring turns to L or R. 300m after crossing/fording shallow stream reach road, and turn L then immediately R on another gravel road down the side of an electricity substation. Cross/ford another stream, continue ahead, cross three fields, then a fourth. Continue first on walled lane, then on gravel road, reaching tarmac road (**Via del Menhir**) by a small golf course/sports field on R (*picnic area to R at start*), on outskirts of

5.5km Filetto (480/476) 163m

You have now passed the halfway point on the Italian section of the Via Francigena.

Turn R then immediately L on **Via S Genesio**, with chestnut woods to either side (*picnic area to R at start*). Pass **Chiesa di San Genesio** (*with covered porch and seats*), veering L (*rte on L and also to R*), and reach bigger road. Turn R onto **Viale Italia** (*shop on corner, bar opposite*), but to visit church (*this was formerly an ospedale*) turn L under arch and then retrace your steps. (*A longer off-road variant route also goes this way, rejoining this one in Terrarossa, but is not described here*). 1km later reach junction with SP62 in

1km Villafranca in Lunignana (481/475) Pop. 4613, 135m

Shops etc. B&B in Villa Magnolia, house No 33 near crossing with SS62 (338.3859648). Camping Castagneto, Via Nazionale 2, 1/4–30/9 (0187.493492, reservation essential). Remains of Castello del Malnido, built to control the traffic on the Via Francigena. Trenitalia.

Cross over, KSO ahead on **Via Roma** (*Chiesa di San Francisco to R*) to railway station. Turn L (**Via della Stazione**), then turn R (**Via Ponte Magra**) under railway

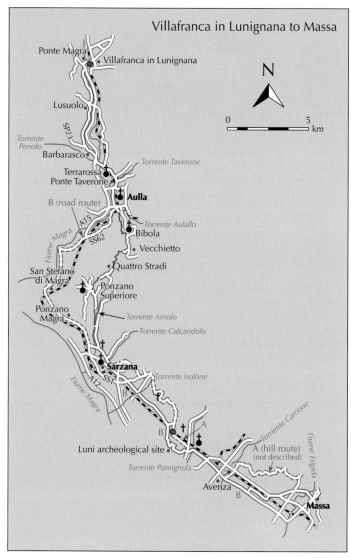

Villafranca in Lunignana to Massa

N

0   5 km

Ponte Magra
Villafranca in Lunignana
Lusuolo
Torrente Penolo
SP23
Barbarasco
Terrarossa
Ponte Taverone
Torrente Taverone
Aulla
B (road route)
A15
SS62
Fiume Magra
Bibola
Torrente Aulallo
Vecchietto
Quattro Stradi
San Stefano di Magra
Ponzano Superiore
Ponzano Magra
Torrente Amolo
Torrente Calcandolo
Sarzana
A12
SS1
Fiume Magra
Torrente Isolone
B
B
Luni archeological site
Torrente Pomignola
A
Torriente Carrione
A (hill route)
(not described)
Fiume Frigida
Avenza
B
Massa

line, then turn R and L on other side. Cross bridge over the **Fiume Magra** and then turn L on other side (signposted 'Lusuolo 3').

KSO, cross motorway, going mainly gently but steadily uphill, woods to both sides. After 3km the road (*very quiet*) levels off and reaches junction with road from Campoli in

5km Lusuoli (486/470) 179m

Walled village with castle (contains Museo della Emigrazione della gente di Toscana), B&B Lusuolo Centro 7 (0187.493174).

KSO(L) ahead then go through arch (*tap at side*). Go down street to another arch at end, go down flight of steps, KSO(L) ahead on unsurfaced road downhill and join tarmac road coming from back R. Road zigzags steeply downhill then continues alongside motorway until it winds its way up to the junction with the SP23 in

3km Barbarasco (489/467) 113m

Shop, bars, banks etc. Rte/Albergo Rolando (X Wed), Via Roma 193 (0187.477371 and 339.8611760).

Turn L. Go over motorway, go over a river with a very long bridge, continue on **Via Barbarasco** and enter

2km Terrarossa (491/465) 70m

Shops, bars etc. Ostello comunale in Castello Malaspina (0187.4749427), built in the 16th–17th centuries, which dominates the town.

Turn R at T-junction onto **Via Nazionale**, veering L by public garden. Turn R at junction opposite castle onto **Via Nazionale Cisa**. KSO. Cross the **Torrente Civiglia** and KSO. Road becomes **Via Ponte Taverone**. Cross the **Torrente Taverone** and enter

3km Aulla (494/462) Pop. 10,406, 64m

All facilities. OP – ask in museo/parish office of San Caprasio, but try to arrive before 7pm (otherwise there are phone numbers on the door – 0187.420148 and 339.6380331). Fortezza La Brunella, up on the hill in the Parco La Brunella, has hostel-type accommodation (X Mon, 0187.409077). **Hotel Pasquino, Piazza Mazzini 22 (0187.420509), ***Hotel Demy, Via A Salucci 9 (0187.408370). TO Piazza 8 Marzo (0187.409474). Trenitalia.

AULLA E LA FORTEZZA DELLA BRUNELLA

Old illustration of the Fortezza La Brunella

The Abbadia di San Caprasio, one of the oldest stopping places on the route, was found by Adalberto, Marquis of Tuscany, in 884. Originally dedicated to Santa Maria, it changed its name after the remains of the fifth-century saint were transferred there later.

Stage XXX (Aguilla, 30) in Sigeric's itinerary.

KSO on road then, opposite house No 252 and with a pedestrian crossing, turn R under railway line. Turn second L onto **Viale Lunignana** on other side and follow road round, veering L at big junction. After a petrol station and before a shopping complex cross to RH side, then veer R to pass behind a big store to continue on Viale Lunignana again – a long straight avenue with a wall to R and river beyond it. KSO. Pass the bus station (on L), shortly after which the Viale Lunignana runs into the **Via XXV Aprile**. Continue to **Piazza dell'Abadia** and the **Abbadia di San Caprasio**.

Pass to R of church to **Piazza dell'Abbadia**, then turn R immediately down **Via M Andrea** (a very short street), continue ahead between buildings, then turn L and go down four steps, after which the road bridge becomes visible ahead. Go towards it and turn R onto the SS62 (road KM15) to cross the **Fiume Magra**.

Note *The section from Aulla to Sarzana is only 17km, but allow plenty of time as the route is very steep and the paths are often rocky. Loose stones and surfaces that are difficult to walk on make it hard to move at your normal walking speed. (This is another of the sections waymarked by the CAI.) It is almost all in woods and so is shady, but there are no facilities of any kind between Aulla and Ponzano Superiore (where there is only one simple bar, but no food), so go prepared. Option A, below, is the normal route, but in bad weather/visibility it is suggested that you continue from Aulla to Sarzana on the road (14.5km), despite all the traffic (see Option B below).*

OPTION A – NORMAL ROUTE

At bend on other side of the **Fiume Magra** turn L down minor road (marked 'Bibola'). At second bend fork R uphill on narrow tarmac road, then just before houses on L turn L on FP along side of wall, marked 'Passaigo pedonale'. Continue uphill, through woods, and at junction with gravel track KSO(R) ahead through vines, uphill past house to road. Turn R here and then immediately L up path opposite house No 4 (although if this is very overgrown you will have to stay on the road here all the way to Bibola).

The FP winds its way uphill through woods, shortcutting all the bends in the road. However, 600m before a wide gravel track a huge tree had fallen lengthwise along the track at the time this guide was written, completely blocking it, so you will need to investigate the best way of getting round it. Then, 300 after that, two large trees had fallen across it at waist level. The gravel track then turns R uphill. 500–600m later reach four-point junction of gravel tracks and KSO(L) ahead. Then, 400–500m later watch out for a wayside shrine on your R, up some steps. Fork R here (up some steps) uphill, and then go down to gravel road 400m later. Turn R, veering L, and then turn R at tarmac road (or KSO if you want to visit the village and then retrace your steps – castello above you) into

3.5km Bibola (497.5/458.5) 378m

Hilltop village with a castello perched on top.

Veer R by bus stop to gravel road downhill.

Tarmac road joins from back L. KSO(R) ahead. KSO (*good views of the Castello de Bibola behind you*) to village of

1.5km Vecchietto (499/457) 269m

KSO(R) at fork at entrance, passing in front of church and veering R to continue through village. Continue ahead through archway, veering L, and fork R part-way down. Go under archway over the street, veering L uphill, veer L at top and continue on gravel track after last house, forking R to pass large wayside shrine (*with limited shelter*). KSO, with the path winding its way uphill. Pass second similar large wayside shrine and KSO uphill. The track then continues as a wide FP, becoming gradually narrower and rockier as it climbs.

If you walk in the autumn it may seem very colourful to walk through a carpet of variegated fallen leaves, but you can't see what the surface is like underneath. Sharp loose stones? A smooth earth track? Loose scree? Be careful!

1km later reach a wide earth track and turn L along it, then 300m after that reach a clearing with stony FP to R – turn R uphill (both options meet up). Path zigzags steeply uphill, then levels out for a while, then goes downhill a little. Ford/cross stream, then veer L uphill again on other side. Continue uphill, then after a while track levels out, winding its way along side of hill.

Cross another stream (probably dry) and continue on other side, mainly level, and 600m later reach clearing and wide gravel track crossing at right angles. This is

2.5km Quatro Stradi (501.5/454.5) 532m

KSO on FP straight ahead on other side here, and KSO, ignoring turns to R and L, for 1.5km. On reaching a junction in a clearing KSO ahead down rough FP. KSO(L) at fork and KSO, downhill all the time for 1km more, after which, by first houses, you come out of the woods onto a gravel road (still downhill). *Panoramic views of whole area.* Turn R at end onto tarmac road, then L, passing cemetery (*Via Mantero*), to a piazza in

3km Ponzano Superiore (496.5/451.5) 257m
Bar, B&B La Costa, Via Marion Baria 11 (338.8080166).

You are now, until you reach Luni, in the regione of Liguria. Stage XXIX (Sce Stefane, 29) in Sigeric's itinerary was in Santo Stefano di Magra, to the west of here, now a town on the SS62 (visited in Option B, below).

Turn L into **Via Orsini** (*unmarked bar at corner*), veering L (*fountain*), and the road becomes a grassy track downhill, veering R. 200–300m later go over a concrete bridge, then turn R then R again onto an old concrete lane which becomes a VS. Follow it downhill, mainly gradually. KSO(L) at fork. At end (*very last house*) 1.5km later, reach open gravel area. (*Good views back to Ponzano to rear.*) KSO(R) ahead up very rough stony track, then KSO downhill on FP, following it uphill and down to an archeological dig/excavations – I Rudieri del Castello de la Brina (ninth century). *Panoramic views, including over to the sea.*

Make your way through the dig (well waymarked, but very fiddly and very rough underfoot) then go downhill on a very rough FP. At the bottom continue ahead on a better path, through trees. KSO, uphill and down, ignoring turns to L and R, until you reach a fork with two wide tracks ahead, one uphill, one down. Fork L, downhill, and the path becomes narrow and rough again. Turn L by house with sheds, then reach tarmac lane by next house and follow it downhill. Turn L at the bottom into **Via Lago**, cross bridge over the **Torrente Amolo** and turn R onto the main road (*seat*).

1.5km later reach junction (**Via San Gotardo** to R; *pizzeria on corner, X Wed*) and turn L. KSO, then turn R down **Via Turi**. Turn L ahead into **Via Cisa**, cross the **Torrente Calcandolio** and go through an archway to enter the pedestrianised centro storico in **Sarzana** (see box for Sarzana below).

OPTION B – ROAD ROUTE (BAD WEATHER/VISIBILITY)

Turn R over the bridge over the **Fiume Magra** as described above, but instead of turning L to Bibola on the other side, KSO ahead on the SS62. *There are some old VF waymarks along the way, and the route is more or less flat. Note that although you would normally walk on the LH side of the road to face the oncoming traffic, because there are a lot of bends you will often have to cross (carefully) over to the RH side (and then back again) so that you can see – and be seen – by the vehicles coming towards you.* KSO until you reach

8km Santo Stefano di Magra

Shops etc. Hotel Rte Il Ciambellino, Via Cisa Sud 394 (0187.631480), Albergo Elicrim, Via Alessandro Volta 23 (349.3513386). Public garden at bend on L of SS62 is a useful place for a rest. Old part of town to L uphill on entry.

Stage XXIX (Sce Stefane, 29) in Sigeric's itinerary.

KSO on road again. *The route is almost all built up from here to Sarzana, so there is quite a lot of pavement and/or hard shoulder to walk on, but it is also very noisy.* Continue through Ponzano Magra (4.5km) and for 2.5km more to enter the centro storico in

6.5km Sarzana (509/447) Pop. 20,1226, 28m

Shops etc. TO Piazza San Giorgio (opposite railway station, 0187.614225/614312). OP in Convento San Francisco di Assisi, Via Paci 8 (next to church, 0187.620356; mass 6pm). Albergo La Villetta, Via Sobborgo Emiliano 24 (0187.620195). Trenitalia.

At the time when Sigeric was travelling through this part of Italy Sarzana was no more than a simple castle built up on the Sarzanello hill dominating the whole area. However, it gradually increased in size and importance as the ancient Roman colony in Luni declined, when the port there (the entrance and exit point for, among other travellers, pilgrims journeying to and from Santiago de Compostela) silted up. Sarzana became a city, and in the second half of the 15th century Lorenzo di Medici built circular ramparts and a ditch surrounding the town, and also demolished the original castrum to build the present Fortezza di Sarzanello on the same site. The town's other sights include the Cattedrale di Santa Maria Assunta (built on the site of the former parish church of San Basilio after the episcopal seat was transferred from Luni to Sarzana, although the building was completed only in 1474), the Pieve di San Andrea (12th century, but possibly earlier), the Museo Diocesano and the Casa Torre Buonaparte (Napoleon's family originally came from Sarzana before they moved to Corsica).

At this point there are two routes from Sarzana. One, almost flat, leaves from behind the railway station and goes alongside the sea via **Marina**, **Luni Mare** *and* **Marina di Massa**, *but this is not yet waymarked and so is not described here. The other, described below, goes via the archeological site in Luni and then Avenza, and the two join up again on the southern outskirts of Massa (see below).*

To leave Sarzana continue ahead on **Via Bertolini**, cross the **Piazza Matteotti** and KSO on Via Mazzini to **Piazza Niccolo V**. *For pilgrim accommodation turn L behind the Duomo, continue on Via Castrucci and then on Via Paci. (The following morning you do not need to go into the town centre, but turn L here on Via San Francesco to continue and then go L opposite the wayside shrine by house No 51.)*

KSO ahead on **Via Mazzini**, go through archway at other end of town to a roundabout. Turn L here (road not named at start, but a signpost indicates 'Via

Francesco'). Turn R by a wayside shrine by house No 51 up a tarmac lane, passing a large property (on L) called 'La Missione' (*a former school but now a community facility*) and then KSO uphill on a wide grassy track. This becomes cobbled, zigzagging steeply uphill (*good view back over Sarzana as you climb*).

Reach a junction at the top (*tap*). You have arrived here via the **Via Montata di Sarzanello**, and the Fortezza Castracani is now above on your L. Turn L downhill again, then KSO. 100m later fork (not turn) R down the continuation of the Via Montata di Sarzanello, veering R downhill into a built-up area – this is **Sarzanello** (*bakery*).

At a crossroads at the bottom cross a small river and KSO ahead. Continue ahead on **Via Canalburo**, a very long street, following it ahead as it twists and turns and then goes uphill to a T-junction with a bigger road at the top. Turn L here (*bar, bakery and alimentari to R*).

KSO ahead to reach a parking area on L and cross a bridge over the **Torrente Isolone**. KSO ahead, reach junction with a road to R shortly afterwards, and KSO ahead on **Via Canipavola**. Pass public garden (*seat*) on L at bend shortly after that, and KSO(R) here on **Via Montecchio**, downhill. Cross bridge over another small river, reach a T-junction, turn R then immediately L (placename board for Colombiera) and continue (still on Via Montecchio) to junction with **Via Provinciale** in **Colombiera** (*bar, shop etc*). Turn L (straight ahead leads to the SS1, the Via Aurelia) down the Via Provinciale, then 100m later turn R into **Via Paradiso**. At the end turn R into **Via Bologna**. 200m later reach a junction with a bigger road and turn L, veering L past sports stadium, and enter **Molicciara**.

KSO ahead, veering R to a junction and turn L here, marked 'Centro Sociale'. 200m after that turn R into **Via Piedmontana**. KSO(L) ahead at junction and reach a 'stop' sign at crossroads (*bar – does meals – farmacia, tap*).

Carrara, marble quarries

Continue ahead on **Via Molino del Piano**, enter the frazione of the same name, but fork R at bend (by fountain). Then turn R into **Piazza Gugliemlo Marconi** and a large grassed area/dried-up river bed with picnic tables. KSO(R) ahead here on a raised tree-lined path. Cross road at the entrance to **Palvotrisia** (bridge to L), continue on other side, then 50m later turn L over a stone bridge. Turn R on the other side along **Via Olmarello**, then after house No 32 turn R into **Via Corta**. Cross canal, then turn L along its RH side. Pass bridge (to L) and KSO ahead. Pass another bridge, KSO, and the path becomes a minor road.

Pass a fourth and then a fifth bridge, and a sixth by a 'stop' sign, and KSO, still on the RH bank of the canal, which has become a grassy path again. Pass the sluice gates, then at the next bridge turn R into **Via Orti**, a wide tarmac road, in **Palvotrisia**. At a 'stop' sign turn L (into the **Via Palvotrisia**), veering L (only 5km from Sarzana by the main road!) to the **Via Aurelia** at

9km SS1 (road KM391) near Stazione FS Luni (518/438) 14m

There are two possible options here, which rejoin into a single route before Avenza.

OPTION A – BAD WEATHER/VISIBILITY

If you are short of daylight or the weather is atrocious, you can take the old route (2.5km shorter) and turn L here for 300m along the SS1 to **Luni railway station**. Cross over, go under the underpass under tracks, and then turn L immediately on the other side onto a quiet tarmac road that continues parallel to the railway (on your L). At the end turn R to the group of trees by the FB over the **Torrente Pomignola** and continue as described below. **>**

OPTION B – VIA LUNI

The waymarked route takes you on a detour – to get off the SS1 – around the perimeter of the archeological site at Luni, although apart from the amphitheatre it is only possible to get a general idea of the size and scale of it all, not the detail. *Luni is recorded as being one of the stages in Sigeric's itinerary (Stage XXVIII; Luna, 28), but it is now thought that it was not here, but located further over to the west, nearer the sea.*

Cross the SS1 and continue ahead on **Via Provasco**, which then becomes the **Via Appia** (*near the end, the Carrara marble quarries are visible ahead to the L*).

1.5km later cross the **Via Braccioli**, go towards the entrance gates to the archeo-logical site, but then (unless you have time to visit it – entrance fee) turn L along its perimeter wall. Turn R along its bottom side, cross a road, and just after some houses watch out for a RH turn alongside metal grille fencing. At the end turn L onto a tarmac lane, veering L past the amphitheatre (fenced in) – this is the **Via Appia** – then turn R at a fork. Turn L onto **Via Caleina**, R onto **Via Marina** and again at junction (to R) onto **Via Padule**.

KSO ahead ('no-entry' sign) to a T-junction with a bigger road, cross over to four large trees (where Option A joins the route) and **〈** go up slope or steps to cross a FB over the **Torrente Pormignola**. Continue on the other side on **Via Carlone**, then **Via Pormignola**, to a big road coming from the R and leading under a railway line.

Cross over and continue ahead on **Via Provinciale**. KSO ahead, entering **Avenza**. 1km later reach a large roundabout at a junction. Cross over and KSO ahead again on **Via Giovanni Pietro**. Go over the **Torrente Carrione** and reach the **Torre** (*La Rocca, partial remains of a tower*) and the Chiesa di San Pietro in

7km Avenza (525/431) 9m

All facilities. OP in Ostello 'Antonio Mazzi' in Piazza Finelli (opposite the Chiesa di San Pietro, 0585.857203, 338.8333413, 366.8084564). Hotel Carrara, Via Petacchi 21 (0585.857616).

Town of Roman origin on the Via Aurelia linking Rome to the north, with the remains of its 13th-century castle. The Chiesa di San Pietro was first men-tioned in a Papal Bull of 1187, but much of the present building dates from its 17th-century reconstruction. Originally a building with a single nave and transept, the church also housed the Ospitale di San Antonio (for pilgrims and other travellers) in a former wing of the church.

There is now a choice of routes. *Option A (not described) is longer and more scenic; Option B is flatter and more direct. They join up on the far side of Massa.*

OPTION A – HILL ROUTE

The waymarked route leads off the Via Aurelia on a very hilly, lengthy, sinuous 'loop' away from Avenza, and joins up with Option B by the town exit boards on the outskirts of Massa. To take this option (4–5km longer, but not described here) turn L by the **Chiesa di San Pietro** under an archway, then L again, to continue, skirting **Massa** on a minor road. **〉**

OPTION B – NORMAL ROUTE

This older route is still waymarked with yellow and white stickers, and is often noisy in places for short distances. But if the weather is bad, or if you have come all the way from Canterbury and are tired of 'scenic detours' aimed more at the Sunday walker than the long-haul pilgrim, you may prefer this option.

From Avenza, with the **Chiesa di San Pietro** on your R, continue on **Via Gino Menconi**, then KSO(L) at fork on **Via Passo Volpe** (not marked at start, and despite VF signs to R). Pass a public garden on L and KSO for 1.5km more, through a very dusty industrial area with marble factories, recycling plant and so on. Reach a 'stop' sign on the boundary of Avenza with a road coming from back R and KSO, reaching a railway line embedded in the road. 200m after this turn L for 150m along a very busy road (no name) towards a railway bridge. However, instead of going under it, turn R immediately before it on **Via Gotarda** (name only at end), continuing alongside the railway (now above you on your L) for 1km.

At the end cross a railway line. *The next section of the route was closed at the time of writing (see below for alternative route), but is described here.* Turn L over more lines by the **Massa Zona Industriale** railway station. Then turn L on the other side, then R alongside a factory on **Via Caselotto di Sopra** (not named at start). After that turn R at the end, veering L, to return to the SS1 (Via Aurelia) and continue on the cycle track on its RH side.

Alternative route After crossing the railway line, the level crossing ahead, through the railway station, is currently closed 'per lavoro', so until it reopens turn R here on **Via Casalotto di Sotto** (*tap*) and then first L onto **Via Bordigona** (not named at start). *This is very long, industrial road, but as a large part of it is lined on both sides with variegated flowering bushes it is less unpleasant than you might expect.* Continue to a T-junction at the end (*bar to L, supermarket to R*) and turn L under a railway bridge onto a busy road (pavement/hard shoulder). Cross another busy road (traffic lights), and after 1.5km reach the SS1 at a roundabout. Turn R along it on its cycle track to rejoin the main route.

The **main route** continues on cycle track for 1.5km more (*bars etc at intervals along the way*), crosses the long bridge over the *Fiume Frigida* (and the marble factories below it) and enters the centre of

9km Massa (534/422) Pop. 67,576, 54m

All facilities. Trenitalia.

The older part of the city, mainly 16th century, is dominated by the earlier fortified La Rocca. The name 'Massa' used to refer to what is now San Leonardo, to the west of the present town, with its hospice set up by the Knights of Saint

Massa cathedral

John of Jerusalem. Cattedrale dei Santi Pietro e Francesco was begun in the 15th century, with successive alterations (the facade dates from 1936).

Continue on **Viale G Puccini** on other side. KSO (cross junction via under-pass) on **Via Democrazia** (lined with orange trees and marked 'Ospedale pedi-atrica') and continue on **Viale Risorgimento**. KSO and pass the exit boards for Massa (town) and the hospital (on L) (this is where Option A from Avenza joins from back L, on Via Bargello). ❮ KSO, enter **Turano**, KSO again. Then pass the exit boards for Massa province (road KM376/viii), and 200m later enter **Montignoso/Le Capanne**. Fork L here onto **Via Sforza** (the SS1 continues R ahead here). At T-junction at end, 1km later, turn L. Continue along street ahead, and just before a farmacia fork L onto **Via Santa Maria**, past church. At end KSO ahead, joining main road coming from back R, leave Le Capanne and enter

3.5km Prato (537.5/418.5) 80m
Shops etc.

Continue up **Via Giorghetto**, then 100m later cross the FB over the **Torrente Montignoso**. Turn L on other side, then by shady sitting area and fountain (*note scallop shells*) turn hard R up **Via Palatina** uphill. KSO. *Views of sea as you climb.*
This area is badly waymarked. In theory you can shortcut a long 'loop' in the road via a 20m FP to L, but although this was indicated the first time this route was researched, it was not on two subsequent occasions.
KSO and pass viewpoint on R (*seats*), a restaurant and a junction where the LH option goes very steeply uphill. KSO(R) ahead here (passing an advertisement for The Secret, a B&B 50m further on on the R), gradually descending. Leave the province of Massa-Carrara, enter the province of Lucca, and the road becomes **Via Casone**. KSO ahead, downhill all the time.
Go through **Strettoia** (*shop on L, 2 bars*), after which the road becomes Via Strettoia, and then enter **Ripa**. Here you can either continue (*the old route, shorter*) until you reach a crossroads with traffic lights and a bigger road and KSO on other side on **Via Foccola**; or turn L into **Via Pigone** (waymarked), then turn R into **Via della Chiesa** to junction with bar and shops, then continue ahead on **Via della Pace** and L into **Via Foccola**, where both options reunite. At more traffic lights at a crossing at the end cross over and veer L to cross the bridge over the **Fiume Versilia** in

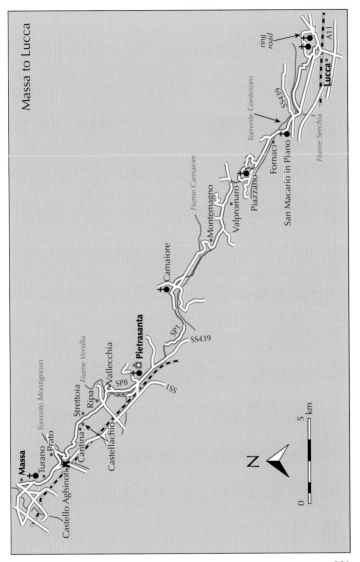

Massa to Lucca

7.5km Vallecchia (545/411) 24m

Pieve di San Stefano.

Follow road round to R. KSO on the SP8 and at the end, opposite a church ▼, turn R onto the **Via Prov. Vallecchia** (the SP8) at the entrance to the town.

A short waymarked variant route starts just after the church, to L, onto Via Solaio, returning to the SP8 again at a bend. Here it crosses over to the RH side, goes alongside the Fiume Versilia for a short distance, goes towards the railway line and then returns to the SP8 again shortly before the entrance to Pietrasanta.

KSO(L) in **Piazza Matteotti** (on R) and pass **Piazza dello Statuto** (on L) and TO (*in booth*, also on L) and go through an archway into **Via Mazzini** and into the **Piazza del Duomo** in the old part of the town in the centre of

Pietrasanta cathedral

3km Pietrasanta (548/408) Pop. 24,469, 21m

All facilities. OP in La Rocca, a convent uphill above centre of town at Via della Rocca 10 (0584.793093 and 0584.793095). Albergo/Rte Stipino (at entrance to town on L, Via Prov. Vallecchia 50, 0584.71448). TO (0584.283284) in booth in Piazza dello Statuto, a square between the Via Prov. Vallecchia and the start of Via Mazzini.

Town founded in 1255 on the site of the pre-existing (sixth–seventh century) Rocca di Sala (a fortress) and taking its name from the *podestà* (mayor) of Lucca, one Guiscardo Pietrasanta. 13th-century Duomo di San Martino, 14th-century Chiesa di San Agostino. Relief sculpture of Saint Roch on the cathedral facade.

From the **Piazza Duomo** pass to RH side of cathedral, then KSO down **Via Garibaldi** and continue to reach the cemetery (on R). Here (in theory, at least) you have two options (both of which join up 2.5km later in Cannoreto), but read ahead first.

OPTION A

The official (CAI/AEVF) route turns L here, up **Via Valdicastello Carducci**, passing the Romanesque **Pieve dei Santi Giovanni e Felicità** (*on L, founded in the sixth century but enlarged in the 13th*) shortly afterwards. It then KSO, and just over 1km later turns R up **Via Regnalla**, crosses a river, veers L, then turns second R up **Via Orticeto**. It then reaches a three-point junction by a sawmill/woodyard. However, on the occasions this route was checked the waymarks fizzled out here and all the paths were over grown. It is therefore suggested that you take Option B.

OPTION B

This is the old route and is no longer waymarked, but is very easy to follow. KSO ahead here past the cemetery on the **Via Sarzanese** (very heavy traffic) until just after road KM2, then turn L up a minor road, the **Via Cannoreto**. KSO uphill for 1km to **Cannoreto** (a hamlet), veering R to cross a bridge over a river. The bend here is where Option A joins up with this one, after which the usual red and white waymarks reappear, although only just adequately.

Both routes
Veer R at junction. Follow the road round, turn L at T-junction (this is still **Via Cannoreto**) and at the top reach slightly bigger road.

Turn L here, but then immediately R (*view of sea ahead in distance*), then 20m after that turn L down FP, steeply. 300m later reach gravel road by electricity tower and turn R. Road becomes tarmac (**Via delle Pianore**), veering L at end to junction by the **Instituto Cavanis**. KSO(L) ahead here on tarmac and cobbled lane that leads down to a crossing of tarmac roads. KSO ahead here (**Via la Stretta**), gradually uphill, then at crossing with wayside cross, KSO ahead, downhill. (*Message underneath cross reads 'Indulgenza di 40 giorni a chi reciterà un pater e ave' – 40 days of indulgences for those who [stop here and] recite an 'Paternoster' [Lord's Prayer] and an 'Ave Maria'.*)

KSO(L) at next junction, on **Via Dietro Monte** (coming from R), cross bridge and turn L (*note impressive number of glass greenhouses sloping down mountainside over to L*). Reach junction with traffic lights and there turn L along the busy **Via Italica**. 200m later turn R over bridge (Via delle Capanne) over the **Fiume Camaiore** and turn hard L at end. Then fork R up embankment to continue on FP above river, parallel to road over to the L. KSO. Path becomes wider as you proceed, and then becomes tarmac road by wayside shrine (*seats*).

Continue until reaching two bridges close together. Cross the first one, then cross the main road via pedestrian-controlled traffic lights and go down the **Via Carignoni** ahead. Turn R at the end along **Via G Ordenani**, passing a public garden (on L) and a large supermarket (on R). Turn L after the police HQ into **Contrada Santa Croce**, R into **Via IV Novembre**, first L into **Contrada La Rocca**, then R into **Vitt Emmanuele** in

9km Camaiore (557/399) Pop. 30,502, 36m

All facilities. OP Oratorio Il Colosseo, Tanarrani 26 (335.8026290 and 339.1832857). Hotel Locanda Le Monache, Piazza XXIX Maggio 36 (0584.984282).

Walled town with two pilgrim hospices, of which one, attached to the Pieve di Santa Maria Assunta, was built in 1278. Chiesa di San Michele, of Romanesque origins, was completely rebuilt after the Second World War.

Stage XXVII (Campmaior, 27) in Sigeric's itinerary.

KSO on Vitt Emmanuele to end on **Via Roma** (cycle track to start with). *At the very end, on L, is a Chiesa di San Rocco with a sculpture of the saint in a niche over the door, with the dog and a stick in his RH, and wearing boots; but unusually, instead of indicating his wound with his LH, it points away to the R.*

The **Via Roma** then joins the SP1 coming from back R. Cross over to the other side of it, then turn R immediately onto **Via Tori**, which then becomes an unsurfaced road. Pass a sports stadium, go alongside a dyke and reach a road opposite a house with a sundial on it. Turn L here into **Via XXV Aprile**. KSO almost to the SS1, but then turn R along **Via Bottaro**, parallel to the main road but separated from it by a small river.

Just before a farm turn R onto **Via Trinitá** (marked 'Strada privata').100m later, just before the road (unsurfaced) bends L, turn L over a small bridge over a ditch onto a small FP, marked 'Ponte Mazzori'. Continue ahead, reach a house by a T-junction with a small tarmac lane, and veer R then L onto a track into woods, with irrigation channel to R; but you then cross this to continue on its RH side. KSO.

Pass a small wayside shrine (*with seat*), veer R past a sports field then L to a road, and continue to a junction with the **Chiesa dell'Ascenzione** (*seats*). Turn R here to continue, along the **Via della Fornace**, gradually uphill. Pass sign to a B&B en route (Le Gusciane, 333.2708752).

KSO, pass house with FB/terrace over the road (ie go underneath it) and pass (disused?) chapel on LH side. At a junction immediately afterwards KSO(L) ahead on a stony track, and 150m later reach the SP1 at road KM20. Turn R, then at a sharp LH bend KSO(R) ahead up a steep stony track, zigzagging your way uphill to reach the junction with the SP1 and the **Via del Lecchio** at the beginning of

4.5km Montemagno (561.5/394.5)

2 bar/rtes, 2 other bars. A 'balcony' view of the surrounding area.

KSO ahead on the SP1, gently downhill all the time, and 1.5km later reach a turning to Viareggio. *War memorial perched up above the road to the R is a good place for a shady rest.* KSO ahead here, but at road KM16/v fork R off the road onto a track, then back again at KM15. Continue on the road into

3.5km Valpromaro (565/391) 170m

Bar, shop. (**Note** After this there are no bars or shops on the route until Lucca.) OP in former priest's house next to the Chiesa di San Martino (0584.956028 and 327.6948204), which formerly had a pilgrim hospital.

Fork R at entrance to village. At end of village do not return to SP1 but KSO(R) ahead between houses on small tarmac lane. KSO, parallel to road, which becomes a grassy track then a gravel lane, to reach bridge over the **Torrente Fredono**, turning R.

Turn R onto minor road (ie coming from bridge). 60–70m later either continue on road (in wet weather) or, at bend, KSO(R) on stony/grassy track into woods, gradually uphill. Turn (not fork) L at junction and continue on uphill. At a T-junction of paths turn L and continue steeply uphill to a road by a small church on L.

This road is the Via delle Gavine, where you can turn R, missing out Piazzano, and zigzag down to the Chiesa di San Michele Arcangelo ❯ below.

To continue on the main route turn L (not R) here and KSO at junction on **Via della Chiesa XII**, following road round into

2.5km Piazzano (567.5/388.5) 192m

Chiesa di San Frediano e ospedaletto (12th century, but rebuilt in the 18th). Sundial on tower (and many on houses in this area). There were also, formerly, a lot of ospizi/ospedaletti in this area.

Continue through village, veering R at a junction down to the church and war memorial. Continue on road to cemetery, then at a junction with a wayside shrine and picnic table turn R down a clear stony track, which becomes steeper and narrower as it descends.

However, in wet weather this track will be extremely slippery, so in bad weather continue ahead here along the road (Via Lupignalla), which will bring you out (slightly longer) just after the small Chiesa di San Michele Arcangelo ❯ (see below), where you then turn L to continue.

Take middle track at junction and KSO, downhill, the track becoming FP, and reach a minor road (**Via Gavine**) by a small wayside cross and turn L. Continue ahead along it, with the **Torrente Contesora** to R below, passing the Chiesa di San Michele Arcangelo on R.

The church was founded in 1175 by donations from two private citizens. The ospedale, a two-storey building on the opposite side of the road, was in use until 1730, when it was closed by the Bishop of Lucca because one of the staff working there was killed by one of the inmates. The building itself was demolished during the Second World War by the retreating German army.

❮ KSO ahead here to the outskirts of

5.5km San Macario in Piano (573/383) 17m

Lucca, looking out over the Chiesa di San Frediano

Pass town entry boards (*the Via Francigena does not enter the town, but only skirts it*). Continue ahead at junction and KSO. When road bends R KSO(L) ahead to the 12th-century **Chiesa ed ospedale di San Jacopo** (now a civilian building). At next junction KSO(R) ahead, veering R and then L past sports ground, then continue on road with high embankment of a dyke (**La Cherchia**). At junction with road from **Ponte San Pietro**, coming from back R (*there was a pilgrim hospice here, founded in 1140*), fork R ahead towards a church (exit boards for Ponte San Pietro at junction), veering R past a small hotel on R (*Il Ponte; advertises rooms, rte but no bar, 0583.329815*).

Turn L (**Via di Poggio**) over bridge over the **Fiume Serchio**. On other side turn L along cycle track for 3km (*seats at intervals along the way*), ignoring the first two RH turns. Go under the new suspension bridge (tarmac starts here) and fork R, veering L and then R on **Via del Tiro a Segno**. Turn L into **Via dei Cavaletti**, passing park with shady seats on R, and continue for 1km to junction with **Viale C del Preto** (a ring road).

If you want to sleep in the youth hostel and go straight there, turn L here along the Viale C del Preto and pass a large supermarket (on L). Then, just before the junction with the Via Tinivella (on L), cross over to RH side of road at pedestrian-controlled traffic lights, and 50–60m later turn R (marked 'Ostello San Frediano') on a path towards the town walls. Cross small bridge over a dyke, then go through tunnel under the town walls. Veer L on other side towards the Piazza del Collegio and Chiesa di San Frediano, turn L in front of church, and the hostel is 30m further on, on the LH side of the street.

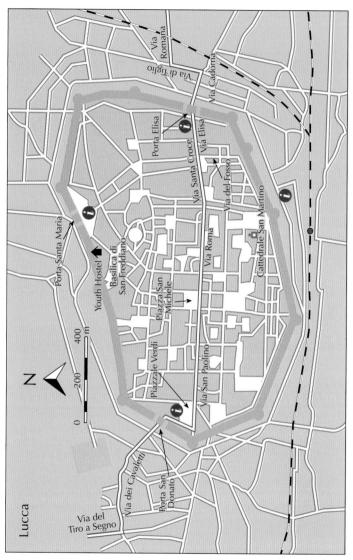

Lucca

To continue to Lucca, cross over the ring road (at the junction at the end of the Via dei Cavaletti) and enter the town by the Porta San Donato.

8km Lucca (581/375) Pop. 81,995, 22m

All facilities. 3 TOs: Porta San Donato (0583.583150), Porta Elisa (0583.495730) and Porta Santa Maria (0583.919931). Trenitalia. Accommodation in all price brackets. YH San Frediano, Via della Cavaliera 12 (between the Basilica di San Frediano and the Porta Santa Maria, 0583.469957) – to go to the hostel directly see description above, but note that during Nov–Feb it may be open only at weekends, so phone well ahead. OP in Convento dei Frati Cappuccini, 3km outside the town to the north in the frazione of Monte San Quirico, Via della Chiesa 87 (essential to phone ahead, 0583.341426 and 339.1118421). Hotel da Elisa, Via Elisa 25 (0583.494539), ***Albergo Diana, Via del Molinetto 11 (near the Duomo, 0583.492202), Alla Dolce Vita, Via Fillungo 232 (near Porta Santa Maria; rented rooms with use of kitchen, 329.5825062). Hotel Stipino, Via Romana 95 (0583.495077), and **Hotel Bernardino, Via Tiglio (0583.953356), are both outside the walls on the way out of Lucca.

Chiesa di San Frediano – detail of facade

A town dating from Roman times, Lucca had at least 35 hospices for pilgrims and other travellers in the Middle Ages, annexed to the main church buildings, with 13 recorded in the 13th century. It was also a prosperous commercial centre with a thriving silk industry. Sometimes referred to as 'la citta delle cento chiese' (city of one hundred churches) Lucca currently has 23 churches (of which seven have regular services). The town's main sights include the Romanesque churches of San Michele in Foro, San Frediano, Santi Giovanni e Reparata, Santa Maria Foris Portam (outside the walls), the Duomo di San Martino (containing a relief sculpture of a labyrinth, symbol of pilgrimage) and the Piazza Anfiteatro. Pilgrims interested in music may like to visit the Museo Casa Natale di Giacomo Puccini (his birthplace).

Labyrinth in the cathedral, symbol of pilgrimage

This was Stage XXVI (Luca, 26) in Sigeric's itinerary.

The waymarked path through Lucca leads through the town from the gate you enter by (Porta San Donato) to the one from which you exit (Porta Elisa), but it may not always be easy to spot the stickers. Pick up a street plan in the TO (you pass one) in order to make any detours to places that interest you. A very 'touristy' town, but nonetheless a good place for a rest day if you feel like sightseeing. Its 4.6km of continuous town walls to walk/cycle round date from the 16th–17th centuries and give a good overview of Lucca.

LUCCA TO SIENA

Looking down on San Gimignano from the Torre Grande

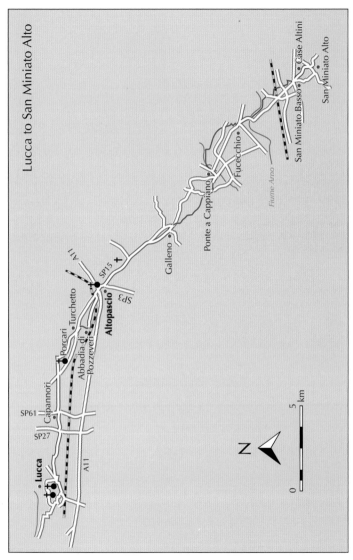

Lucca to San Miniato Alto

SECTION 4
Lucca to Siena (120km)

Pensioners on the city walls, Lucca

In Lucca, after going through the **Porta Donato** pass to LH side of a children's playground, turn R, pass TO (on R), and at **Piazza G Verdi** turn L into **Via Paolino**. Cross **Piazza San Michele** at the end, continue on **Via Roma** (turn L at end into **Via Fillungo** for YH) and continue on **Via Santa Croce**. Continue to end of Via Santa Croce, passing Piazza Santa Maria Foris Portam on the way, and go under archway (**Porta San Gervasio**). Cross **Via del Fosso** and canal, continue on **Via Elisa** and leave via the **Porta Elisa**.

Cross the **Piazza Don Antonio Mai**, KSO on **Viale Cardona** and then turn L into **Via di Tiglio**. Turn first R into **Via Romana** (*Hotel Stipini on L*). Go over level crossing and KSO (this is the SP23).

1.5km from the centre of Lucca, opposite house No 1425, watch out for fork R onto **Via Paladini**, by wayside cross on corner. Veer R then L to continue on a much quieter street parallel to the SP23, which is now over to the L. KSO. 1.5km after that pass the mainly Romanesque **Chiesa di San Michele di Antraccoli** (on L). *This was founded in AD777, but replaced by a larger building in the 12th century and then modified in the 16th. Fresco of Saint Michael in the centre of the apse, with Saint Peter to L and Saint Paul to R.*

KSO. Cross **Canale Ozzeri**, cross SP23 (it having bent R), and then, by wayside shrine, turn L onto **Via Francesco Banchieri**, veering R and passing in front of what was formerly a pilgrim hospital dedicated to San Lorenzo. KSO ahead, passing 15th-century **Chiesa di San Rocco** on L. Veer R near end, and then turn

213

L onto **Via G Piaggia** and reach the Chiesa dei Santi Quirico e Giulitta in the centre of

6.5km Capannori (587.5/368.5) Pop. 42,747, 15m

Shops etc. Chiesa dei Santi Quirico e Giulitta. There was formerly a leprosarium here.

The waymarks direct pilgrims to cross the Via Romana to continue ahead on Via Cardinale Pacini then, at T-junction at end, to turn R onto Via Colombini; but when the tarmac ends, so do the waymarks. So instead, unless you find waymarking to the contrary, turn R onto **Via Romana** and KSO for 2.5km. Then, at large roundabout 1.5km before the town, KSO ahead (*seats at intervals nearly all the way into the town centre*) into

4km Porcari (591.5/364.5) 14m

Shops etc. Bar La Rotonda at big oval traffic island on entry has rooms (0583.298242). Hotel da Rino, Via Pacini 23 (0583.299377).

Stage XXV (Forcri, 25) in Sigeric's itinerary.

Chiesa di San Rocco, Altopascio

Turn R in centre onto **Via Roma**, below church, and then continue on **Via Provinciale Romana Est** (rooms at No 20; 0583.228269 and 333.9306400).

KSO. Cross river/canal and KSO. 1.5km later cross **Torrente Tazzera** by exit boards for Porcari and entrance boards for **Turchetto**, then fork R onto **Via Serchio**. At end cross the **Strada Provinciale** opposite a large supermarket and continue on other side (behind the store) on **Via Pistoresi-Tappo-Turchetto**. On reaching the last building (on your L), before tarmac stops by a sign indicating 'strada dissesta' and before the last street light, turn R on grassy track towards woods ahead and continue in a straight line ahead, passing deserted house (overgrown) on R. KSO through woods, pass to RH side of cemetery and reach a minor road in front of the

2.5km Abbadia di Pozzeveri (594/362) 19m

Abbey dedicated to Saint Peter, but now empty. It was founded in the 13th century by monks from the Congregazione Camadolese (an order following the Rule of Saint Benedict) and built on the banks of the dried-up Lago di Bièntina (much of the area between Lucca and Altopascio was malarial swamp land in the Middle Ages).

Turn L in front of it, then KSO (*Via della Chiesa*) to a crossroads with wayside shrine at the entrance to

0.5km Bodia Pozzeveri (594.5/361.5) 19m

Bar/Rte at entrance with menu fisso.

Continue ahead on **Via Catalini** on other side, passing modern church on L. 2km later road veers L, and after passing the town entrance boards turn R onto **Via Francesca Romea** into

3km Altopascio (597.5/358.5) Pop. 13,650, 19m

All facilities. Trenitalia. OP in the municipal foresteria – ask in library (Biblioteca Comunale, Piazza Vitt Emanuele 23, which also doubles up as tourist office, 0583.216455) in building up steps to LH side of municipio. They also have a large pilgrim stamp which is a replica of a (large) original medieval seal. Note, however, that it is **essential** to phone ahead if you want to sleep there on either a Sunday or a public holiday (0583.216280 in working hours, 334.6821060 at other times). Albergo Paola, Via Romea Francesca 24 (0583.276453).

Town situated between two very large marshlands, the Bièntina and the Fucecchio, Altopascio developed around its medieval ospedale, which resembled a fortress from the outside. Mother house of the Knights of the Tau, the hospice remained active until 1780. Altopascio was not one of the stages on Sigeric's itinerary, as the hospice was built only in the late 11th century – after he made his pilgrimage. Its Romanesque bell tower is well known for its bell, known as 'La Smarrita' ('the lost'), which tolled to summon pilgrims lost in the mist of the two swamps. Chiesa di San Jacopo Maggiore, Chiesa di San Rocco. You are now in the province of Firenze (Florence).

At entrance to town go over level crossing by station (to L), under motorway and KSO ahead on **Via Cavour** (municipio on L), passing parish church (**Chiesa di San Jacopo Maggiore**). Pass to RH side of the **Chiesa di San Rocco** and then KSO ahead for 5km. Just after passing **Chimento** (*bar, supermarket*), then the exit boards for the province of Lucca and the entry signs for the province of Firenze, fork R onto a wide VS, with sections of the original Via Francigena (*picnic tables and marker stones for the route at the start*). Pass the **Casa Greppi**, a former hospice (12th century). *An information board relates that Filippo Augusto passed by in 1191 on his way from the Third Crusade. A very nice quiet, shady section.* KSO along this for 1.2km, passing **Termini 13** (a boundary stone) on R. After crossing a sturdy wooden FB, the **Ponte a Greppo**, enter the town on **Via della Chiesa** and continue to the 'square' in

6km Galleno (603.5/352.5) 39m

Shops etc. Cartolibrería Felix in square has a timbro (stamp) and pilgrim book.

Continue through village on SP15 (*sitting area on L*) and 1km later, 100m after a junction with a split roundabout, turn R onto a VS. Shortly afterwards KSO(L) at fork, just before house on R, and the way becomes a grassy track into woods. Continue past horse-riding establishment (large enclosed area) on R, veering R and then immediately L downhill to a small asphalt road (metal barrier to L) and turn R.

On reaching an open tarmac area (car park for a night club?) KSO ahead uphill (not obvious at first – don't go L, marked 'Centro Ippico'), then veer L at T-junction. Fork R at fork shortly afterwards uphill. At top KSO at five-point junction, KSO ahead at first junction, KSO(L) at fork, and then turn L at T-junction (*note old milestone for Fucecchio on R of track*), continuing on heathland. KSO, ignoring turns to L or R until you reach a busy tarmac road at a bend coming from back L (5km from Galleno), and KSO(R) ahead on it. At junction 400m later turn L downhill (marked 'S Croce'), then 200m later turn hard L downhill on a stony track. This becomes a grassy track, and at metal gates to a large property KSO(R) ahead. At end (more gates) join small tarmac road (**Via dei Medici**) and follow it down to main road 400–500m later. Cross over, then continue ahead on **Via della Palagina** to the main street and **Piazza Donnini** in

---

6.5km Ponte A Cappiano (610/346) 19m

Ostello Comunale Ponte dei'Medici, Via Colombo 237 (on bridge, 0571.297831). Bakery, bar (does snacks). 16th-century bridge over the Usciana, which was formerly a river port.

Stage XXIV (Aqua Nigra, 24) in Sigeric's itinerary.

Turn R over bridge (the first part open, the second half with buildings on it) over the **River Usciana**, then turn off it to the L after start through brick pillars to a car park (*sitting area ahead*). KSO(L) ahead on an embankment alongside the river (now on the L) and KSO.

After 1km watch out for a RH turn down a similar banked-up grassy track, veering L 400m later to pass the end of a concrete FB over a dyke on the R. Turn R over this, then L on the other side to continue on the RH side of the canal. Reach a road bridge (at right angles) 300–400m later, and KSO ahead again on RH side of canal. KSO ahead again at the next bridge, continue for 1km more alongside the canal, and reach the SP11 on the outskirts of Fucecchio, after which the waymarks lead you on a tour of the old part of the town before descending to its more modern part.

Cross the SP11 (carefully as it is a busy road, but there is no zebra crossing) and continue ahead on **Via Ponte del Rio**, veering R to reach a junction with a busy road and a wayside shrine opposite. Cross over, continue ahead on **Via Sotto la Valle** and then turn first R up **Via Sant-Antonio**. Go uphill up a long brick staircase and continue ahead on **Via F Bracci**. Reach a small square at the top, then turn L along **Via Castruccio**. Turn R at the end down **Via San Giorgio** to the **Piazza Garibaldi**, then KSO(R) ahead along **Poggio Salamartano** (with a 'balcony view' of the surrounding area). Reach a brick 'square' (actually a triangle) in front of the **Abbazia di San Salvatore**.

Pass to the LH side of the monastery down steps to the **Piazza Vittorio Veneto**. Cross it diagonally towards the **Museo di Fucecchio**, then continue down **Via Borgo Valori**. Turn R, downhill, on **Via Donateschi** to the **Piazza Montanelli** in the modern part of

5km Fucecchio (615/341) Pop. 21,621, 20m

Shops etc. Accommodation in Abbazia di San Salvatore (0571.20325; reserve 2 days ahead). Hotel Campagnola, Viale Cristoforo Colombo 144 (0571.260756).

Crossing point over the Fiume Arno. (Fucecchio was formerly a river port, as the Arno was navigable as far as Pisa in the Middle Ages.) Abbazia di San Salvatore (founded in the 10th century, rebuilt after flooding in 1105 and restored and extended in the 16th–18th centuries). 11th-century collegiate church of San Giovanni Battista, former Villa Corsini (now the town museum), Palazzo del Podestà.

Stage XXIII (Arne Blanca, 23) in Sigeric's itinerary.

KSO ahead on **Via N Sauro**, cross **Via Cairoli/Via C Battista** and KSO ahead on **Via Roma**, which becomes **Viale Gramisci** then the **Via Saminiatese**.

Cross the **Fiume Arno**, and then there is a choice of routes to San Miniato Basso.

<hr>

OPTION A

KSO on other side of the Arno into **San Pierino**. Go through the village, but because of motorway works to LH side of road watch out for new road layout. KSO ahead on the road all the time until you reach the entrance boards for San Miniato Basso. Fork L ahead (*useful plan of how to get to the refuge accommodation in the Casa della Misericordia on LH side of road – but make sure you stand on the LH side of the crash barrier before you start to study it*). KSO, go under railway line (station to L), KSO on **Via Marconi**, go under motorway, and at traffic lights in centre either KSO to continue or turn L, then R into **Via Porto** and R into **Piazza Vicente Cuoco 9** for OP in the **Casa della Misericordia**.

OPTION B

Watch out for a newly waymarked path along the river bank, which then turns R onto minor roads and leads under the railway line and then the motorway, and emerges in San Miniato opposite the **Casa della Misericordia**.

Looking down over San Miniato Alto

6km San Miniato Basso (621/335) Pop. 5994, 28m

Shops etc. Trenitalia. OP (donation) in the Casa della Misericordia (a hospital, with 6 beds plus mattresses for pilgrims, shower, 0571.418444). **Albergo Elio, Via Tosca Romagnola 485 (0571.42010), in centre.

Both routes

KSO at junction on **Via Aldo Moro**. At bend by house No 76 KSO ahead uphill on paved driveway, which then becomes a grassy track and later a FP. *All this section, until leaving the town, is very badly waymarked.* Emerge on the road again higher up, 400m later, just above a bend. KSO as road winds its way very steeply uphill to

2km San Miniato Alto (623/333) Pop. 26,787, 139m

Shops etc. TO. Accommodation in Convento de San Francesco, Piazza San Francesco 1 (0571.43051). Hotel San Miniato, Via Aldo Moro (0571.418904), Hotel Villa Sonnino, Via Castelvecchio 9–11 (0571.484033), Albergo Miravalle, Piazzetta del Castello 3 (0571.418075).

The town is named after Saint Minias (San Miniato), a Christian martyr, probably of Greek or Armenian origin, who left his home to make a pilgrimage to Rome. He arrived in Florence about AD250 and took up life as a hermit, but fell victim to the persecutions of the Emperor Decius and was beheaded. Legend has it that, after his decapitation, he picked up his head, put it back on his shoulders, crossed the River Arno and returned to die in the cave on the Mons Fiorentinus where he had lived as a hermit and where the Basilica di San Miniato al Monte now overlooks Florence.

14th-century Chiesa di San Domenico. 12th-century Duomo dell'Assunta e di San Genesio – its bell tower, the Torre di Matilde, was originally built for defensive purposes before being incorporated into the church. 13th–14th century Chiesa di San Francesco, Palazzo Vescovile, built 13th century, restored in 17th century. Brick Oratorio dei Santi Sebastiano e Rocco – this was built in 1524, at the time of a plague epidemic, as both Saints Rocco and Sebastian were invoked to help plague victims. Torre della Rocca, 192m high, has splendid views of the whole of the surrounding countryside. The area is well known for its white truffles.

After entering town turn L up cobbled street and go under tunnel-like archway, veering R to Piazza with TO opposite **Chiesa di San Jacopo e Lucia**. KSO(L) ahead, then KSO(R) at fork on **Via Augusto Conti** and go under another archway into a square where all the buildings have medallions on their facades (**Piazza della Repubblica**). (Turn L up flight of steps to **Piazza del Duomo** to visit cathedral, then retrace your steps.) Go out at other end, continue ahead, then fork R down **Via dei Mangiadori**, passing the municipio, to **Piazza Buonaparte**. KSO(R) ahead here, passing the **Oratorio dei Santi Sebastiano e Rocco**.

Most of the section between San Miniato Alto and Gambassi Terme (strenuous) is on ridges with splendid views all round on a clear day, although there is little shade for long stretches. Stage XXII San Genesio (Sce Dionis, 22) in Sigeric's itinerary has now disappeared, but was thought to have been somewhere in the area between San Miniato Alto and Coiano (Stage XXI).

Continue up **Via Paolo Maioli** to **Piazza Venti Settembre**, then either: **a)** turn L (the waymarked route) just before **Piazza Venti Settembre**, turn R into **Vicolo Borghizzi**, veering L under archway, turn L at end then R onto **Via Francesco Ferrucci** and continue as described below; or **b)** KSO(R) ahead into **Piazza Venti Settembre**, then KSO(R) ahead on **Via Francesco Ferrucci**, then continue on **Via Calenzano** – uphill again! 1km later pass **Centro Studi i**

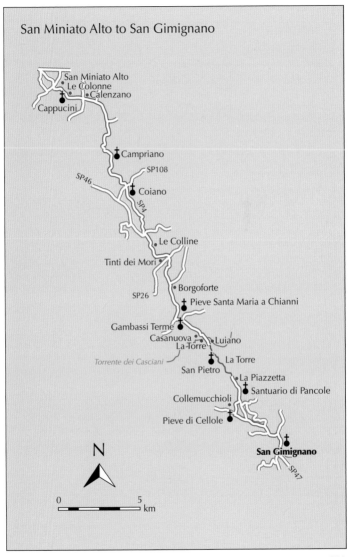

San Miniato Alto to San Gimignano

San Miniato Alto
Le Colonne
Calenzano
Cappucini

Campriano
SP108
SP46
SP4
Coiano

Le Colline

Tinti dei Mori

SP26
Borgoforte
Pieve Santa Maria a Chianni
Gambassi Terme
Casanuova
La Torre
Luiano
Torrente dei Casciani
La Torre
San Pietro
La Piazzetta
Santuario di Pancole
Collemucchioli
Pieve di Cellole

San Gimignano
SP47

N

0   5 km

Cappuccino on R and KSO (*splendid views all round*) – road has now become **Via Montegrappa** – to

3km Calenzano (626/330) 157m

Bar with small shop on road has pilgrim stamp from church (Chiesa di Santa Lucia). Note that there are no facilities after this point until the bar at Borgoforte, 3km before Gambassi Terme (9km).

KSO through village, veering L (below church) to leave on **Via Castelfiorentino**. KSO. At junction by swimming pool (to R) and LH turn to 'Ponte A Elsa' KSO(R) ahead. KSO. 2.5km later, when road bends sharp L, slightly downhill, turn hard R onto a VS (gravel but becomes earth track later), veering R and then L to continue ahead on your previous line of travel. *All this is on a ridge, with splendid views if there is no haze.*

Pass a deserted house. KSO, ignoring turns, to a T-junction by house at top of hill and KSO(L) twice. Pass another notice board about the formation of La Guardia Svizzera Pontifica (*1506–2006; the Swiss Guard that guards the Vatican*). After this the track bends R, and at junction turn hard L to continue. KSO. 1km later veer L by an isolated farm; this is

6km Campriano (632/324) 160m

The way after San Miniato Alto

Turn R here onto gravel road (**Via de Meleto**), veering L. KSO, passing a small cemetery to R (*steps useful if you want to sit down*).

1.5km later, at junction at entry to **Borgo Fontana**, turn L on **Via della Poggiarella** onto gravel road. KSO, veering L at fork. Turn L by gates of large property. Pass signpost to large red house on L (*tower-like castle*) signposted 'Bertini 0.2', but also, curiously, 'Monaco 285, Oslo 1780, Tunis 760'! KSO ahead. Reach tarmac road (**Via Coiana**) in

3km Coiano (635/321) 176m

Pieve (parish church) di Coiano (and staircase), currently being restored, and mentioned as a stopping place/halt on Sigeric's journey in AD990. Stage XXI (Sce Petre Currant, 21) in his itinerary.

Cross road and KSO on other side, uphill and down. KSO at crossing by farm and KSO. Pass large square house with barn next to it, and 100m later fork R downhill, with vines to L.

KSO(L) at fork. Enter woods. KSO at junction on leaving them, re-enter woods briefly, then KSO on grassy track along side of hill. *Olive groves to L.* Turn R at next crossing, with a 'balcony' view of the countryside to L below, veering R and then veering L round the sides of two hills. At next junction KSO(R) ahead past small wood, veering L round side of hill. Follow tarmac road until you reach two houses, pass between them, and then turn L in front of them on gravel track (**Via Orlo**) leading down to asphalt road (*picnic tables*) below a modern house, **La Vrigne**. KSO(L) uphill on road.

200m later, just before small lake below to R, turn hard R uphill on gravel lane (**Via dei Praticelli**) on ridge, leading to three houses (**Le Colline**). Pass in front of them, and then KSO ahead on grassy lane beside small plantation of trees and barn, veering L.

KSO and pass to L of two houses, then KSO(L) on gravel track coming from back R. KSO at junction by shed and continue on down to house above road, turn R down tree-lined road, **Via della Maremmana** (*this area is Tinto dei Mori*), and reach a 'stop' sign by a two-laned asphalt road. KSO(R) ahead for a short distance on track to RH side of road, then turn L at gap in crash barrier, cross via pedestrian crossing, and go down another gravel lane on other side.

Turn R over bridge, turn L on other side (*this is private land but the owners have given their permission*) and pass house. Then continue ahead on grassy track between fields at first and then uphill between vines, in more or less a straight line, up towards a large building ahead. Turn R below it, on broad track, veering L

223

uphill at end of line of trees. KSO, following track (**Via della Meliano**) uphill (*picnic table*). Pass cemetery, and 150m later, by wayside shrine (*seats and tap behind it*), reach SP4 coming from back L. Turn R uphill into

9km Borgoforte (644/312)

Bar/Rte on road.

Go through village/hamlet, KSO, and 2km later on LH side of road reach the

2km Pieve Santa Maria a Chianni (646/310)

Romanesque church on the outskirts of Gambassi, just before the entrance boards to the town, and once a separate parish in its own right. Here the parrochia in Gambassi has converted the former priest's house, empty since the late 1990s, into the Ostello Sigerico, a place where pilgrims can spend the night, whether on their way to Rome, Santiago or Assisi. (Go round the back to the L to find the entrance.) There is dormitory-type accommodation (sleeping bag required) in a separate building, single rooms in the main house, and evening meals and/or breakfast are available if required. Phone ahead – 0571.6382422 or (Anna) 339.7832270. Open all year except January.

This was Stage XX (Sce Maria Glan, 20) in Sigeric's itinerary.

Continue uphill, and at junction with traffic lights turn L onto **Via Volterrana** in

1km Gambassi Terme (647/309) 320m

Spa town with shops etc. Ostello Sigerico (see above). Albergo Osteria Pinchiorba, Via Volterrana 3, has rooms (X Mon, 0571.638188). Chiesa dei Santi Jacopo e Stefano.

Turn L opposite church (**Via Franchi**) marked 'Certaldo'. *(However, if you want to go into the town, KSO here then retrace your steps to continue.)* At junction 800m later KSO ahead ('Luiano 3'), downhill. Pass small wayside chapel. KSO(L) and pass Casanuova, a farm selling wine and olive oil. *A notice announces that from here it is 279km to Rome, 842km to Brindisi (for those continuing to*

Jerusalem), 1426km to Canterbury and 2036km to Santiago de Compostela…
Pass **Torre**, cross the **Torrente dei Casciani** and go uphill to a farm. This is

3km Luiano (650/306) 154m

Picnic table (but no shade).

After that KSO on earth track. Go over wide brick bridge over the **Torrente dei Casciani** again and turn R on other side. Turn L along side of field (hedge to R), then turn L again along its top edge. Turn R at end uphill. KSO, and near top of the hill turn L, veering R towards barn then L onto gravel road. Then turn R uphill, following road round, veering L through tree-lined section to a large house, **San Pietro Fattoria** (*a restaurant*). Pass to RH side of it on wide gravel road. KSO, following road round, pass the Pieve (*now in private hands, an agriturismo*) and reach a T-junction with tarmac road in hamlet of

2.5km San Pietro (652.5/303.5) 235m

KSO(R) ahead here to

1.5km Pancole (654/302) 252m

Village dominated by the Santuario di Pancole, built 1670, destroyed in 1944 by German bombing and rebuilt 1949. This is the place where the Virgin Mary appeared to Bartholomea Ghisni, a young deaf-mute girl, and cured her. She is venerated as the mother of Divine Providence – flour, oil, wine and so on (life's basic essentials).

KSO for 900m through village of Pancole itself, reach the santuario, then fork L downhill under archway and KSO uphill. When road levels out a bit (1km after the santuario), and opposite a roadside grave to L and pumping station to R, turn R up earth/gravel road uphill. *San Gimignano visible ahead.* KSO(L) uphill at fork, and 500m later go through hamlet of **Collemuccioli** and out under archway. KSO to the **Pieve di Santa Maria a Cellole**, first documented in 1109 but finished only in 1238 (normally open every Saturday, 10am–6pm, June to mid-Sept, but closed for repairs at the time of writing; mass first Sunday of month at 6pm.)

Santuario di Pancole

Continue past church downhill, reach SP69 500m later and turn L. KSO for 2.5km, downhill, passing former **Chiesa di San Biagio** on R (now part of a private house) and reach large roundabout. KSO(R) ahead, then at fork 700m later KSO(R) up **Via Niccolo Cannici**. Veer R at top, cross road and go through archway (**Porta S Matteo**) into

6.5km San Gimignano (660.5/295.5) Pop. 7283, 314m

A very 'touristy' town with shops etc. TO in Piazza del Duomo 1 has list of affittacamere – rooms for rent (0577.940008). OP in Convento San Agostino, Piazza San Agostino 10 (0577.907012) – to go there turn L immediately after going through the archway into the town, then first L again, but note that the church is closed daily 12–3pm, so avoid arriving between these times. Accommodation in Convento San Girolamo, Via Folgore (0577.940573). B&B Casa dei Potente, Piazza delle Erbe 10 (0577.943190), B&B Fabio, Via delle Vergene 2 (0577.938838 and 348.4125486), B&B Giovanna, Via San Giovanni 58 (0577.940419). Campsite (Il Broschetto di Piemma), 2–3km outside the town (but on the Via Francigena itself), which also has a mobile home for rent – phone one day ahead for this (0577.940352), although no need to if you have your own tent.

Walled hilltop town dating back to 929, which developed with the establishment of numerous monasteries and hospices for pilgrims and other travellers. Its main sights include the Romanesque Duomo di Santa Maria Assunta with two series of 14th-century frescoes inside, the Romanesque Chiesa di San Agostino with a series of 15th-century frescoes depicting the life of Saint Augustine, the Piazza del Duomo with seven towers, the 13th-century Palazzo della Podestà and the 13th–14th century Palazzo del Populo, the Piazza della Cisterna with its large 13th–14th century dwelling houses, and the 13th-century Porte San Giovanni to the south, by which you leave the town.

Stage XIX (Sce Gemiane, 19) in Sigeric's itinerary. Stage XVIII (San Martino Fosci, 18) in Sigeric's itinerary is difficult to locate nowadays, but it is thought to have been somewhere between here and the Colle di Val d'Elsa (see below).

San Gimignano, sundial on Chiesa di San Agostino

Continue along **Via Matteo** to the **Piazza del Duomo** and then the **Piazza della Cisterna** (adjoining). Leave via RH corner and go down **Via San Giovanni**, go through the **Porta San Giovanni** and continue with large public garden (**Piazza Martin Montemaggio**) to R. Go down steps to L (marked 'bus checkpoint'), and then turn R into **Via Baccanella** to roundabout.

Continue ahead on other side, but then turn L immediately, marked 'S Lucia 2.3'. KSO. *Good views back to San Gimignano as you go (SP47).* KSO. Pass a campsite (on L) and 100m after that a caravan/motorhome site, then watch out for a sharp RH (waymarked) turn by a wayside shrine (just before a sports ground).

227

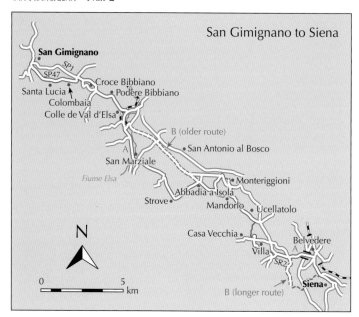

This is a variant route, whose advantage (according to a notice) is only 5 per cent asphalt as compared to 45 per cent on the road straight ahead. Note, however, that it is not immediately apparent that there is a choice of routes here. This variant is 7km longer than the main route and much hillier, designed more for the Sunday rambler than the long-haul pilgrim. So KSO ahead here, past a large children's playground (*seats*) into

3.5km Santa Lucia (664/292) 260m

KSO(R) at fork. Pass sports ground (L), then fork L by another wayside shrine, gradually downhill at first then steeply. 1.5km later (after Santa Lucia) reach tarmac road opposite metal gates and turn L. 200m later reach SP1 and turn R, then 100m after that, at fork, KSO(R) on SP36 (marked 'Colle Val d'Elsa 6').

Cross bridge over river and 100m later, just after bend, turn L onto earth track. *This next section was badly waymarked on the occasions that this guide was researched.* KSO ahead on grassy track, gently uphill, then on FP through woods. Turn R onto track that passes in front of **Croce Bibbiano** (a farm). Veer R and L in front of it and KSO uphill all the time until a tarmac road by a house labelled 'Podere Bibbiano' is reached.

Turn R here, then 200m later, just past house No 16, fork then turn L onto gravel road which becomes an earth track along ridge (*splendid views on a clear day*). KSO ahead for 1km to an oval brick building on L (cypress trees) and big villa (Podere Borboni) to R. Turn L, steeply downhill at first then level, and KSO for 2km (this is the **Strada di Vallebuona**). At fork at bottom KSO(R), cross old railway lines (*which look as though they are being made into a cycle track – if so, you could turn R along them instead of the SP68*) and turn R onto the SP68 (**Via Gramisci**) at the entrance to the town. Continue ahead for 900m (road becomes **Via Stefano Masson**) until a shady square at the end (**Piazza Bartomomeo Scalo**) is reached in

8.5km Colle di Val d'Elsa (672.5/283.5) Pop. 20,110, 145m

All facilities. TO in Piazza Arnulfi di Cambio 9 (0577.921334). OP in Seminario Vescovile, Via San Francesco 4 (0577.587083). **Albergo Il Nazionale, Via Garibaldi 20 (0577.920039).

Hilltop town on a ridge. Duomo, Museo Archeologico, Museo d' Arte Sacra, Museo Civico. Stage XVII (Aelse, 17) in Sigeric's itinerary.

Relief sculpture of Saint Peter, Duomo

Go shopping for food here if you don't want to eat out in Monteriggioni, which has no proper food shops (only places selling specialist local produce). After Monteriggioni, if you take Option B (the longer route to west of Siena) before you reach the Pian del Lago (see below), there are no facilities until Siena. So stock up on food in Colle di Val d'Elsa and water in Monteriggioni.

There are two routes out of the Colle di Val d'Elsa, roughly the same length, which reunite before Monteriggioni. *The more recently waymarked one (Option A) goes via Strove and Abbadia a Isola, while the older one (Option B) is less picturesque, crosses the river straight away and then continues all on minor roads.*

OPTION A – VIA ABBADIA A ISOLA

Continue ahead here, then nearly 1km later turn R at junction into **Viale dei Mille**. Continue ahead on this for 2.5km to cross the **Fiume Elsa** and reach **San Marziale** (175m). Turn L here into the **Strada delle Ponelle**, cross a tarmac road some 600–700m later, then continue ahead on a track, passing a lake on R part-way along, to reach another junction 3km later. Turn L here onto the **Strada delle Cerreta**, veering R, and KSO for 2km more to reach

7.5km Strove (680/276) 260m

Ostello Comunale La Sosta (0577.300000 and 338.2506902).

Turn L here onto the SP74 and KSO to reach

2km Abbadia a Isola (682/274) 205m

Cistercian Abbazia dei Santi Salvatore e Cirino, founded in AD1001 on a hilltop in a swampy area, hence its name 'Isola' ('an island'). It accommodated pilgrims right from the start until its decline in the 14th century. It has now been restored, and the Confraternità di San Jacopo provides pilgrim-only accommodation in the Ospitale dei Santi Cirino e Giacomo from the Thursday before Easter to the beginning of October, run by resident ospitalieri from their association. Donation (329.6593778).

Stage XVI (Burgenove, 16) in Sigeric's itinerary.

Continue for 300m to reach the **Strada Valmaggiore**, a gravel track, and here turn R to join Option B coming from your LH side. ❯

OPTION B – OLDER ROUTE

This section is not well waymarked, but is easy to follow. To visit Colle di Val d'Elsa KSO ahead here and then retrace your steps. Turn L here down **Via dei Botroni** and then **Via Cennini** to the **Piazza Arnulfi**, a very large square. Turn L past tourist office (ask for street plan), turn L and then R on **Via Spugna**, and then turn L downhill to cross the bridge over the **Fiume Elsa**. KSO ahead, uphill, on other side and KSO(R) at fork (uphill again).

Reach a large roundabout with factories and KSO on the other side (this is the SP5). KSO ahead, then at bend to R (road KM7/vii) KSO ahead uphill instead.

Duomo, Colle di Val d'Elsa

KSO at a crossing, go over grassed area, then rejoin the SP5 again 700m later, coming from back R. Reach large roundabout (the rotatoria Belvedere) at entrance **to Belvedere** (KM5/ix; *bar/rte to R*), then KSO ahead on other side. *All this section is very tedious, with nothing but factories and mini-industrial estates interspersed with flat fields; there is quite a lot of traffic, but there are almost no houses, bars, cafés or shops, and few features along the way.*

Pass bar/osteria (*meals*) on L at road KM3/vi and KSO. Pass entrance/exit No 16 to the **Zona Industriale Casone**, and just before road KM22/iv (7km from Colle di Val d'Elsa) turn R into **Strada Casone**, veering L (*view of Monteriggioni ahead*).

Cross the SP74 1km later – this is where Option A joins from the R (*the village over to the R is Abbadia a Isola*). ❮ KSO on other side on gravel track (this is the **Strada Valmaggiore**), veering L and then R past a house to start with. KSO.

At the end, 1km later, after last houses, the gravel track becomes an earth one, and 250m after that reach a T-junction with two similar tracks. (To continue without visiting Monteriggioni, turn R here and join up with the route again 1km later at Mandorlo. ❯)

To visit Monteriggioni turn L here and continue on shady lane. Emerge from the woods and 300m later continue on gravel lane with houses to either side. Turn R at end, and 50m later reach SP5 again at **La Colonna** (*bar/rte at corner*). Turn R

231

Monteriggioni

onto SP2 (**Via Cassia Nord**), and 200m later turn L up gravel track that wends its way steeply uphill into

3.5km Monteriggioni (685.5/270.5) 267m

Small completely walled town with 14 square towers (two sections of the walls have walkways open to the public), but very 'touristy'. Bars/rtes (some also have rooms), but no bars open early. TO in Piazza Roma 23, with OP behind it in the Casa per Ferie Santa Maria Assunta (bunks, kitchen with materials for self-catering breakfast, opens 3–6pm, but phone ahead: 0577.304068). One or two shops, but these sell only expensive local products, so if you intend to cook you will need to bring supplies with you.

Chiesa di Santa Maria Assunta, dating back to 13th century, once the headquarters of a canonical community.

Enter town by **Porta Nord** (Porta San Giovanni), continue on **Via I Maggio**, go through **Piazza Roma** and leave by **Porta Sud**. Turn R then L and continue along road ahead, downhill. Just before reaching the SP2 (the **Via Cassia**) turn L and go behind a large building with a football pitch, veering R to road. Cross it (pedestrian crossing), then turn R along the pavement and L onto **Strada del Galinaio**, passing the town exit boards, unsurfaced. 200m later turn R uphill (marked 'Il Mandorlo') between fields, olive trees and then woods, veering R, L and then R to a junction in Mandorlo (where the route that avoids Monteriggione joins up again). *This is the site of a former inn for travellers (17th–18th centuries).*

❮ Turn (not fork) L here, onto shady walled lane. Continue downhill, ignoring turns to L and R. At junction with **Ponte a Rosso e Camminata** (a bridge) KSO ahead. KSO, uphill all the time, passing house (on L), to arrive at to a junction with another similar road, a few houses and a sign (pointing back R) to 'Bracciano', and horse-riding field to R. This is **Ucellatolo**. KSO ahead here.

At next junction (not waymarked), 70–80m after a gas appliance in a metal cage on your L, turn R along clear gravel track leading uphill between fields to **Casa Colonica**, a large deserted farm building visible some 200–300m ahead. This is **Cerbaia** (4.5km), an old medieval village. *(If you do not turn R, but KSO ahead at the three oak trees, you will return to the Via Cassia – SP2.)*

Turn L here (before reaching the houses) on earth track alongside woods, veering L at end, and then turn R onto short shady lane and reach **Casa Vecchia**. (When you emerge the Castello de Villa is visible ahead.)

Turn L downhill here on unsurfaced road, veering R. Turn R at junction – this is **Villa** (2km) – then veer L with wall on R, below a large house.

Cross tarmac road and continue on other side on **Strada della Chiocciola** (gravel), passing in front of the **Castello della Chiocciola**. *This dates from the 14th century, and its name ('snail') derives from the spiral staircase contained inside the unusual cylindrical tower rising on its eastern side.*

When the **Strada della Chiocciola** bends R, turn L onto earth track, passing very large (and very deep) stone water tank to R. Reach tarmac road and turn

Via Francigena after Monteriggioni

L. 150m later turn R past **Castello della Villa** (on L), a square tower with a large medieval building next to it, then turn R past a circular building, veering R and then L downhill on walled lane, downhill all the time. KSO(R) at fork by entrance gates to private property, downhill again, then KSO(R) at next fork, still downhill. KSO.

At junction with track to L KSO alongside field, then at end, by small stone bridge ahead, reach the junction of two options.

7.5km Division of routes (693/263) 260m

Here the waymarks now indicate that you should turn right. However, there are two choices here for the route to Siena. The older route (Option A), to the L, still waymarked, is mainly on minor roads with little traffic. It enters Siena from the north and has some facilities en route. The more recently waymarked Option B, to the R, is at least 3–4km longer, but a quieter, shadier route. It goes on a long detour via La Grande Traversata and the Pyramide to enter Siena from the west, but note that there are no facilities whatsoever on this option until well into the town itself.

OPTION A – OLDER ROUTE TO NORTH OF SIENA

KSO ahead over the small stone bridge and then continue across a vast open space, the **Pian del Lago**, veering L towards some large sheds and reach the road (the SP101). *This area is marked (a bit further on) as a 'zona militare', but seems to be an area where a lot of local people take their dogs for a long walk – so you will see quite a lot of people walking here.* On reaching the yellow building (and the car park) go to the road and turn L to a junction, ▼ after which the waymarks are picked up again. At another junction shortly afterwards, when the SP101 bends L, KSO(R) ahead, uphill, on the **Strada del Pian di Lago** marked 'Siena'. (It is 3km from here to the entrance to the town.)

Alternatively, if it is raining or very wet – all this area is reclaimed swamp land – from the small stone bridge at the start of the route continue R to the SP101 and then L along it over the road bridge to reach this junction (very slightly longer).

1km later reach junction (*bar shortly afterwards*) with the SR2, turn R and KSO. Then, at a junction with a large roundabout 2km later, KSO(L) past a petrol station and a MacDonalds (on L) and enter **Siena** on **Via Fiorentina** (*youth hostel at No 89, on R, was marked 'chiuso per riconstrutturazione' (closed for* *alterations) at the time of writing).* At the very end of the Via Fiorentina the two options meet, Option B joining you from the R. KSO here on **Viale Cavour** and then continue as described below (see 'Both routes').

OPTION B – LONGER ROUTE TO WEST OF SIENA

At the small stone bridge turn R and reach the SP1 at the end by a road bridge (on your L), after which turn right along it (not L, as you would expect). KSO, and do not be deterred by the signposts indicating that you are going away from, not approaching, Siena – as explained above, this is a detour from the 'straight and narrow' of the older route.

At a junction nearly 2km later turn L (marked 'Montebuccio 5') onto **Strada dell'Osteriaccia**. KSO. 1km later turn L by a house, then fork L off road and KSO ahead on FP through woods. Come out into open fields and reach the **Pyramide**, a monument erected in honour of all those involved in the land reclamation work that was done in this area to convert the former swamps to arable land. *Picnic table nearby.* KSO(R) ahead here. Reach gravel track, turn R onto it, then cross tarmac road immediately afterwards (pedestrian crossing) and KSO through woods on other side. Cross field diagonally and continue on FP on other side, veering L to bigger track and turning R along it. KSO, turn R at T-junction, then watch out for another one and turn R there too. 200m later watch out for LH turn leading gradually downhill to large, low modern building, and turn R in front of it on gravel road then on a tree-lined lane. Pass cemetery, and at bend reach a road.

Turn L downhill, then up again, then at junction at the top turn R on **Strada delle Coste**, heading along a ridge to the hamlet of that name. At end veer R then L downhill, passing lake on R, go under the motorway, and KSO on other side, steeply uphill, to enter **Siena** (still on Strada delle Coste). Reach junction with **Via G Milanesi** and turn R, steeply uphill again. Turn L at the top and continue downhill, passing a modern church on L. At a T-junction turn L to a roundabout at a junction with the **Via Fiorentina**, coming from your L (this is where Option A joins Option B). To go to the youth hostel (at No 89) turn L here *(youth hostel was marked 'chiuso per riconstrutturazione' (closed for alterations) at the time of writing)*.

Both routes

To continue into the centre of Siena, turn R here and continue on **Viale Cavour**. Reach a roundabout and a fork, then KSO(L) ahead (still Viale Cavour) to reach a large archway. Continue ahead to reach a very large brick gateway (**Antiporto di Camollia**). Go under it and continue ahead on **Viale Vitt. Emanuele II**. KSO to reach the **Porta Camollia** and enter the walled (and pedestrianised) part of the town.

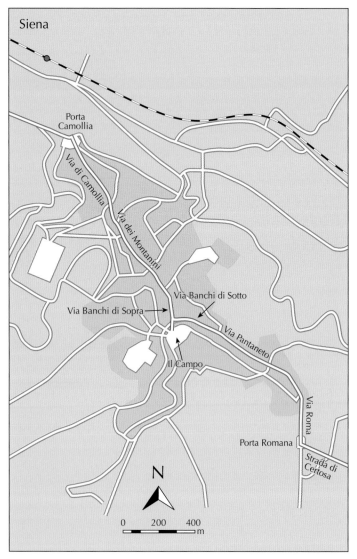

KSO(R) on **Via Camollia**, going through another very large gateway, then at the end of that continue on **Via dei Montanini** and, when that ends, on **Via Banchi di Sopra**. Turn L at end, then 1km after the Porta Camollia go through **Vicolo S Pietro** to **Il Campo**, a very large square, in the centre of

8km Siena (701/255) Pop. 54,370, 341m

Torre di Mangia, Siena

All facilities. If you are having a day off the tourist office (Piazza del Campo 56, 0577.280551) has a useful leaflet in its 'Trekking Urbano' series, which takes you on a 6km walk around the alleys and gardens of the Torre. Pilgrim accommodation in Accoglienza Santa Luisa Via Girolamo 8 (0577.284377 – reservation essential) near end of town. Hotel Alma Domus, Via Camporeggio 37 (0577.44177), Hotel Tre Donzelle, Via Donzelle 5 (0577.280358). Rooms at La Magioni di Camollia, Via Camollia 179, Via dei Termini 13 (339.6699143 for both). 'Pullman' (long-distance coaches) to Rome (Stazione Tibertina), Florence and other destinations. Trenitalia. After Siena the road signs (finally) start pointing to Rome.

Perched on three hills separating the Val d'Elsa from the Val d'Arbia, with its *terzi* (three districts) of San Martino, Camollia and the centre, Siena is one of Italy's most important medieval cities and the one most influenced by the passage of the Via Francigena. There were numerous hospices accommodating pilgrims and other travellers, such as the famous Spedale di Santa Maria della Scala, while in 1288 there were 90 innkeepers recorded in the town. There is a lot to see in Siena, and it is worth having a day off here to visit and rest up before undertaking the last 250km or so of your journey.

Siena's main sights include the late 12th-century Duomo, with its black and white marble facade and Battistero adjoining it. Opposite is the Spedale di Santa Maria della Scala, begun in the 9th and 10th centuries, in whose Sala del Pellegrinaggio ('pilgrimage room') there is a series of frescoes depicting daily life in the hospice in the 14th and 15th centuries. (There were 34 other ospedale in Siena in medieval times.) Brick Oratorio di San Rocco, built 1511, has with a statue of Saint Roch in a niche on the facade; the adjacent Cappella di San Rocco houses a polychrome terracotta statue of the saint and a cycle of frescoes depicting his life. There are numerous other interesting churches and important civic buildings, such as the Gothic Palazzo Pubblico, now housing the Museo Civico, but probably Siena's best-known sight is its Piazza del Campo. Today, as in the past, the heart of the city is this very large square, where every two years on 2 July and 16 August the famous Palio (horse racing event) takes place.

Stage XV (Seocine, 15) in Sigeric's itinerary.

SIENA TO ROME

Collegiate church of Santi Quirico e Giulitta, San Quirico d'Orcia

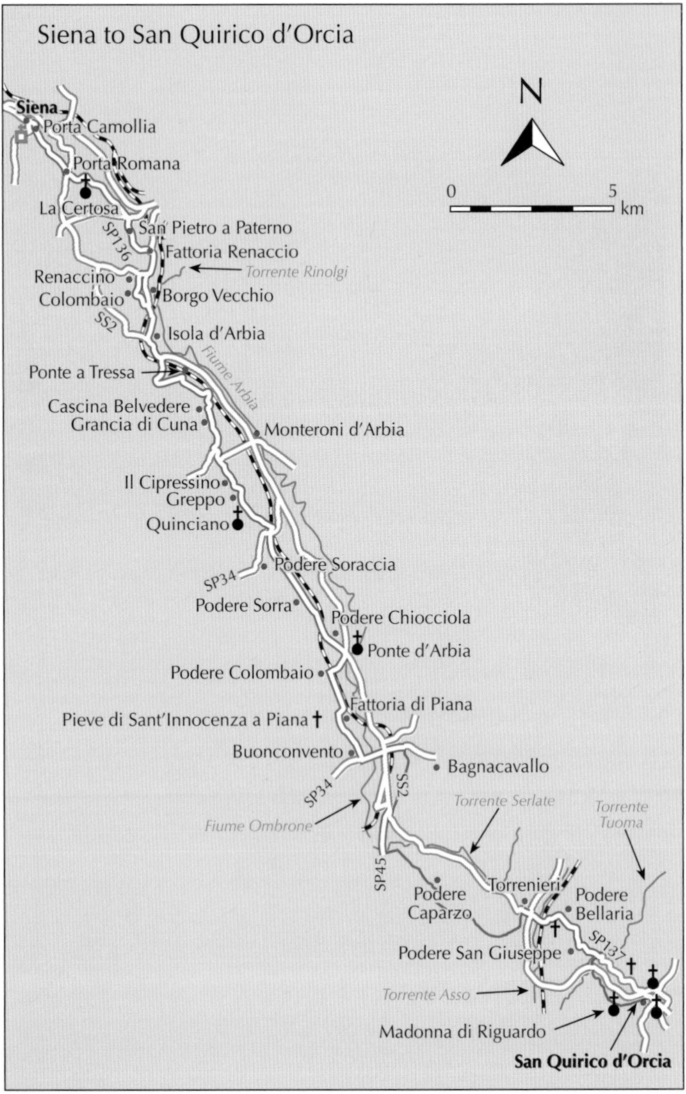

Siena to San Quirico d'Orcia

N

0   5
km

Siena
Porta Camollia
Porta Romana
La Certosa
San Pietro a Paterno
SP136
Fattoria Renaccio
Renaccino
Torrente Rinolgi
Colombaio
Borgo Vecchio
SS2
Isola d'Arbia
Ponte a Tressa
Fiume Arbia
Cascina Belvedere
Grancia di Cuna
Monteroni d'Arbia
Il Cipressino
Greppo
Quinciano
Podere Soraccia
SP34
Podere Sorra
Podere Chiocciola
Ponte d'Arbia
Podere Colombaio
Fattoria di Piana
Pieve di Sant'Innocenza a Piana †
Buonconvento
Bagnacavallo
SP34
SS2
Torrente Serlate
Torrente Tuoma
Fiume Ombrone
SP45
Podere Caparzo
Torrenieri
Podere Bellaria
SP137
Podere San Giuseppe
Torrente Asso
Madonna di Riguardo
San Quirico d'Orcia

SECTION 5

Siena to Rome (255km)

Piazza del Campo, Siena

From **Piazza del Campo** in Siena retrace your steps and turn hard R down **Via Banchi di Sotto**, then continue on **Via Pantaneto** and **Via Roma**. Continue to the end of Via Roma, then go through the **Porta Romana**, turn immediately L down a flight of steps (on the **Strada di Certosa**), cross **Via Girolamo** (shop on LH corner) and continue again on Strada di Certosa on other side.

Continue ahead on Strada di Certosa. Stay on it when it bends R 800m later, and stay on it for 5km more (after a while it becomes unsurfaced) to reach the junction with the SP136, just after KM3 by the **Fattoria Renaccio**, a big farm. *A nice ridge walk, with good views.*

Turn R here (*bar/rte 200m further on, on L*) and KSO for just over 1km. Cross the **Torrente Rinolgi**, go over a roundabout, and then, 300m later, turn L at road KM1/viii onto **Strada di Rennacio**. Continue ahead, passing to RH side of a farmhouse, then KSO(R) ahead on gravel lane past horse enclosures. At top reach gravel road and continue on other side on track, passing behind a house (on L) then veering R downhill, up between fields and alongside hedge (on L). At top turn hard L onto grassy track coming from R.

200m later turn R at junction onto gravel road. Go through barrier at end, and two sets of waymarks are visible to both L and R. *(The RH option is a variant route, which does a very big 'loop' before rejoining the main one 1.5km after Isola d'Arbia.)* To continue on the main route turn L here (despite signs saying 'propri-età privata') and then turn R after going through gateposts. Pass between buildings on the outskirts of

9km Borgovecchio (710/246) 195m

Veer L and then R in front of house No 13, then continue ahead on grassy track (railway line and road visible ahead). Turn L by empty building on R (this is **Strada di Borgo Vecchio**) and cross, as best you can, a new road (*under construction at the time this guide was prepared*) and then the railway line.

Turn R on other side, neither a good nor a very clear track, but continue to **Zona Industriale** railway station (big industrial estate to R). Turn L into car park and then R to continue ahead, parallel to tracks, on partly surfaced road leading, after bending L, to the SS2 (**Via Cassia**) on the edge of

1.5km Isola d'Arbia (711.5/244.5) 173m

Bar, shop and rte at junction. Romanesque Chiesa di San Ilario.

Turn L on SS2, then turn R into **Via della Mercanzia** (*public garden on L, seats, fountain*), veering L. Continue to end, veering L to return to the SS2, and then turn R under railway line, just after bar/rte Il Pino on **Traversia di Isola d'Arbia**.

The next section, as far as Ponte d'Arbia, is very up and down and full of twists and turns as it is designed to keep pilgrims off the Via Cassia, which is often visible below to the L.

Continue ahead (on the other side of the railway line) on other side on unsur-faced road, cross a small river, and then veer L and then R uphill past houses on R. At T-junction at top of the hill turn L. Turn L again, at fork, downhill, and KSO. The road becomes tarmac at junction by seats. Continue downhill – this is the **Via del Poggio** – and you are now on the outskirts of **Ponte a Tressa**, although the Via Francigena does not go into it. Instead, turn R onto **Via di Villa Canina** (opposite house No 290).

At the end of houses (new) KSO ahead on an unsurfaced road between fields. At T-junction at top (*seat*) turn L (this is still the Via Villa Canina). 250m later turn L down a track that veers R uphill towards

4km Grancia di Cuna (715.5/240.5) 175m

This is a rare example of a fortified farmhouse that remains almost intact today. The nearby small 13th-century Chiesa di San Jacopo has a 15th-century fresco depicting the scene of the 'hanged unhanged'. This is reminiscent of the story of a pilgrim on his way to Santiago who was condemned to the gallows for stealing. Innocent of the crime, he was found hanging, but still alive, by his parents on their return journey.

Turn R at crossing and pass below the fortified farm (to its RH side). 200m later reach a crossing with a wayside cross and seat and KSO ahead. This is the **Strada di Belvedere** – KSO(L) ahead along it at the junction with the **Strada della Fornacina** (*small wayside cross on L*). 150m later KSO ahead again at another junction.

Just below the top of the hill, opposite houses Nos 571 and 573, turn R uphill. At fork 400m later turn hard L towards the transmitter on the belvedere

Street in Buonconvento

243

(viewpoint) at the top (214m). *From here there are 360° views – back to Siena on the one side and then, suddenly, a plunging view of Monteroni d'Arbia to L ahead below.* Continue ahead downhill on a rough track, then 250m later, by a pond to L, turn hard R uphill and reach a road by a post marked KMVII/0. Cross over and turn L along a horse-riding track on the other side until it comes to an end, then continue on the road (very little traffic) – this is the **Strada Villa Littoria** – uphill.

500m later turn R at T-junction (this is still the Strada Villa Littoria) and KSO. Pass pond on R, then fork L at junction by barn (on L). KSO at next junction shortly afterwards, and then KSO(R) at fork, downhill. KSO – this is now the **Strada di Greppo** – and go past a small group of houses in

5km Greppo (720.5/235.5) 199m

KSO at junction at end (*seat*) and reach the hamlet – *note very realistic scarecrow (spaventapasseri) working in field on R just before it* – of

1km Quinciano (721.5/234.5) 174m
Chiesa di San Albano.

Go through hamlet, then turn R downhill on **Via del Castello**, veering L. KSO(L) at fork, veering L down to the SP34, at KM5/vi. Turn L along it for 200m, then turn hard R down a slope, veering L to continue on a track to the RH side of the railway line (this is just after it has come out of a tunnel). KSO for 3.5km, passing road bridge over the railway opposite the entrance to the **Podere Sorra** (on your R). KSO ahead again, and 800m later (after bridge) reach metal gates preventing you from continuing (with 'Fondo chiuso' (closed – from here) sign), and turn L over level crossing. Turn R on other side, on smaller track at first then KSO, gradually veering L away from railway lines. 1.5km later (after level crossing) enter

6km Ponte d'Arbia (727.5/228.5) 145m
Shop (limited range), 2 bar/rtes (one with bank machine). Pilgrim refuge in Centro Cresti, a cultural centre in yellow building on other side of the bridge (on L) with 20 beds, kitchen, shower; donation; key from house No 18 opposite (contact Massimo: 348.6021256 and 0577.370096; or Patrizia

327.7197439; or 328.617840). First house on R after bridge has rooms (X winter). It is often very foggy in the mornings in this area.

Stage XIV (Arbia, 14) in Sigeric's itinerary.

Enter town on **Via degli Stagni**, by large children's playground (on L), cross **Via Magi** and continue past football ground (on R). At end, at T-junction with **Via Magistrato**, either turn L (to visit town, bar and shop) and then R to cross the bridge over the **Fiume Arbia** for refugio (retracing your steps the following morning), or turn R (at the T-junction) to continue.

Cross bridge over small river. KSO, then immediately after crossing the railway line, 1km from Ponte d'Arbia, turn L onto a wide gravel road and continue alongside it. 1.5km later the road veers R to skirt the **Fattoria di Piana** (a large farm). At junction with wayside cross KSO(R) ahead on road coming from back R. *Pieve di Sant'Innocenza a Piana, over to your R, on a hilltop.*

Reach the SP34 and turn L. Cross the **Fiume Ombrone** and 800m later enter

5.5km Buonconvento (733/223) Pop. 3190, 146m

Shops etc. Large supermarket on L at entry has useful street plan in its car park. Hotel Ghibellino (0577.809112). Rolling landscape with either a large farm or a castle on every available hilltop! 13th-century city walls, mainly intact, but with only two gateways into the town. In the past the town had numerous inns and hospices. Chiesa parrochiale di Santi Pietro e Paolo.

Continue past supermarket to junction, where there is a choice of routes. Option A is a shorter, flatter route, while Option B very hilly and quieter, but 1km longer. In either case make sure you have enough to eat and drink with you before you leave Buonconvento.

OPTION A

Turn R on **Via Dante Alighieri** to continue (alternatively, to visit the centro storico turn L first on Via Roma and then retrace your steps), then either continue on it to road KM200 or, 700m later, fork R along a railway line. Just over 1km after that turn L at a level crossing, and 500m later reach the **Via Cassia** (SR2) at road KM199 and turn R along it.

OPTION B

Turn L onto **Via Roma** (marked 'centro storico') and then turn R onto **Via Percena**. Cross the SR2 (the Via Cassia). Continue ahead on other side, go over level crossing, cross the **Via I Maggio** (*public garden on L*) – this is still the Via Percena – and go steeply uphill ahead.

At the crossing at the top turn R (uphill again!) onto a gravel road that then veers L and levels out. Follow it along a ridge, and 2km later reach a farm. This junction is not marked, but fork either L in front of it or R behind it (they join up) and continue down to the **Via Cassia** at KM199 (still only on the outskirts of Buonconvento) and turn L along it.

Both routes

400m later turn R at road junction onto the SP45 (marked 'Montalcino 10'). KSO. 1.8km later, having crossed the **Torrente Serlate**, turn L uphill at a crossing with a wayside shrine up above to the R, onto a VS. Veer R near the top towards a large property and a chapel slightly further on on the R. KSO, mainly downhill, pass the tree-lined drive to the **Agriturismo Altosino** (on R) and KSO ahead.

KSO, uphill all the time, to reach a walled enclosure at the top with seven trees (*shady place for a short rest*). KSO, then pass **Caparzo** (*agriturismo – vignobles, wine-tasting, sales*) and KSO ahead again, uphill all the time. Pass another farm (on R) and reach a junction with another track coming from back L. Pass a farm (on R), and 400m later turn L on gravel track leading uphill.

KSO, uphill continuously, until eventually the track levels out. KSO again. Pass **Comunità Incontro** (on R) and KSO again. At top of hill KSO ahead, ignoring turns to L and R, and KSO ahead. 2km later, at T-junction, turn L towards Torrenieri (visible ahead). 1km after that reach a junction, turn R and continue to a junction by the church in

12km Torrenieri (745/211) 254m

Shops etc. Useful street plan in supermarket car park. 13th-century Chiesa di Santa Maria Maddelena, Madonna della Misericordia Patrona della Via Francigena. 10th-century Chiesa di San Rocco has modern sculpture (2000) of two feet outside the building, entitled 'Monumento al Pellegrino'.

Stage XIII (Turreiner, 13) in Sigeric's itinerary.

Sculpture of pilgrim feet outside the Chiesa di San Rocco

Continue ahead at junction on SP137, go over level crossing, then cross the **Torrente Asso** and continue past cemetery (R). This (SP137) is the **Via Cassia Vecchia**. Continue uphill for 2km, and after that, on the descent to cross the **Torrente Tuoma**, San Quirico d'Orcia is visible up on the skyline ahead. There are now two alternatives.

OPTION A

After crossing the Torrente Tuoma, go up hill again and KSO. On reaching road KM1/i, just before a RH bend, it is possible to short-cut a loop in the SP137 by continuing ahead at the bend up an earth track leading up to the cemetery (whose wall is visible uphill ahead). Then turn L to rejoin the SP137 again (coming from back R) and KSO ahead along it. On reaching a Y-junction (at the end of SP137) KSO(R) ahead on SP146, going over the main road. Turn R at the end, by a wayside cross, turn L, and just before the archways ahead turn L again up a long flight of steps leading to the road at the top. KSO ahead here on **Via Dante Alighieri** to the **Collegiata dei Santi Quirico e Giulitta** in San Quirico d'Orcia.

OPTION B

Shortly after crossing the Torrente Tuoma, near road KM2/vii, follow the way-marks indicating that you turn R over a stream onto an earth track. This then goes under the **Via Cassia**, turns L uphill, does a lengthy 'loop' and enters San Quirico d'Orcia from the west (rather than the north). *This is waymarked, if you want to take it, and isn't on tarmac, but is not a lot quieter than Option B, since the old Via Cassia isn't very busy anyway.* At the end go up a long flight of steps and continue ahead on the **Via Dante Alighieri** as described in Option A.

7km San Quirico d'Orcia (752/204) Pop. 2521, 408m

Shops, banks etc (but there are only 'touristy' shops in the old part of the town). OP run by the parish in Piazza Chigi 18; phone ahead 9am–4pm (347.7748732) or ask at priest's house (No 1 outside main church door); 20+ beds, shower, kitchen. Albergo-Rte Il Garibaldi, Via Cassia 17 (0577.897236), Hotel Palazzuolo, Via Santa Caterina 43 (0577.897080).

Small town that grew up along the Via Cassia; the Via Francigena entered by the Porta Senese and left by the Porta Romana, and four hospices were recorded in the 15th century. Romanesque Collegiata, Chiesa di Santa Maria

Vitalete, Chiesa di Santa Maria Assunta, Palazzo Chigi (the present-day Horti Leonini, now a public park, was formerly part of the palazzo's grounds).

Stage XII (Sce Quiric, 12) in Sigeric's itinerary.

Both routes

KSO along **Via Dante Alighieri** to reach a junction after the third church, and turn R up **Via G Matteotti**. When this bends R KSO(L) on **Via Garibaldi**, which then becomes **Strada Ripa d'Orcia**. At fork after town exit board KSO(L) ahead, uphill, after which the road becomes sterrata/gravelled. *The information boards along the way are in both Italian and English.*

At fork near top of hill KSO(L) ahead (marked 'Vignoni', 'Bagno Vignoni'). KSO. On finally reaching the top of the hill (*splendid views*) continue ahead downhill, ignoring turns. 100m before reaching the castle KSO(L) at fork (do not turn R, marked 'Bagno Vignoni 1.7') and reach the castle in

3.5km Vignoni Alto (755.5/200.5) 481m

Tap by tower. 11th-century castello, originally belonging to the Abbadia di Sant'Animo. Chiesa di San Biaggio.

Town walls, San Quirico d'Orcia

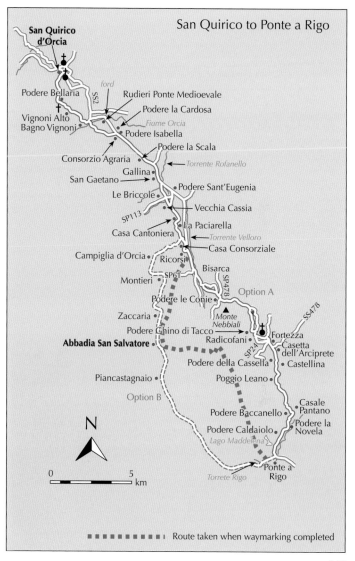

San Quirico to Ponte a Rigo

San Quirico d'Orcia

Podere Bellaria

ford

Rudieri Ponte Medioevale

Podere la Cardosa

SS2

Vignoni Alto
Bagno Vignoni

Fiume Orcia

Podere Isabella

Consorzio Agraria

Podere la Scala

Torrente Rofanello

Gallina

San Gaetano

Podere Sant'Eugenia

Le Briccole

Vecchia Cassia

SP113

La Paciarella

Casa Cantoniera

Torrente Velloro

Casa Consorziale

Campiglia d'Orcia

Ricorsi

Bisarca

Montieri

SP61

SP478

Option A

Podere le Conie

▲ *Monte Nebbiali*

Zaccaria

Podere Chino di Tacco

Abbadia San Salvatore

Radicofani

SS478

Fortezza

Casetta dell'Arciprete

SP24

Castellina

Podere della Cassella

Piancastagnaio

Poggio Leano

Option B

Casale Pantano

Podere Baccanello

Podere la Novela

Podere Caldaiolo

Lago Maddelena

N

Ponte a Rigo

0   5 km

Torrete Rigo

■ ■ ■ ■ ■ ■ ■ ■ ■ ■ ■ ■ Route taken when waymarking completed

Ahead, laid out like a ribbon on the landscape, is the Via Cassia, which (not all that busy in this section) pilgrims will be following for 6km to Gallina. Also visible, on the horizon, is a dome-shaped hill with a clear tower on top – this is Radicofani, 25km away!

Turn L and then R through hamlet to church (at end). Leave via the **Porta Est** (archway) and then turn R on path leading down to the cemetery (and on the RH option where you forked L). Turn L downhill, and at next fork, 300m later, KSO(L) ahead, downhill all the time. On reaching a car park (on your R) ▼ turn R alongside it and then continue alongside a public park (on L). Continue ahead between houses to reach the *sorgenti* (thermal springs) in Bagno Vignoni.

Alternatively, to bypass Bagno Vignoni, continue directly ahead and then turn L onto a path. Continue alongside the Fiume Orcia to the site of the former medieval bridge, where pilgrims have to ford the river. This is no problem in summer, but in the spring, autumn and winter you will have to remove your boots and wade across in sandals. After this, rejoin the Via Cassia (SR2) at road KM176/viii, turn L along it and continue to Gallina to rejoin the main route.

1.5km Bagno Vignoni (757/199) 254m

Thermal spa, characterised by its *piazza d'acqua*, a big open reservoir with sulphurous water coming out of the ground at 50°C, one of Tuscany's main hot springs in the Middle Ages. Several rather touristy bars/rtes around it.

Thermal pool, Bagno Vignoni

After visiting the terme retrace your steps to the public garden, turn R alongside it, turn R to a parking area and then L downhill on road (pavement). Just before the road bridge on the SR2 (**Cassia**) turn hard R and then L to cross the **Fiume Orcia** over the restored bridge, now for pedestrians/cycles only. Continue ahead on other side, veering L and then R to a junction, then KSO downhill to the junction with the **Via Cassia** and continue ahead along it – now signposted 'Roma'!

Continue along it for 200m, then just before the road bridge over the **Torrente Onsola** the (waymarked) Via Francigena turns R up towards the hills for a long diversion in the form of a big C-shaped 'loop' to keep pilgrims off the Via Cassia. There is also a more direct route that follows the Cassia, and the two options meet up again at Le Briccole, beyond Gallina. *The diversion (not described here) is 4–5km longer, and there are a lot of 'ups and downs', so your decision will depend on issues such as how much traffic there is on the Cassia (very little early on a Sunday morning, for example), how energetic you feel, and how much time/ daylight you have if you are intending to sleep in either Radicofani or Abbadia San Salvatore.*

For the **direct route** KSO on the SR2 (*no shade, but a wayside cross on R, opposite road KM174/vi, is a good place for a short rest*). KSO for 6km more. Just before the village the road from Chiusi joins from the L; pass church (on L, *seats*) and enter

6.5km Gallina (763.5/192.5) 315m

2 bars (first one, X Mon, has rooms and a restaurant with three differently priced menus – for tourists, motorcyclists and workmen!).

From Gallina to Radicofani (841m) it is 17km, continuously (and relentlessly) uphill…

In **dry weather**, continue through village on the road, and at the first bend, to the L, KSO ahead up a gravel lane. Then turn L by a house onto a grassy track through fields, continuing with a hedge on the LH side. Then, 100m before a road bridge to L, visible below, fork L downhill (*this is where the long diversion joins the direct route*) towards the road immediately before the bridge over the **Torrente Velloro** at road KM172/i. Then turn R immediately after that onto a gravel lane coming from behind the crash barrier to your L. Veer L and R to cross a small river (stepping stones) and then continue L uphill between fields, joining a wide gravel road coming up from back L. 100m later fork L towards an abandoned podere (farm): this one (di Sotto) and the one higher up (di Sopra) form the hamlet of **Le Briccole**.

However, if it has been very **wet weather**, fording the small rivers will be very difficult, so another option (but with the disadvantage of missing out Le Briccole) is to stay on the SS2 from Gallina for 2.5km more as far as its junction with the SP113, marked 'Campiglia d'Orcia' at road KM167/ii. Turn R here, then at a fork 200m later KSO(L) ahead on the **old Via Cassia** (although this is not marked as such). 1km later reach the junction with the track coming (from back R) from Le Briccole, by the now abandoned **casa cantoniera** on your L. ❭

2km Le Briccole (765.5/190.5) 340m

Chiesa di San Pellegrino (L), abandoned, but door is open. Le Briccole was mentioned as 'Abricula' by Sigeric. The hospice of the Briccole was a major resting site along the Via Francigena and in the late 13th century was mentioned as 'Ospitale San Pellegrino de Obricolis'. There are Romanesque traces, such as ashlars in base and portal with architrave surmounted by rounded arch; today, however, the building seems to be used mainly as a barn.

Stage XI (Abricula, 11) in Sigeric's itinerary.

KSO ahead. Cross the SP137 and KSO on other side, crossing another two small streams, and then continue between fields and then next to woods on wide grassy track to reach the **Cassia Vecchia** coming from back L by the casa cantoniera (where the wet-weather route rejoins) (road KM169,938). ❬ KSO ahead here for 2.5km, gradually uphill, to reach a junction (to R) with a local road leading to **Campiglia d'Orcia** (*visible perched up on a hilltop over to the R*).

View from Radicofani

Here there is a choice. *Continue L ahead to Radicofani (Option A) or turn R here to go to Abbadia San Salvatore (Option B, not yet waymarked but very easy to follow). The two options meet up again the following day in Ponte A Rigo (see below). Originally all pilgrims went via Abbadia San Salvatore, but from the 12th century onwards they began to divert onto the much hillier and more strenuous (but better-defended) route via Radicofani. The first mention of this route is in the account written by the Icelandic Bishop Nikulas von Munkhatverà of his journey to Rome in 1154.*

OPTION A – VIA RADICOFANI

KSO(L) ahead at junction and 1km later reach

7km Ricorsi (772.5/183.5) 404m

Former halting place on Via Francigena (with two buildings, chapel and medieval bridge), the ancient village of Formone. Post building from 13th century, renovated 16th century, similar to other post stations on the Strada Regionale Romana restructured by the Medici.

Reach the **Via Cassia (Nuova)** and turn R along it for 1.2km. Then, after the petrol station (*with Hotel Beyfin, bar and rte, 0577.872877*), turn L onto the SP478 (marked 'Radicofani 8'). KSO, uphill all the time (not much traffic). Just after road KM32, VF waymarking indicates a turn R here for an off-road option on a track (very slightly shorter), which returns to the SP478 again at road KM30/ii (turn R here along it to continue).

KSO ahead all the time. At junction at road KM30/ii KSO ahead, and then at next one 200m later KSO(L), still uphill all the time. *Picnic tables at KM29 if you want a rest (good views on a clear day).*

On reaching road KM25/iv turn L up **Viale O Lucini** into

8.5km Radicofani (781/175) Pop. 1229, 814m

Shop, bar, OP in the Spedale di San Pietro e Giacomo di Radicofani, run by the Italian Confraternità di San Jacopo at No 2 Via della Spedale (just behind the main church), 18 beds, kitchen, shower, donation, open all year, with resident ospitalieri (wardens) June–August. For key telephone Fausto (Confraternità della Misericordia, 338.7982255) or Don Elia Sartori (parroco, 0578.555614 and 338.9240307). Albergo-Rte La Torre, Via Giacomo Matteotti 7 (0578.55943).

Strategically placed on top of a hill, dominated by the remains of a castle and fortifications, and with a commanding view of the whole area Radicofani played an important role in the past in controlling traffic to and from Rome. Romanesque Chiesa di San Pietro, Chiesa di Santa Agatha (patron saint of the area) opposite, with Gothic facade.

Stage X (San Peitr in Pal, 10) in Sigeric's itinerary has now disappeared, but was originally on the site where the Casa Vòltole (a farm) now stands, just below Radicofani.

Modern painting of Saint Peter being nailed onto the cross (upside down), prior to his crucifixion, Chiesa di San Pietro

Fork L up slope at fork then KSO(L) into **Via Renato Magi**. KSO down this street, then on **Via Roma**. Go through town gate (archway) – *another bar on L* – and then turn L onto SP24 (**Viale Matteotti**). 400m later, at junction, cross the SP478 and KSO(R) (marked 'Roma 159'), then 200m after that, at bend, KSO(L) ahead, downhill on gravel road. Continue ahead, mainly gradually downhill – *a very nice walk in the early morning light*.

KSO. At first junction, with 'Agriturismo Pantano' sign, KSO(L) downhill, then KSO(L) again 150m later. On passing the Agriturismo Pantano KSO(R) at fork and KSO again. Pass two farms by road – one with a lot of dogs, the other with a chapel (on R) – and KSO again, downhill gently all the time. At fork close to the river (to your L) KSO(R) ahead to reach the **Via Cassia** (KM146) in

10.5km Ponte A Rigo (791.5/164.5) 293m

Bar to R on Via Cassia (does food). Villa San Ermanno, 2km further on on historic route, at KM144/ii has pilgrim-only accommodation (sleeping bag needed, kitchen, donation, 329.1644501).

OPTION B – VIA ABBADIA SAN SALVATORE

This option has been included because of the historic importance of Abbadia San Salvatore and because the off-road waymarked route is expected to be ready very shortly.

At present, however, pilgrims on this option have to go by road (little traffic). The route is not yet waymarked as there are problems with rights of way, but when the proposed off-road itinerary is approved it will start from Ricorsi (a couple of kilometres further on than the turning to Campaglia, in the direction of Radicofani) and use vie sterrate, leading to Petronieri, then Zaccaria, and from there to Abbadia. When this waymarked route is ready there will be an explanatory notice at the bivio (fork) in Ricorsi, indicating the two options.

So, for the time being, turn R onto a local road (at 437m) in the direction of Campiglia d'Orcia, the village perched on a hilltop ahead on the skyline, and KSO ahead, relentlessly uphill, to reach

3.5km Campiglia d'Orcia 704m

Shop, bar, bank, B&B Tre Rioni, Campotondo 1–2 (0577.872015). Chiesa di San Biaggio.

Cross road ahead and continue on **Via della Chiesa** on other side, passing the **Chiesa di San Biaggio** on R. Continue to the end of this street, then KSO ahead on **Via IV Novembre**, forking L uphill at a junction marked 'Abbadia 13km'. At next junction turn L into the **Via Guiseppe Verdi**, the SP18/d, which leads round the side of the hill, the route being level or gently undulating, shady and with very little traffic. KSO.

Continue through the hamlet of **Montieri** (3.5km) and KSO for a further 3km to **Zaccaria** (another hamlet), where a junction with the SP18a is reached (marked 'Abbadia'). KSO ahead on this all the time to reach the outskirts of the town. Pass the **Hotel Gambinus** on L, after which the pavement starts.

Continue on **Via Esasseta** then on **Via Trento**, passing a large Coop supermarket on L. Reach the hospital (also on L), veer L and then continue along **Via Cavour**. Turn L into **Via Cellini** and reach the **Piazza XX Settembre** and the **Abbazia San Salvatore** in

13km Abbadia San Salvatore Pop 6722, 818m

All facilities. 2 OPs – in the monastery, donation, essential to phone ahead

Detail of crypt, abbey church

(7.30–8.30am or 12.30–1.30pm, 0577.778083); and Parrochia Santa Croce, Casa per Ferie (0577.778310 and 338.562312482). Albergo Roma, Via Matteotti 34 (0577.7780125), Albergo Pensione Cesaretto, Via Trento 37–39 (0577.778198 and 340.3146827).

Medieval hilltop town on the eastern slopes of the Monte Amiata, an extinct volcano rich in deposits of cinnabar, which takes its name from the Abbadia San Salvatore. This was founded in AD743 by the Lombardian king Ratchis and handed over to the Benedictine order, who maintained it until the abbey was suppressed in 1783 by Leopold, Emperor and Grand Duke of Tuscany, and transferred to private ownership. Pilgrims to Rome passed through the town and were accommodated here until the 12th century, by

which time they had begun to opt for the route via Radicofani. In 1939, however, Cistercian monks returned to live and work in the abbey, which then became a monastery again, but today there are only two monks left.

The Romanesque church (today just a parish church) dates from the 11th century (restored in the 16th) and still has its eighth-century crypt. Most of the abbey archives were transferred to the Biblioteca Medicea

14th-century reliquary bust of Saint Mark Pope

Laurenziana in Florence at the time the monastery was suppressed, including one of the three copies of Saint Jerome's Vulgate version of the Bible, made by monks in the abbeys of Jarrow and Wearmouth (Northumbria) during the late seventh and early eighth centuries. The Codex Amiatinus (the original is now in the library in Florence) is the only surviving one of these three copies, and was on its way to Rome as a gift to Pope Gregory II when it somehow found its way to the Abbadia San Salvatore in the late 9th or early 10th century. It is an extremely large codex, consisting of 1030 sheets, measuring 540x345x253mm, and weighing nearly 50kg, and is illuminated throughout. Today, however, an exact (anastatic) copy of this Bible can be seen in the abbey treasury, along with, among many other interesting exhibits, a 12th-century reliquary bust of Saint Mark Pope in gilded bronze.

The town of Abbadia San Salvatore has always been an important mining area and was, for a long time, one of the most important sources of cinnabar in the world (a mineral from which mercury is extracted.) At the end of the 19th century a German industrialist installed a vast complex for its extraction and processing here, attracting workers to the area, and this activity continued until the mines were finally closed in the 1970s. The Parco Museo Minerario, housed on the edge of the town, provides a good idea of Abbadia's former industrial activity.

In the maze of small streets in the medieval part of the town, many of them criss-crossed with arches, there are a number of Gothic and Renaissance buildings, including the 15th-century Palazzo della Potestà, as well as the early 10th-century Chiesa di Santa Croce. Today Abbadia San Salvatore is a popular destination for summer holidays and winter sports.

To leave Abbadia pilgrims once again have to continue by road for the time being. *Eventually the waymarked route will lead, via the SP39, towards the SS Via Cassia, where it turns R, shadowing the SS2 Via Cassia via Voltole – Stage X (San Peitr in Pal, 10) in Sigeric's itinerary – and Voltolino down to a junction with the SP18 just west of Ponte A Rigo.* At present, though, continue through the town on the **Via Roma**, and then continue on the road through **Piancastagnaio** to reach the junction with the SP18 just west of Ponte A Rigo.

10.5km Ponte A Rigo (791.5/164.5) 293m

Bar to R on Via Cassia (does food).

Abbey church, Abbadia

Both routes

Here again there is a choice. *Option A continues on the historic route along the road; Option B is a very long C-shaped loop (waymarked) designed to keep pilgrims off the Via Cassia, which goes via La Cacina and Proceno. The two meet up again just after the Ponte Gregoriano, either 10.5km (Option A) or 16.5km (Option B) later, and both enter Acquapendente on the Via Cassia Vecchia.*

OPTION A – THE HISTORIC ROUTE

Turn L over the **Torrente Rigo**, then cross over to the RH side to walk on an earth track parallel to the road for 2km. Return to the Via Cassia just before **Villa San Ermanno** (on RH side), then KSO(L) at fork onto the old road (**Ex-Cassia**). Continue on this for 2km more, veering R back to modern road at KM142/ii, but do not join it here. Instead KSO on old road to its LH side for 500m more and then continue on the new one. Cross the **Torrente Alvella**, leaving the regione of Toscana to enter that of Latium, and then turn R immediately into

5km Centeno (796.5/159.5) 278m

B&B Cascina Centeno at first house on R at entry (333.4798958).

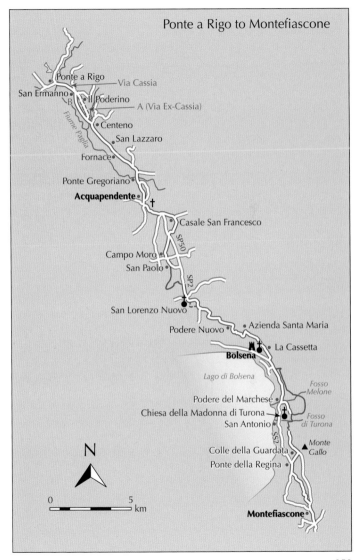

Ponte a Rigo to Montefiascone

Go through hamlet and return to SS2. KSO (*bar, X Sat, after KM140*) for 5km to cross the **Fiume Paglia** by the

---

5.5km Ponte Gregoriano (802/154) 258m

The construction of the original bridge here was ordered by Pope Gregory XIII after a ferry crossing he made in 1578. The Paglia was a particularly difficult and dangerous crossing in medieval times, as the river changed course frequently, and numerous pilgrims had drowned as they attempted to cross it before this bridge was built.

OPTION B – VIA PROCENO

For the longer option via Proceno (OP Parroquia San Salvatore, 340.2265595) turn R along the **Via Cassia** here (past bar), then 600m later turn L onto the SP18. (This option is not described here.)

Both routes

At junction on other side (*fountain*) KSO ahead uphill (ie turn R then immediately L uphill on the **old Via Cassia**) and KSO, uphill all the time. Rejoin the modern **Via Cassia** at KM133/iii and continue ahead uphill. Turn L part-way up into **Via G**

Duomo del Santo Sepulcro, Acquapendente

Marconi and KSO to **Piazza G Fabrizio** and **municipio**. Turn L into **Vicolo delle Volte**, continue ahead on **Via G Fabrizio**, then turn R onto **Via Roma**. KSO to very end, pass **Basilica del Santo Sepulcro** and return to the SS2 again at the end of

3km Acquapendente (805/151) Pop. 5768, 398m

All facilities. 2 OPs – very simple accommodation run by the Confraternità di San Rocco in the Casa del Pellegrino San Rocco, Via Roma 51, next to the church of Santa Caterina (which has a large statue of San Rocco with halo, stick, dog and two large scallop shells on shoulders), 9 beds, shower, microwave; donation), telephone either Sig.ra Amelia (347.1662919) or Don Luigi (parroco, 339.8499965); and Casa di San Lazzaro, Via Capuccini 23 (kitchen; donation), telephone Suor Amelia (0763.73177). To get to Casa di San Lazzaro either continue on the Via Cassia before you go into the town itself and then turn R up Via Capuccini 300m after the 'Total' petrol station or continue through the town as described and then, on reaching the Via Cassia again by the Basilica del Santo Sepulcro, turn R along it and then L up the Via Capuccini.

Hotel Aquila d'Oro, SS Cassia KM133 (0763.734175), Hotel Toscana, Piazza N Sauro 5 (0763.711220), Hotel La Ripa, Via Cesare Battisti 61 (0763.730136). TO, Via Torre Julia de Jacopo (0763.730065).

Town of probably Etruscan origin, which grew up around the borgo of Arisa with its Pieve (parish church) di Santa Vittoria in the 9th and 10th centuries. The modern town's most prominent sight is the 10th-century Basilica del Santo Sepulcro, near the Porta Romana on leaving the town. When Queen Matthilda of Westphalia (895–968) was on her way to Rome with a caravan of mules loaded with gold to build a church there dedicated to the Holy Sepulchre, and was about to leave Acquapendente, the animals are reported to have stopped there, knelt down and refused to go any further. During the night she is said to

Casa del Pellegrino (pilgrim hostel)

Banner, Confraternità di San Rocco

have had a vision in which she was told to build a church there, on that spot, and inside the building she had a chapel constructed that is an imitation of its namesake, the Church of the Holy Sepulchre in Jerusalem.

Other churches include the 12th-century Chiesa di San Francesco, the Chiesa di San Agostino and the Monasterio di Santa Chiara. Acquapendente also has various interesting civic buildings such as the Bishop's Palace (now the town museum), the Town Hospital (one of at least six reported in 1588), the palaces in the Via Roma (Nos 6, 33, 50 and 82–86), the Palazzo Viscontini and the main square (Piazza Girolamo Fabrizio), the Palazzo Viscontini, the town hall, the Torre Julia de' Jacopo (one of the last vestiges of the medieval town walls) and the Torre di Barbarossa.

On his way to Rome Saint Roch (San Rocco) stayed in a hospice near Acquapendente, where he then remained to look after the sick, particularly plague victims, and where he effected miraculous cures until he was turned out of the hospice and continued his journey to Rome.

Stage IX (Acquapendente, 9) in Sigeric's itinerary.

After passing the **Basilica del Santo Sepulcro** (on L), continue to the top of the hill (KM131) then turn L onto a local road, veering L uphill. 1km later, at top, fork L by industrial buildings (**Casale San Francesco**) to a more minor road, then 300m after that turn R onto a VS, following it round for just over 1km back to the **Via Cassia** again. *(If there is very little traffic, such as early on a Sunday morning, an alternative is to simply turn L along the Via Cassia – a lot shorter – and follow it all the way to San Lorenzo Nuovo.)*

Cross over the **Via Cassia** and continue on another VS on the other side, passing a 'solar panel orchard'. KSO, veer L, reach a large deserted house and turn L onto a small tarmac road. Then almost immediately turn R onto another VS 600m later, at T-junction, where there are two sets of waymarks.

Here there is a choice of routes to San Lorenzo Nuovo. One option is to KSO ahead, returning to the **Via Cassia**, where you then turn R along it to **San Lorenzo Nuovo**. Alternatively, turn R (1.5km longer) onto similar track and KSO for nearly 2km to a T-junction. Turn L here, and then almost immediately L again by a small stone hut, then 200m later fork R. Follow track round as it winds L and R (*passing modern stone seat on L*) for 700–800m more to return to the **Via Cassia** by the town entrance boards. Turn R along it for almost 1km to the centre of

10.5km San Lorenzo Nuovo (815.5/140.5) Pop. 2131, 490m

Shops etc. Ostello Francigena, Via Cassia Vecchia (0763.7268211 and 338.7154144). Albergo/Rte Bar Italia, Via dell'Ospedale (339.2774533), campsite 'Mario'. Chiesa di San Lorenzo Martire. Town on the largest European lake of volcanic origin, Lago di Bolsena. The town is 'Nuovo' because the original San Lorenzo was nearer the lake and therefore marshy and less healthy, so the town was later moved higher up the hill to its present location.

Continue through the town on SS2 – *sudden view of the Lago di Bolsena from the main 'square' (which is, in fact, round)* – veering L above the lake (which is below to R). (Watch out for waymarks to take you off the SS2 to the R, if you want to, until 200m before the LH turn described below.) KSO for 1.5km, then just after road KM122/vii turn L onto wide gravel road, uphill at first. KSO ahead all the time, sometimes gravel, sometimes tarmac, ignoring turnings to L and R, uphill

View over Lago di Bolsena

and down. Pass **Podere Sterta** (a farm, on R), go uphill and pass behind it to R and in front of a big red quarry. Go downhill and tarmac stops, giving way to a red gravel track between vines.

After that the track passes between open fields, then turns R downhill, passing the entrance to the **Agriturismo Poderaccio** (on R). Reach a junction, 4km after leaving the Via Cassia, with a 'solar panel orchard' (also on R), where you turn L towards some woods. Follow the path as it twists uphill and down, past **La Roccaccia**, round the bottom of a field, then veer R and then L to pass in front of a new house. Continue past **Azienda Santa Maria (Podere Nuovo)**, with the lake over to your R all the time.

After a second building similar to the Azienda Santa Maria turn L up a track alongside a fence and KSO for 1km to a junction by farm buildings. Turn R up a sunken lane, continuing, undulating, between fields after that. At junction 600m later by deserted stone building turn R onto earth lane and KSO for nearly 2km, until the track becomes tarmac and reaches a T-junction. Turn L here (*views over the Lago di Bolsena, to R*), and 500m later pass a turning to L with a very large wayside shrine (this leads to the Ostello Comunale Gazetta, see below for details), then veer R uphill to the SP53 coming from behind you. KSO along it, veering R at junction, pass **Volsini archeological site** (on R) and enter the town, continuing to junction by a church (on L) and the **Piazza Monaldeschi**. Cross road and go down stepped street to the L of **La Rocca** (a tower), then either continue down **Via del Piage**, turning R and then L down to the **Piazza Matteotti**, or turn first L into **Via degli Adami** and then continue down the stepped (and curving) **Via del Castello** to the **Piazza Matteotti** and the Chiesa di San Francesco (now a theatre) in the centre of

11.5km Bolsena (827/129) Pop. 4083, 348m

Shops etc. TO in Piazza Matteotti. Pilgrim accommodation with the Suori del Santissimo Sacramento, Piazza S Cristina 14 (0762.7990582). Foresteria Ex-Convento Santa Maria del Giglio (Ostello Comunale Gazetta), Via Madonna del Giglio 49 (0761.799066 and 328.6027357). Pensione Italia, Via Cavour 53 (0761.799193). ***Hotel Zodiaco, Via IV Novembre 8 (0761.7978791). 2 campsites on leaving town, both near road KM111 on SR2 (on R, near lake).

Bolsena was the birthplace of the third-century martyr Santa Cristina, by whose name the town was known at the time that Sigeric made his journey. Her father, unable to accept her conversion to Christianity, tied a rope round her neck, attached it to a large rock, and threw her into the lake.

The rock floated to the surface, however, marked with the imprint of her
footsteps, and was placed shortly
afterwards in the chapel dedicated to
her. The first (paleo-Christian) church
was built in the fourth century, and
enlarged and rebuilt in the 11th.

Chiesa di Santa Cristina

The town is also known for the
Miracle of Bolsena, which is similar
to an event which took place along
the Camino de Santiago in the small
hilltop village church in O Cebreiro,
as the route enters Galicia. In 1263 a
German priest on pilgrimage to Rome
was celebrating mass in the church
in Bolsena, but was very sceptical
as to whether, during the consecration of the bread and the wine, they were
actually transformed into the body and blood of Christ. He saw though, to
his great astonishment, that blood was gushing out of the consecrated host.
Pope Urban IV was present in the church at the time, witnessed the miracle,
and as a permanent commemoration of the event instituted the annual feast of
Corpus Christi (Corpus Dominum in Italian), observed on the Thursday after
Trinity Sunday. As a result the Chiesa di Santa Cristina became a popular pilgrimage destination in the succeeding centuries. It also contains a large free-
standing statue of San Rocco, both as saint (with halo) and pilgrim, wearing
red 'Wellington boots', with scallop shells on clothing, hat on the ground, stick
(to which somebody has added a wine gourd), plus dog and a loaf of bread.

Apart from this church (whose chapel houses the saint's relics, and from
where there is access to the catacombs) Bolsena's other main sight (inside
the town walls) is the Rocca Monaldeschi della Cervara, with the Museo
Territoriale del Lago di Bolsena.

Stage VIII (Sca Cristina, 8) in Sigeric's itinerary.

There are two waymarked routes out of Bolsena – the older one (described
here), which continues out of the town for 3km on the SS2 before turning L into
the countryside, and the other, some 2–3km longer, which does a big loop to the
west, up and downhill, to keep pilgrims off the Via Cassia. The two join up 4km
(via the road) after Bolsena.

To take the **longer route** go through the **Porta Romana** and turn second L, opposite a public garden, onto **Via Acqua della Croce**, joining the other route 5km later. **〉**

For the **older route** KSO along **Via IV Novembre** and then join the **Via Cassia**. KSO ahead along this, passing large supermarket on R, for 3km. Immediately after crossing a bridge, and a few metres before road KM110, fork L uphill on small tarmac road, veering R uphill. Follow it round, and then, on L, pass turning onto a gravel track (signposted 'Meridiano 12 Agriturismo', *which has accommodation, 347.1084298*). This is where the longer joins up. **〈** KSO ahead here (or turn L if you came from the longer route). 1km later tarmac stops, and at fork KSO(R) ahead.

Continue downhill, and at the bottom turn R by a small bridge over the **River Turona**. *You are now in the Parco di Turona, an area was settled as early as the 16th–15th centuries* BC. *Fountain on R 100m after turning, and access to picnic tables in woods to R.* Shortly afterwards reach the very small

5.5km Chiesa della Madonna di Turona (832.5/123.5)

More picnic tables – a good place for a short rest.

To continue, turn L on path just before the church and continue on a track through woods. Then, as the route starts to go downhill, watch out for white arrows leading off onto a small FP on the R, veering L, while the main (normal) waymark ahead has an 'X' over it. This is because it was thought easier (and slightly shorter) to ford the **Torrente Arlena** higher up, but in practice the traditional guado (ford) is no more difficult and has a better (although longer) path leading down to the river bank.

So KSO ahead here, gradually downhill on a clear path, continuing R ahead at a fork near the end. Reach the river bank, and it should normally be possible to cross without any difficulty, as there are large well-placed stepping stones (*a stick is a big help to keep your balance*).

If the ford is completely impassable, retrace your steps to the small church and continue ahead on that track for some 800m–1km to the SS2. Turn L there and continue along the SS2 to reach KM105, the Ponte Regina, and there pick up the waymarks again, coming downhill from the L.

On the other side of the **Torrente Arlena** veer R in front of a house and then, at a crossing shortly afterwards, turn R uphill. KSO, veering L, and on reaching some buildings turn L in front of house No 22 onto a fairly long section of original Roman paving (a *strada basolata*) – you are now on the **Via Cassia Antica**. KSO

Via Cassia Antica after Bolsena

along it for nearly 2km, ignoring turns to L and R, until just before a junction with a tarmac road coming up from your R at a bend, where you have a choice.

Either **a)** turn R down an earth track (waymarked), which leads down to the road just before the **Ponte Regina** on the SS2 (this is to keep pilgrims off a very short section of tarmac road, which has very little traffic anyway, but this track has a very bad surface to walk on); or **b)** continue a short distance further on to a bend with a road coming up from bottom R; turn R downhill here to the SS2 (the modern Via Cassia) at road KM105 by the **Ponte Regina**.

Both routes Turn L along the SS2 for 700m and just before KM104/iii fork L off it onto a VS and KSO ahead up it for 2.5km, ignoring turns to L and R. At the top another VS joins from the L – KSO(R) here, gently downhill. KSO then go uphill, steadily. Near the top pass the **Fontane del Sabuco** (*with seats*) on R, and 200m later pass junction with similar road coming from back R. KSO(L) ahead here, uphill (yet again!) before levelling out and reach a 'stop' sign by a bigger road coming from L. Turn R. Houses start here. 500m later reach the SS2 and turn L along it.

200m later turn L (signposted 'Orvieto' and then 'San Flaviano'), veering R uphill (*bar near top, on R*). Continue ahead, going downhill, then after passing the HQ of the local carabinieri (painted bright pink) turn L at a T-junction onto **Via Santa Maria delle Grazie** (not marked at start), signposted 'Viterbo'. Turn R at 'stop' sign and continue uphill (to L) on **Via Orvetiana** (pavement on L), pass a petrol station and reach the **Chiesa di San Flaviano** (on R). Turn R here (to LH side of church) on **Via Flaviano**, veering L uphill to the **Piazzale Roma**. Cross over and go through the archway into the **Via Cavour**, uphill, and at the top reach the **Piazza Vittorio Emanuele** in

8.5km Montefiascone (841/115) Pop. 12,823, 582m

Shops, banks, bars etc. Trenitalia. Monasterio San Pietro, Via Garibaldi 31 (0761.828066, donation, meals possible), Centro di Spiritualità Santa Lucia Filippini, Via Santa Maria in Arce 11 (0761.826088, April–September, donation), Accoglienza Raggio di Sole, Via San Francesco 3 (347.5900953).

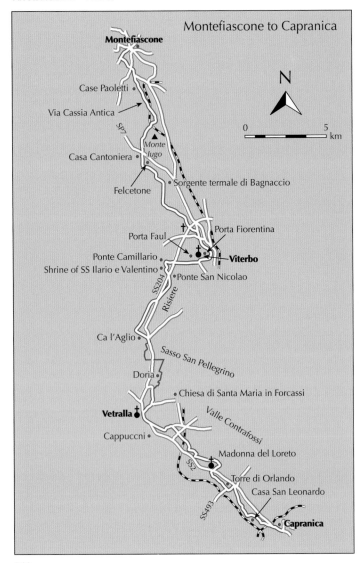

Montefiascone to Capranica

N

0   5 km

Montefiascone

Case Paoletti

Via Cassia Antica

SP7

Monte Iugo

Casa Cantoniera

Felcetone

Sorgente termale di Bagnaccio

Porta Faul   Porta Fiorentina

Ponte Camillario   **Viterbo**

Shrine of SS Ilario e Valentino   Ponte San Nicolao

SS204

Risiere

Ca l'Aglio

Sasso San Pellegrino

Doria

Chiesa di Santa Maria in Forcassi

Vetralla

Valle Contrafossi

Cappuccni

Madonna del Loreto

SS2

Torre di Orlando

Casa San Leonardo

SS493

Capranica

Albergo Dante, Via Nazionale 6 (0761.825015), Hotel Urbano V, Corso Cavour 107 (0761.831094). Hotel Rondinella, KM100 on SS2 (0761.824995). TO Piazza Vittorio Emanuele.

Medieval town with 12th-century Basilica di San Flaviano, best known, probably, for housing (in the third chapel on the L) the tomb of a certain German nobleman, Johannes Defuk (or Fugger), on which is inscribed (reportedly the work of his servant): 'Est, Est, Est per troppo est qui giace morto il mio signore Giovanni Deuc' ('here, on account of too much [drink], my master lies dead'). The story goes that, as he travelled, the nobleman sent his servant on ahead to mark with 'Est' all the establishments where good wine was served. When he arrived in Montefiascone the servant found somewhere where it was of such good quality that he marked it 'EST, EST, EST', upon which his master is said to have imbibed so much that he drank himself to death. Late 15th-century Cattedrale di Santa Margherita, with the third largest dome in Italy after St Peter's in Rome and Santa Maria del Fiore in Florence.

Stage VII (Sce Flaviane, 7) in Sigeric's itinerary.

From the **Piazza Vittorio Emanuele** go under the arch ahead to **Largo del Plebicito** and the **Chiesa di Santa Lucia** (on L). Go up steps ahead, veering L to public garden, and continue ahead to the **Rocca dei Papi** (Papal residence 12th–16th centuries) and the **Torre del Pellegrino**. Leave (no waymarks) down steps on RH side (facing the Rocca and with the Lago di Bolsena to your R) leading to a car park, and continue (also not waymarked) along the street ahead. Turn R into **Largo Barbarigo** and the road below (*Piazza Luigi Boccadoro ahead on other side with good view over lake*) and turn L downhill (**Via di Pini**).

At the junction at the bottom with **Via Verentana** (coming from the L) watch out carefully for waymarks. Turn slightly L, cross over and go downhill steeply on a VS by a VF noticeboard and the ruins of the **Chiesa della Madonna del Riposo** (*seats*). 200m later fork L, downhill all the time. At the end (1.5km from the Torre Pellegrino) reach a 'stop' sign and cross over to the other side of the road, marked 'Stazione'.

200–300m later fork R onto a grassy track. At the end KSO on track which has extensive sections, for the next few kilometres, of its original *basulato romano, one of the best-preserved examples of Roman road on the whole Via Francigena*. At a junction after that (with asphalt road to L) KSO ahead on gravel road.

200m later, at bend with wayside shrine, fork L onto another paved section, gradually uphill. KSO, ignoring turns to L and R, pass house at **Case Paoletti** and

KSO, gently downhill all the time (*the paved section stops and starts from time to time*). Reach railway line (on L), and 200m later turn L under railway line, and then turn R on other side. KSO for 1.5km, then go back under it again. Turn L on other side, veering R uphill – this is the **Strada Montejugo** (*look back for a view of Montefiascone as you climb*).

At the top, track levels out. KSO, pass fountain on L (*view of Viterbo ahead L*) and 400m later reach SP3. Cross over and continue ahead on gravel road on other side (**Strada Cassetta**). 300m after that pass another fountain (L) at crossing and KSO(L) ahead. 300–400m later, just before a house ahead, turn L on similar track and KSO.

Pass turning to R and then one to L (*this whole section was badly waymarked at the times this guide was prepared*) and KSO, veering R towards a group of trees. At junction when you reach the trees turn L (trees are now on your RH side) and continue for 300m to a junction with a bigger track. Turn R here, passing the **Sorgente termale del Bagnaccio,**

11km Bagnaccio (852/104) 320m

Open-air thermal springs with 3 pools for 8–10 people at a time.

Pilgrim quarter, Viterbo

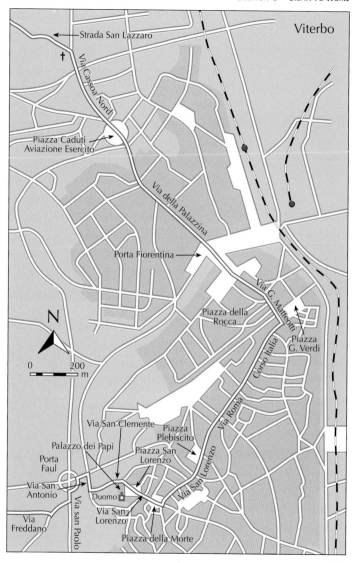

Viterbo

Strada San Lazzaro

Via Cassoa Nordi

Piazza Caduti
Aviazione Esercito

Via della Palazzina

Porta Fiorentina

Piazza della
Rocca

Via G. Matteoti

Piazza
G. Verdi

Corso Italia

N

0   200
         m

Via Roma

Via San Clemente

Piazza
Plebiscito

Palazzo dei Papi

Piazza San
Lorenzo

Porta
Faul

Via San
Antonio

Duomo

Via San Lorenzo

Via San
Lorenzo

Via san Paolo

Via
Freddano

Piazza della Morte

Turn L into the thermal area to visit (*seats*) and then KSO ahead past it to continue.

This was Bullicame, Stage VI (Valentine, 6) in Sigeric's itinerary.

KSO past the terme (on your L), continue ahead for 1.5km, and then, opposite a stone gateway on R, turn L along **Strada San Lazzaro**. KSO ahead, go under motorway 2.5km later, and pass cemetery on R (*parts of it look more like a cross between futuristic blocks of council flats and an industrial estate than a traditional burial ground*). 500m later reach the **Via Cassia** (*petrol station to L with bar*). Turn R here past cemetery entrance then go under the ring road.

KSO, cross to LH side, and 400m later reach a big roundabout, the **Piazza Caduti Aviazione Esercito**. KSO ahead on other side on **Via della Palazzina** (pavement on RH side) up to the **Porta Fiorentina** and go under it (*useful street plan with index just inside on R*) to reach the **Piazza della Rocca** in

---

7km Viterbo (859/97) Pop. 59,860, 327m

All facilities. Trenitalia. OP in Nuovo Ostello di Viterbo, Via Giovanni Derollato 1 (335.1621652, 15 March – November, 12 pl., donation). Residenza Nazareth, Via San Tommaso 26–30 (0761.321525). Instituto Adoratrici Sanque di Cristo, Viale 4 Novembre 25 (0761.341900). Hotel Trieste, Via N Sauro 32 (0761.341882/347110). 2 TOs – Via Romiti (near Viterbo Porta Romana station, 0761.304795, infoviterbo@apt.viterbo.it) and Via Ascenzi 4 (0761.325992, infotuscia@libero.it).

Town of Etruscan origins that was already of considerable size during the Middle Ages – its walls were 5km long in the 13th century. Viterbo has numerous Romanesque churches, and many had hospices annexed to them – San Lorenzo, for example, Santa Maria Nuova (note its 12th-century outdoor pulpit), San Luca, Santo Stefano and others – as well as civic buildings dating back to that time. Its other main sights include the Cattedrale, the Palazzo dei Papi adjoining it, the ninth-century Chiesa di San Sisto (built on the remains of a Roman temple and much frequented by pilgrims), the Chiesa di Santa Rosa and the medieval district of San Pellegrino. Good place for a final rest day before you reach Rome.

12th-century pulpit outside the Chiesa di Santa Maria Nuova

Duomo, Viterbo

Given the labyrinthine nature of the streets in the old part of Viterbo, and depending on where you slept, you may prefer to leave the town by the **Porta Fiorentina** then turn L immediately alongside the (outside of) the town walls on **Via del Pilastro** to the **Porta Faul**. ❯

Otherwise, cross the **Piazza della Rocca** and continue on other side down **Via G Matteotti** to the **Piazza G Verdi**. Turn second L along the **Corso Italia**, KSO(R) ahead along the **Via Roma** and reach the **Piazza del Plebiscito**. Continue ahead along the **Via San Lorenzo**, a very long street, to the **Piazza della Morte**, then veer R (still the Via San Lorenzo) to the **Piazza San Lorenzo**, with the **Duomo** and the **Palazzo dei Papi**.

Facing the cathedral go down the steps under the archway to your R and turn L at the bottom (this is the **Via di San Clemente**, although it is not marked until the end). Turn R into **Via San Antonio**, and 100m later reach the Porta Faul and ❮ turn L.

Here there is a choice. *The new route goes via the Terme dei Papi, but is not yet waymarked and involves 2.5km on a very busy road, not always with a pavement. The older route (described here) misses out the terme, but is much quieter. The two join up after the first 4km.*

At the roundabout outside the Porta Faul turn L and then immediately R onto a minor road, then fork R immediately after that – this is the **Strada Freddano**, but is not marked at the start. KSO – very quiet – for 1km, then KSO(R) ahead at fork

273

onto the **Strada San Ilario e Valentino**. KSO ahead, cross over the motorway (*in this section, most of the way to Vetralla, you are playing 'hide and seek' with the motorway, crossing, recrossing it…*), veering L on other side behind its service station, and KSO. Pass a tall *edicola* (*wayside shrine dedicated to Santi Ilario e Valentino, placed near the spot where their martyrdom took place; seats*). Turn L (this is where the route via the Terme dei Papi joins up) (*now on the Itinerario della Fede – Etruscan, Roman, Christian, marked with 'Stations of the Cross' type picture frames*) and reach a tall grille-type gate that looks as though it is firmly locked and impossible to pass through. It is not immediately evident, but there is a pedestrian gate set into its LH side, which is normally only bolted shut (not locked with a key). ▼ Go through it, shut the gate behind you and continue ahead – this is private property.

In the unlikely event that both big and small gates are locked, retrace your steps back over the motorway to the junction where you forked R and turn down what would have been the LH fork instead – the Strada Freddano. KSO ahead, cross the motorway by the next road bridge, and 400m afterwards pick up the waymarks again where the route leaves the field with the Etruscan tombs and turns R onto a minor road (which you are now on).

Shortly afterwards the track bends R, but KSO ahead here on a small FP (the Itinerario della Fede), which then turns L alongside a tall fence on L. Turn R at end, pass Etruscan tombs (*seats*), go through a small gate, KSO ahead and emerge onto a minor road (the Strada Freddano again) and turn R along it. *The landscape is beginning to change and is a lot flatter than before.*

Continue on the Strada Freddano for 200m more, then turn L into *Via San Nicolao* (a VS) and go under the motorway. KSO(R) at fork on other side, uphill and down, ignoring turns to R and L. 700m later turn R onto a tarmac road coming from your L (**Strada Signorino**), and 700m after that, when it bends R at junction with wayside shrine, KSO(L) ahead on a VS, the **Strada Risiere**. Nearly 1km later go under motorway again and turn L on other side on earth track alongside it. KSO for 1km, going under road bridge part-way along, cross the **Strada Paliano** and KSO ahead on other side, gradually going alongside motorway slip road for a while.

1km later turn L under motorway again. Turn R at T-junction 100m later, then 200m after that, at another junction, turn R ahead on minor tarmac road. KSO for 450m then, by two very large rocks on L, turn L through a low gate into a grassy walled lane, straight as a die, gently uphill. 1km later, when a similar track joins from back L, KSO(R) ahead uphill, ignoring turnings to L and R.

Pass a tall abandoned house on L, then 200m later (olive grove opposite) turn L along **Strada Quartuccio**, a gravel road. 500m later cross a bigger minor road, and then cross a bridge over the **Via Cassia**. KSO ahead on other side for 700m, then turn R onto an earth track (large pine tree and mailboxes for houses Nos 5F and 5H at turning). KSO past olive groves, and 800m later reach a small road and turn L along it. 300m after that turn R (olive groves on R) onto earth track, veering L downhill. Then, at the bottom, watch out very carefully – *the whole of the next section, to the centre of Vetralla, was very badly and incompletely waymarked at the time this guide was prepared.*

Turn hard R downhill into the woods – the path is clear and obvious enough, but not the waymarking – then 50m later turn L uphill to be faced with a mesh fence immediately in front of you. Be careful, as it is electrified at the top. Turn R to the corner of this very large fenced-in enclosure (*with CCTV surveillance*), then turn L uphill alongside it. At the very top, some 400m later, there are several farm buildings but no waymarks. Continue ahead to a junction of paths and pass in front of the main house (on your L), then KSO ahead on a track that winds its way up and downhill for some 600–700m to a T-junction with a bigger track, where the waymarks reappear for a while. Turn R and follow the track down to another T-junction with a minor road. Here turn L and KSO for 1km to a further T-junction with the **Cassia Suburbana** (not marked). Here you can do one of two things – either make a detour to visit the Chiesa di Santa Maria in Forcassi before returning to the main route to head into Vetralla or go directly to Vetralla.

Turn L for 250m to see the abandoned **Chiesa di Santa Maria in Forcassi** (there are plans afoot to restore it). This was Stage V (Furcari, 5) in Sigeric's itinerary. Afterwards (this is not obvious from the waymarking) retrace your steps to the junction where you turned L and pick up the main route, described below.

For the main route to Vetralla turn R, then 250m later fork L onto **Via San Nicolao** (not marked), downhill. Cross a bridge and go uphill to a junction, then continue ahead on **Via Selvarella** (also not marked) to **Piazza Mattaoio** (not marked either!), and at the end turn R to traffic lights by the **Via Cassia**. Cross over and continue ahead up **Via della Pietà** (bar on L), veering R at the very top to **Via Roma**, where you turn L. Continue to the **Piazza Carmine** and the **Duomo** in

---

17km Vetralla (876/80) Pop. 12,266, 383m

All facilities. OP in the parish of San Francesco (donation, 0761.478676 and 349.9724493). Bar/Rte Albergo da Benedetta, Via della Pietà 76 (0761.477032). Monasterio Regina Pacis, Via del Giardino 4 (on way out of town, 0761.481519).

18th-century Duomo di Sant'Andrea apostolo, Romanesque Chiesa di San Francesco, Museo della Città e del Territorio.

Via Francigena sign leaving Vetralla

Continue ahead on **Via San Michele** (*supermarket on R*). Cross the Via Cassia via the underpass and KSO ahead on the other side, uphill all the time, on the **Via dei Capuccini**. At the T-junction in front of the **Monasterio Regina Pacis** (see box above for accommodation details) turn L onto **Via Giardino** (and enter *località* of Giardino).

KSO(R) at fork, and at junction with traffic lights KSO ahead, then go under railway bridge (very carefully). At next bend turn L onto earth lane, signposted (twice) to 'Scooby Doo Toeletta per Cani'. KSO on earth track, and at junction KSO(R), then turn R again immediately, uphill. At the top go through (an open) gateway and KSO ahead, with open space to L and orchards to R. Pass a large modern house (on R), KSO ahead towards woods, and then turn R on gravel road coming from your L (**Strada La Scorticata**). Turn L by football field, uphill, passing electricity tower on R, then by blocks of flats at the top turn L into woods, again on an earth track.

KSO ahead for 1.5km. Pass house on R, and shortly afterwards start veering R. When track begins to veer L watch out for a RH turn onto a slightly smaller earth track and turn R. Veer R at gateway 200m later, then turn R at junction 300m after that. KSO, and 600m later reach the **Via Cassia** at road KM61/vi, opposite the chapel (on the other side of the road) of the

7km Madonna di Loreto (883/73) 466m

You have now walked 7km from Vetralla (or 6km if you slept in the Monasterio Regina Pacis), but you are, if you look to the R before crossing the SS2, only just beyond the town exit board! No seats.

Cross over carefully and turn L down the side of the chapel on an earth track alongside a dyke, veering L. KSO ahead (track becomes very faint) to reach a wire-netting fence ahead. Turn L, and then 40–50m later turn R alongside it. 400m after that reach a gravel road, turn L and then immediately R through gateway to another grassy track. (*The Via Cassia is invisible, but not inaudible, over to the L all the time.*) Here you will see the first of some new-style waymarks, a terracotta plaque with the relief sculpture of a pilgrim on it.

KSO ahead, with fence to L and then a line of trees, but when on reaching a grassy track coming up from the R turn L along it, veering R. Reach a gravel track by a farm with a lot of (loose) small dogs. Cross over and reach the **Torre di Orlando**. On reaching a third 'construction' (for want of a better term) KSO ahead through more hazelnut trees, very slightly L, to reach the **Strada Dogonale Oriolese** (the SP493) by the entrance boards to **Vico Malvino**. Turn L along it, back towards the **Via Cassia**.

Just a very few metres before reaching the Via Cassia turn hard R onto a wide gravel track. KSO. Cross a minor gravel road and KSO ahead. After a while the road veers R towards a railway line, which it then crosses, but you don't. Just before the bridge fork L (to the LH side of the fence), veering L to continue parallel to the railway line until, 600–700m later, a gravel road is reached coming from your R from a tunnel underneath the railway. KSO(L) ahead here, veering L away from the railway. KSO, then just over 1km later reach a similar road coming from back R and KSO(L) ahead. 400m later go under the railway line and reach the outskirts of Capranica.

On the other side continue ahead on the **Antica Strada della Valle dei Santi**. KSO at junction. Join **Via Alcide de Gasperi** coming from back R, and at top of hill join SS2 (*bar and pizzeria to L*) coming from back L in

7.5km Capranica (890.5/65.5) Pop. 5646, 363m

Shops etc. B&B Monticelli (on leaving the town, 0761.669692, 345.6178956, 327.0914049).

Town of Etruscan origin, which grew up around the Castello degli Anguillara. Duomo, Romanesque portal of the 12th-century pilgrim hospital, Romanesque Chiesa di San Francesco. Chiesa di San Rocco and Fonte di San Rocco on leaving the town.

KSO (**Viale Nardini**) to **Piazza Garibaldi** and go through arch to **Corso Franca Petrarca**. Go through another arch, KSO on **Via degli Anguillare**, pass **Piazza del Duomo** (on R) and KSO. Pass **Piazza Sette Luglio** (on R) and continue on **Via Vergini Vespi**. Pass **Piazza Santa Maria** (R) and KSO. Go down stepped **Via Castelvecchia**, turning hard L then R through arch to the **Piazzale dei Frati** – a sort of esplanade bending R (*bar and supermarket on road below*).

Turn L then R down slope to road (KM54) and then immediately R (*Chiesa di San Rocco to L, with Fonte San Rocco and sitting area behind church*) onto **Strada Polgliere**, veering L steadily uphill. Follow road round (*fork L part-way up for B&B at Monticelli*) for 2km to reach a tarmac road (**Strada Capranichese**, SP91) and

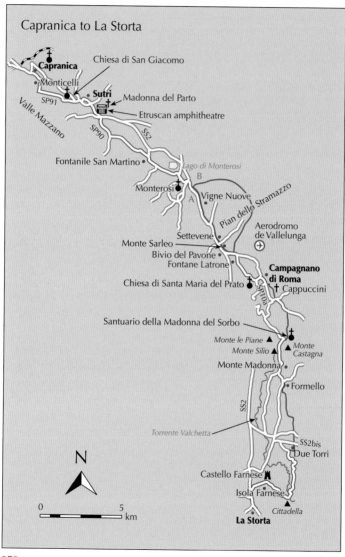

Capranica to La Storta

Capranica
Chiesa di San Giacomo
Monticelli
SP91
Sutri
Madonna del Parto
Etruscan amphitheatre
Valle Mazzano
SP90
SS2
Fontanile San Martino
Lago di Monterosi
B
Monterosi
A
Vigne Nuove
Pian dello Stramazzo
Aerodromo de Vallelunga
Settevene
Monte Sarleo
Bivio del Pavone
Fontane Latrone
Chiesa di Santa Maria del Prato
Campagnano di Roma
SP11bis
Cappuccini
Santuario della Madonna del Sorbo
Monte le Piane ▲
Monte Silio ▲
Monte Castagna ▲
Monte Madonna
Formello
SS2
Torrente Valchetta
SS2bis
Due Torri
N
Castello Farnese
Isola Farnese
Cittadella ▲
0   5 km
La Storta

turn L (*note terracotta pilgrim plaque on milestone*). Road does a sharp bend to R (*Chiesa di San Giacomo visible through trees to L*) before veering L to join **Via Cassia** again just below the entrance to the town.

Turn R along the **Via Cassia** for 300m, then there are two ways into Sutri.

If you want to go into the town straight away or sleep in the Carmelite convent, turn hard L up the **Via della Stazione** then hard R (marked 'Centro') and enter the town through the **Porta Morone**. Continue ahead on **Via Garibaldi** and then **Via Roma** to the Piazza del Comune in the centre of **Sutri**.

Otherwise, continue a short distance further along the **Via Cassia** and then turn L through **Porta Franceta**, veer L up the **Via Porta Vecchia**, cross the **Piazza San Rocco** (*Chiesetta di San Rocco to R*) and continue up the **Via dell'Ospedale** to the **Piazza del Comune**. Then turn R in the centre of

5.5km Sutri (896/60) Pop. 5208, 292m

Shops etc. Pilgrim accommodation in Monasterio Carmelitane Santissima Concezione, Via Garibaldi 1 (0761.609082). **Hotel Sutrium, Piazza San Francesco 1 (0761.600468). TO Piazza del Comune.

Sutri – typical street

Fortified medieval city, perched on a height dominating the road below, was the site of the first hospices for pilgrims. Remains of the ancient town to the southeast on leaving, including amphitheatre, the Necropolis Urbano (with 64 Roman tombs of various types), the Chiesa di Santa Maria del Parto (constructed using one of the numerous Etruscan and Roman cave tombs built into the tufa cliffs and containing a sequence of 14th-century frescoes depicting events from the life of San Michele Arcangelo), the 18th-century Villa Savorelli and the Chiesa di Santa Maria del Monte. Duomo di Santa Maria Assunta (in the town itself), originally Romanesque but altered 18th and 19th centuries. Chiesetta di San Rocco.

Stage IV (Suteria, 4) in Sigeric's itinerary. Stage III (Baccano, 3) in Sigeric's itinerary was somewhere between Monterosi and La Storta, to the west of Campagnano di Roma, but the waymarked route does not pass that way at present.

Section of seating, amphitheatre, Sutri

From the **Piazza del Comune** continue along the **Via Veneto**, the **Via XXIV Maggio** and then the **Via IV Novembre** down to the **Via Cassia**. From here it is possible to cross over and visit **Il Parco Urbano Antichissima Città di Sutri**, containing the amphitheatre, Necropolis Urbano, Chiesa di Santa Maria del Parto, 18th-century Villa Savorelli and Chiesa di Santa Maria del Monte. Afterwards cross back over to the LH side of the **Via Cassia** and continue along the cycle track (waymarked, but ignore the LH turn with a brown VF board) until it stops (by the cemetery). KSO for 600m more to some pedestrian-controlled traffic lights, cross over to the RH side and take the second RH turn (signposted 'Trevignana'), the SP90. Pass cement works on R and KSO for just over 1km, then turn L onto a wide earth track with hazelnut trees to either side. 1km later another slightly bigger track joins from back R, the **Strada Vallicella**. KSO(L) ahead on this for 3km, ignoring turns, to reach a tarmac road by the **Fontanile di San Martino** (*with picnic area*) and entrance to a golf course opposite. Turn R, veering L along side of golf course. 700m later, at RH bend, KSO(L) ahead on gravel lane, marked 'L'Olivaia'. KSO. This is the **Via Sutri Vecchia**.

2km later reach SS2 by a large public clothes-washing area to R (*shady place for a rest*) and small 15th-century **Chiesa della Madonna della Centura** to L. Turn R uphill on **Via XIII Settembre**, which then becomes the **Via Roma**, into

10km Monterosi (906/50) Pop. 2585, 278m

Small town with shops etc, two churches and the Palazzo Cardinalizio (originally a monastery).

Pass 18th-century **Chiesa di Santa Croce** and a bar/bakery with a pilgrim book (both on R), then turn L into **Piazza Garibaldi** along the side of the Chiesa di San Guiseppe (16th century, restored 2002) into **Via Caduti di Tutte le Guerre**. Go over the **Via Cassia** on a FP behind the crash barrier on the LH side, then KSO(L) on FP above the road at fork on 'no entry' road. Continue ahead on FP above the LH side of the carriageway and then on the level, but fenced off from the traffic to your R.

1km later reach a T-junction (to L) with the **Via della Saliviota**, where there is a choice between the older, more direct but noisier route (Option A), which shadows the Via Cassia, and a longer, quieter route (Option B), which loops round some way from the Via Cassia through the countryside on minor roads. Both are waymarked – Option A with yellow and white markings, often with a pilgrim figure; and Option B with the now familiar red and white.

OPTION A

KSO ahead here on the slip road to the **Via Cassia**, separated from it by a concrete partition and with very little traffic (all oncoming). KSO ahead all the time, passing a **casa cantoniera** in a lay-by. KSO, go uphill to go over a road bridge and KSO(L) ahead all the time. After road KM37/viii, by a builders' yard (*the marker posts on the Via Cassia are visible below you to your R*), the concrete partition comes to an end; then continue ahead on a minor road behind the crash barrier (*the old main road*). This ends 400m further on, at which point go down to the Via Cassia and walk on its hard shoulder for 500m, after which a FP starts.

At road KM36/viii (*very large industrial estate to R on other side of the Cassia – this is Settevene*) turn L onto a local road, the **Via Umiltà**, then 100m later, at crossing, turn R (still the Via Umiltà), gently downhill, veering R to return to the Via Cassia, where wide tarmac path starts and which then becomes the **Via Anierina** (*bar on L near FB*). Fork L uphill on slip road leading to a road bridge and go down the other side. Continue on the hard shoulder for 400m more, then fork L, at a 'no entry' sign, down the slip road at the first turn-off to 'Campagnano 4km' – this junction is the

6.5km Bivio del Pavone (912.5/43.5) 196m

KSO(L) ahead at the bottom on the **Via del Pavone** for nearly 2km, passing the end of the **Via di Monte Sarleo** (on R) – this is where the two routes join up. KSO ahead here and continue as described at 'Both routes', below.

OPTION B

Turn L at the T-junction onto a minor road, the **Via della Salivotta**, then 500m after that, at fork (still the Via della Salivotta), KSO(R) ahead. KSO. On reaching a minor tarmac road at right angles, cross over and continue on the other side on the **Via Cascinone**. At the very end, nearly 3km later, reach another tarmac road, the **Via Ronci**, and turn R along it. 700m after that turn R again (still the Via Ronci) and KSO for 1km more to a road junction with the SP16b. *There were no waymarks at the time this guide was prepared, as a lot of trees had been cut down at the crossing.* Cross over and continue ahead uphill, marked 'Monte Sarleo'. Then watch out for a RH turn which leads to the **Via di Monte Sarleo** (leading to an industrial estate). Turn R along it to reach the **Via del Pavone** (SP10a), some 2–3km from the centre of Campagnano di Roma, and turn L along it for a short distance.

Both routes

After road KM19 cross a bridge over a river and then turn R up an earth track, the **Strada de Fontana Latrona**, gradually veering L. 1km later reach the **Fontana Latrona** on R, which looks as though it has recently been restored. Turn L uphill here and KSO. After the tarmac starts, veer L to a T-junction with another road at a bend and KSO(L) ahead, then at the next T-junction KSO(R) ahead. Follow the road round, still uphill (and still the Strada de Fontana Latrona), then 700m later reach a further T-junction with the **Strada Comunale della Vignaccio** and turn L along it (downhill for a change).

Reach a junction at the bottom with the **Via del Pavone** (SP10a) and turn R (*large supermarket on L*). Turn first L for the 'Centro Parrochiale' if you are going to sleep there, but other otherwise follow Via del Pavone round to R and L to a square (**Piazza Regina Elena**) in the centre of

4km Campagnano di Roma (916.5/39.5), Pop. 9387, 283m

All facilities. OP in Centro Parrochiale, Via Dante Alighieri 7, access via priest (06.9041094 and 333.9381576, no beds but mattresses, shower, donation). Albergo da Righetto, Corso Vittorio Emanuele 70 (06.9041036), Hotel Ristorante Benigni, Via della Vittoria 13 (06.904.2671), Albergo Il Postiglione Via Cassia Antica 15 (KM30, 06.9041214).

Chiesa di San Giovanni Battista, built in 1515 on the site of an older structure, with materials from a destroyed paleo-Christian church. Chiesa di San Rocco e San Sebastiano.

To visit the centro storico turn L through archway, then retrace your steps to continue.

Note *There were plans afoot to re-route part or all the way to the Santuario della Madonna del Sorbo (see below), but this had not yet been done at the time of writing; so if there is waymarking that differs from the description given here, and if it looks reliable, follow that.*

KSO(L) ahead (past arch and public garden) on SP10a on **Via Sebastiano** ('no entry' sign), passing small **Chiesa di San Rocco e San Sebastiano** (on R), then 200m later fork (not turn) L into **Via dei Cappuchini** (marked 'cimitero') and follow it round uphill (*waymarks start again part-way up*). KSO, uphill all the time.

At the top, 1.5km later, cross the SP14 and continue on other side (staggered L) on the SP10a (signposted 'Formello') at KM13/vii and the waymarks reappear. KSO until KM12/vi, and then fork R by small wayside shrine up the **Strada di Macchiano**. KSO, on a ridge at first, ignoring turnings. When tarmac stops the road starts going downhill, and the Santuario della Madonna del Sorbo is visible ahead in the trees. Continue more steeply downhill until you come to the last house, No 39, at the bottom.

Fork R here on a small FP to the RH side of the house, which winds its way down through the woods to a T-junction of two *torrenti*. Cross the one on your R, then turn hard R uphill alongside it, veering L, and KSO on FP uphill (not enough waymarks) until you reach a T-junction of tarmac roads (*wayside shrine, seats*). Turn L to visit the

5km Santuario della Madonna del Sorbo (921.5/34.5) 188m

There are two versions of the history and origins of this sanctuary, which has recently been restored and is open for visits.

One is that in the 10th century there was a castle on this site, which contained a chapel within its precincts dedicated to the Madonna. In 1427 it was ceded to an order of Carmelites, who built a convent with a church, dedicated to the Virgin, on the site of the former one. Today all that remains of the convent are the buildings surrounding it, but the church is still used for services, and the icon of the Madonna that spoke to the swineherd in the second version of the story (see below) still stands on the altar.

According to the second, more colourful explanation, a young man from Formello with a mutilated arm kept his pigs on the grazing land near the site of the future santuario and one day noticed a sow running off alone then returning an hour later. He observed the same thing for several days in succession and so decided to follow the animal and see where it went. The sow climbed the hill to a service tree at the top (*sorbo* in Italian – a tree in the rose family and similar to a rowan), where it sat back on its haunches, raised its front legs as if in prayer, and gazed fixedly at the icon of the Virgin and Child nailed to the tree.

The Madonna appeared and spoke to the swineherd, telling him to run back to Formello and tell everybody about the apparition. She said that if they didn't believe him (which they didn't) she would perform a miracle. So when the swineherd put his mutilated arm into his pocket and then withdrew it, it came out complete with the hand that he had formerly been missing. The people of Formello therefore carried out the Virgin's wish that a sanctuary be built on the site of the apparition, keeping the service tree with the icon of the Madonna that had spoken to the swineherd and building the church round it. This new church then became a place of pilgrimage.

Return to the junction after visiting the sanctuary and turn L (or KSO ahead if you didn't visit) down **Via del Sorbo**, going downhill. Cross the torrente (bridge) and the cattle grid, and then continue on a gravel road. Go through another cattle grid and reach a parking lot for the **Parco di Veio**.

KSO ahead, continuously uphill, until you come to a fork (*sitting area on L*) on the outskirts of

2.5km Formello (924/32) Pop. 9435, 270m

Shops etc. Town in existence since prehistoric times, whose main sights include the Chiesa di San Lorenzo (10th–11th centuries), the Chiesa di San Michele Arcangelo, the Palazzo Chigi (now an archeological museum) and the ruined 17th-century Villa Chigi-Versaglia.

At this junction there are two sets of waymarking, as the older route, continuing ahead here along Via Antonio Angelozzi and then on minor roads, skirted the town altogether. Now, however, the Via Francigena has been rewaymarked, taking pilgrims through Formello, the route described here.

Fork L here onto **Via Emilio Bellomi**, downhill, then veer R into **Via Umberto I**. KSO, veering L by a sitting area to go through the archway ahead into the **Piazza San Lorenzo** and the church of that name. Cross the square diagonally and continue along **Via Vente Settembre**. Pass the **Chiesa di San Angelo**, then at the end turn L down some steps – this is the **Salita della Porta da Piedi**. Reach a tarmac road at the bottom, the **Via Regina Elena**, turn R and then KSO(L) ahead on the

Strada Comunale Fontana Rutola, a VS – *note the figure of a pilgrim etched into the road surface at the start.* KSO.

KSO(R) at fork and continue downhill, gently at first and then more steeply. Reach a sharp RH bend ahead, but turn left here uphill on a shady path, veering L and then R uphill between fields, going along the hillside and downhill again. When the wooden railings stop KSO ahead on a clear gravel path along the valley bottom. KSO. Pass two sturdy purpose-built seats, KSO, pass two more seats, then reach a minor road at a bend (*note another pilgrim figure etched into the surface of the pathway*) and turn L uphill (this is the **Strada dei Pantanicci**).

200m later turn R at a crossing along a VS, the **Via della Pietrarella di Monte Aguzzo**. 500m later, at next crossing, turn R onto the **Via del Prataccio**, a minor tarmac road, gradually going downhill. 1km later, at end, reach a bigger road coming from the R. Turn right along it, but then 200m after that turn hard L onto the **Via della Selviotta**, passing a sports stadium on R. 1km later cross a road bridge over the **Via Cassia**.

KSO(R) ahead at fork on the other side, still the **Via della Selviotta**, which quickly becomes unsurfaced. KSO ahead, but then watch out for a junction with a similar track coming from back R and turn hard R along it uphill. This is the **Via Monte dell'Ara**, and the junction at the top is known as **Due Torri** (the name of the house on your R). *This is where the two options from Formello join up.*

Turn L here along the **Via Monte Michele**, which then becomes a VS. Follow it as it winds its way, mainly gently, uphill, continuing on a ridge with splendid views on a clear day and veering mainly R. 1km later go through a hedge and then turn R at the T-junction on the other side, veering round to the L to reach a small junction by a flying club (*for enthusiasts of model – not life-sized – aeroplanes*). Turn L here, veering R, go through gates where the property ends and KSO along another ridge, more or less level – this is the **Vacchereccia**. Continue to a LH fork leading to two large buildings, one of them a pink house with turquoise shutters, where there is a 'dead end' sign.

Fork right here through a gateway onto a small earth track, which descends all the time and becomes narrower until, some 800m later, it reaches the **Torrente Valchetta**, which has to be forded. However, there are large, solid stepping stones above the water level, so you should be able to cross without any trouble.

Continue ahead on a VS on the other side, then some 400m later watch out! There are two sets of waymarks here, one of which, very clearly signed in red and white but with a figure '2', invites you to turn R. Do **not** take this (*a local recreational walking route leading to the cemetery in Isola Farnese by a very long circuitous, hilly path*). KSO(L) ahead here instead, cross a bridge over a branch of the **Torrente Valchetta**, and veer R to continue on the level for 1km more to a junction by a sports stadium on the L. Turn R uphill here (this is the **Via Prato della Corte**) to reach a junction at the end of the **Via Isola Farnese** in

13km Isola Farnese (937/19) Pop. 3902, 89m

Small medieval borgo with the Castello Farnese perched on a hilltop. It takes its name from being an 'island' amid the many water channels in the area, and from the powerful Farnese family who bought the whole town in the late 16th century, complete with its baronial palace and late medieval castle. Chiesa di San Pancrazio Martire.

To visit the borgo turn R here up the stepped **Via Agella**, leading to the Piazza Colonella (*seats*) and the church, then retrace your steps to continue.

Continue ahead (coming from the Via Prato della Corte) and follow the **Via Isola Farnese** as it wends its way continuously uphill for 1km to reach the junction with the **Via Cassia**. Turn L here and continue for 1.5km to reach the junction by the small Cappella della Visione in

4km La Storta (941/15) 170m

Shop, banks etc. Trenitalia. Suore Santa Brigida, Via Cassia KM20 (06.30880272). Also Casa S M degli Angeli, Via della Storta 783 (06.3089080), Instituto Suore Poverella, Via Baccarica 5 (06.30890495 and 335.2746450, small charge).

Cappella della Visione, the small chapel on the RH side of the road (SS2), is so-named because it was the place where Saint Ignatius Loyola, on his way to Rome with two companions in 1537, stopped to pray and had a vision. He saw Christ carrying the cross, and God the Father asking his Son to take on Ignatius as his servant, a vision that had a profound influence on the future activities of the Society of Jesus (Jesuits) that he had already founded. Modern Cattedrale del Sacre Cuore di Gesu e Maria.

Stage II (Johannis VIIII, 2) in Sigeric's itinerary.

From the **Cappella della Visione** (*seats*) continue on pavement on LH side, passing below the cathedral perched up on the hill above on the R, and KSO ahead. 800 later KSO(L) at fork where road splits for one-way system, leave La Storta and enter the comune of La Giustiniana.

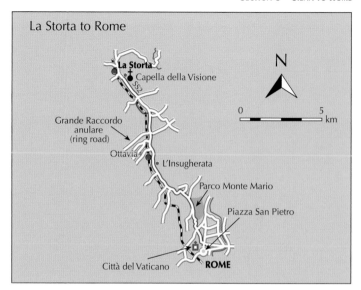

La Storta to Rome

N

0 — 5 km

La Storta
Capella della Visione
Grande Raccordo anulare (ring road)
Ottavia
L'Insugherata
Parco Monte Mario
Piazza San Pietro
Città del Vaticano
ROME

1.5km from the chapel, when the **Torre della Cornace** becomes visible in the trees on a hill ahead, turn R at (old) road KM15 (crossing the Via Cassia very carefully) into **Via della Torre della Cornachie**. Go down under the railway line, then turn L into **Via della Torre di Spizzichino**, with the tower and the railway line now to your L. At the end turn R into **Via dei Casale della Castelluchia**, veering L at fork. KSO ahead on a very quiet, shady road with houses and small-holdings to either side.

1km later pass **Tenutas la Castelluchia** on R, a very large farm property, after which the Via dei Casale della Castelluchia turns L, through some gates (kept open). Turn L here, follow the road downhill and then KSO, veering L and R and then ahead to reach a set of tall locked gates, through which pedestrians can pass to their RH side. Go through more gates (open), turn L into **Via Gioacchino da Fiore**, then 50m later go under the railway line ahead on **Via Guiseppe da Copertino** and then R into the **Via Trionfale** (*shops opposite, waymarks return*). Cross over, and then turn R along it (on pavement on LH side).

100m later pilgrims will, at some point in the future, be able to turn L up the Via Carlo Gherardino, leading uphill to the Via Cassia, and continue on a much quieter (although 5km longer) option into the centre of Rome, the Vatican and the end of their pilgrimage. However, until this route through the Riserva Naturale

287

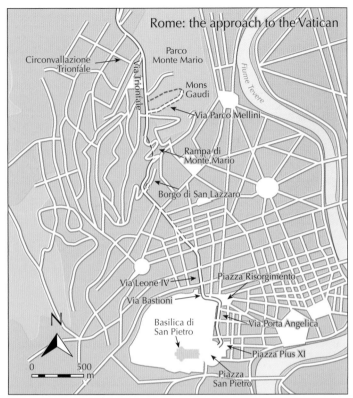

Rome: the approach to the Vatican

Circonvallazione Trionfale
Parco Monte Mario
Via Trionfale
Fiume Tevere
Mons Gaudi
Via Parco Mellini
Rampa di Monte Mario
Borgo di San Lazzaro
Via Leone IV
Piazza Risorgimento
Via Bastioni
Basilica di San Pietro
Via Porta Angelica
Piazza Pius XI
Piazza San Pietro
N
0 500 m

View of Rome from Monte Mario (Mons Gaudi)

Stepped Rampa di Monte Mario

dell'Insugherata (a nature reserve) has been waymarked (without which it would be difficult to follow successfully, added to which there is, at present, no access to the area on Saturdays and Sundays without prior telephoning), pilgrims (unless they want to take a bus) must continue along the Via Trionfale (which has by now split off from the Via Cassia). This was the road preferred by pilgrims and other travellers in the past, as the Via Cassia, running closer to the Tiber, was prone to flooding.

The section from here to the Basilica San Pietro in Rome is probably the noisiest and most tedious section of the whole 1900km journey from Canterbury, and due to the hilly nature of the landscape there appear to be no continuous minor roads or footpaths that could be used as an alternative. The Via Trionfale passes to the RH side of the nature reserve, but is almost continuously built-up, and passes through run-down areas adjacent to the railway line for much of the way. Although there are plenty of bars and shops en route there are almost no parks, public gardens, squares or churches with benches for a sit down and quiet rest. There are also some sections where there is no pavement on either side of the road, so watch out carefully for the (fast) oncoming traffic, as in this section the road has split into two parts, with all the vehicles coming towards you, northbound. This option is waymarked, although somewhat sparsely.

KSO. Pass the railway stations of **Ipogea degli Ottavi** and **San Filippo Neri** and then a big hospital (on R), and at a junction with **Via Barellai** turn R under the railway line and then L onto the **Via E di Mattei** (tree-lined, so shady) as far as the **Piazza Santa Maria della Pietà**. Pass the end of the **Via Chiarugi** (on L), then turn L over railway line by a sitting area, R along the tracks, and L at the end by the **Stazione Monte Mario**. Turn L after that along the **Via della Stazione Monte Mario** and then R back onto the **Via Trionfale**.

KSO ahead to the junction with the **Via Pinetta Sacchetti** (on R). Turn R onto it for a short distance (waymarked), then L until it runs into the **Via Trionfale**, passing the medical school of the **Università Cattolica del Sacre Cuore** (on R). Pass the **Forte Trionfale** (on L) and KSO to the **Piazza Monte Gaudio** (seats), where the Via Trionfale turns R in front of a church (on L). Pass the **Fontanile Pie IX**, below R (who had it built in 1866 for the benefit of the inhabitants of the Borgata di San

289

St Peter's Basilica, facade

Chofrio). KSO (*pavement on RH side, but this section is very noisy*) and reach a square, **Largo Cervinia**. *This is where the route through the nature reserve will meet up with the historic (Via Trionfale) route, once it is fully waymarked.*

KSO downhill here, on the **Via Trionfale**, passing **Casa di Cura Villa Stuart** on L surrounded by a large park, and KSO. Pass the first entrance to the **Parco della Vittoria** (on L). 100m later cross over and turn L through archway (waymarked) up a stepped lane, veering R, then continue on clear FP, veering L, to a viewpoint. *This is the Mons Gaudi of the Via Francigena, the equivalent of the 'Monte de Gozo' on the Camino de Santiago, from where pilgrims can see the Basilica di San Pietro and the whole of Rome for the first time.*

From here retrace your steps. Turn hard R on a tarmac road here, the **Via Parco Mellini**, and return to the **Via Trionfale** at the **Largo Zucchi**, *a junction where the main heavy traffic turns L along the Viale Cavalieri de Vittorio Veneto and so leaves the Via Trionfale (ahead) relatively quiet, although the pavement (to either side) is not very good.*

Turn L (leaving the park), continue down the **Via Trionfale** and KSO. Just after a paved lay-by on L watch out for a LH turn down the **Rampa di Monte Mario**, which shortcuts the loops in the **Via Trionfale** twice. Continue downhill, and opposite house No 81 (on the Via Trionfale) turn hard L along the **Borgo di San Lazzaro** to see the 12th-century **Chiesa di San Lazzaro dei Lebbrosi** (lepers) at No 4 (*usually closed, but there is a mass each Sunday at 10.30am*). Retrace your steps, continue downhill, cross the **Circonvallazione Trionfale** and continue ahead on other side, passing the medieval **Osteria del Falcone** at No 62 on L (*now a trattoria, X Tues*).

200–300m later reach the **Largo Trionfale**. Cross over and continue ahead on the **Via Leone IV**, then the **Via Bastioni**, veering L to the **Piazza Risorgimento**. KSO here along the **Via Porta Angelica**, veering L to the **Piazza Pius XI**, and go through the colonnade into the **Piazza San Pietro** to the **Basilica**, reaching the end of your long journey. (For information on obtaining your Testimonium, see Appendix G.)

15km Rome (956/000) Pop. 2,718,768, 25m

Large capital city with all facilities. Stage I (Urbs Roma, 1) in Sigeric's itinerary.

Transport Two international airports – Fiumincino to the west of the city for main airlines, with flights to numerous destinations worldwide; and Ciampino to the southeast for low-cost airlines, with a wide range of European destinations. Trains and long-distance coaches ('pullman') to all parts of Italy and different parts of Europe, including Paris. Rome has a very comprehensive bus network and a metro system (one price wherever you go) with two lines, one north–south, the other east–west, which intersect only in one place – Roma Termini, the main railway station. (Both bus and metro

St Peter's dome from Monte Mario

tickets must be bought from news-stands or certain bars/cafés before travel-ling, and can be used for 100mins from the time passengers validate them on either the bus or in the metro station.)

Tourist offices There are a number in Rome, many of them in small green kiosks in popular tourist areas, but the main ones are in the following places – Largo Goldoni (Via del Corso, 06.68136061), Piazza San Giovanni in Laterano (06.77203535), Via Nazionale (Palazzo delle Esposizioni, 06.47824525), Piazza Pia (Castel Sant'Angelo, 06.68809707), Piazza Sonnino (Trastevere, 06.58333457), Piazza dei Cinquecento (Termini Railway Station, 06.47825194), Via Marco Minghetti (Trevi Fountain, 06.6782988).

Bookshops Large international bookshop in Stazione Termini, two large branches of La Feltrinelli (a chain of general bookshops with stores all over Italy) in Via Balbuino 39–40 and Via V E Orlando 78–81.

Water There are a lot of drinking fountains in public places in Rome.

Safety A word of warning – there are, unfortunately, a lot of pickpockets out and about in Rome.

Accommodation The Italian Confraternità di San Jacopo now runs a brand new pilgrim-only refuge in the Trastevere area of Rome, only a couple of hundred metres from the river Tiber. Its address is Suore Francisce del Cuore Immaculato di Maria, Via dei Genovesi, Trastevere. Open all year, this is attended by volunteer ospitalieri from June to September. It has bunk beds, toilets and showers and is only for pilgrims with a credenziale (pilgrim passport). There is a maximum stay of two nights. Prior reservation essential (48hrs notice needed): 327.2319312). There is no fixed charge as this refuge operates on a donation basis.

Otherwise there is accommodation in all price brackets, and the following is only a small selection, mainly at the more economical end of the scale. Istituto Suore dell'Addolorato, Borgo Santo Spirito 41 (06.68610767 and 06.6861078), Istituto san Guiseppe della Montagna (delle Madre degli abbandonati), Viale Vaticano 88 (06.39723807), Casa per Ferie Santa Maria delle Fornaci-Padri Trinitari, Piazza Santa Maria alle Fornaci 25 (06.39367632), Casa Accoglienza Paolo VI, Viale Vatican 96 (06.3909141),

Pensione Ottaviano Hotel, Via Ottaviano 6 (06.39738138; metro: Ottaviano) – all of these are within 1km of the Vatican.

Suore del Preziosissimo Sangue, Via Santa Maria Mediatrice (06.631759), Casa Figlie di San Giuseppe, Viccolo Moroni 22 (06.58333896), Istituto Santa Giuliana Falconieri, inizio Corso Rinascimento (Piazza Navona) (06.68803344), Casa per Ferie Oasi di San Giuseppe, Via del Fontanile Arenato 277 and Via dei Brusati 84 (06.660391), Villa Aurelia-Centro Dolean, Via Leone XIII 459 (06.66017458; metro: Valle Aurelia), Casa per Ferie 'Mater Mundi', Via Lorenzo Rocci 64 (06.65740406), Congregazione Figlie dei Santissimi Cuori di Gesú e Maria – Istituto Rovaso – Religiose Missonarie Francescane, Via Pio VIII 10–12 (06.39366582), Suore Oblate del Santissimo Redentore, Via Aurelia 238 (06.39366666), Casa Generalizia Fratelli Scuole Cristiane, Casa La Salle, Via Aurelia 476 (06.666981), Foyer Phat Diem, Via Pineta Sacchetti 45 (06.6638826 and 06.6633630; metro: Cornelia).

Casa per Ferie Villa Maria – Divino Salvatore, Largo Giuovanni Berchet 4 (06.5852031; near Villa Sciarra), Suori Orsoline, Via Dandolo 46 (06.5812150), Suore Marcelline, Via Dandolo 59 (06.5812443), Casa Santa Francesca Romana, Via Vascellari 61 (06.5812125 and 06.5882408) – these four are all in the Trastevere district. Suore Immacolata Concezione (di Lourdes), Via Sistina 113 (06.4745324, metro: Barberini), Monasterio San Gregorio Monaci Romeni, Piazza San Gregorio al Celio 1 (06.7000987; metro: Circo Massimo), Istituto Sacro Cuore, Via Marsala 47 (06.4463353;

Nave ceiling, detail, St Peter's Basilica

near Termini station), Suore Oblate Divino Amore, Viale Marruvio 2/R (06.70475611; metro: San Giovanni).

The next three are all near the Monte Mario and the Olympic Stadium – Ostello Foro Italico (look for the AIG – Italian Youth Hotels – sign), Viale delle Olimpiadi 61 (06.3236267 and 06.3236279), Opera Don Orione-Casa per Ferie Giovanni Paolo II, Via della Camilluccia 120 (06.35404767), Casa per Ferie 'Santa Teresa', Via Vicenzo

Ambrosia 9–11(06.35401142; metro: Cipro; donation basis for pilgrims with a credenziale).

Guidebooks As the present guidebook is for pilgrims, as opposed to general tourists, the main sights, such as the Colosseum and the Forum, are not included here. So if you intend to stay in Rome for more than one or two days you would be advised to purchase a guidebook to the city – a wide variety of these, in a range of languages, is available in bookshops and on many street stalls as well.

For a general guide to pilgrim Rome, both practical and as an introduction to the churches built by Constantine and continuing up to the seventh century, Howard Nelson's *Rome: The Early Church. A pilgrim's guide* is recommended (see Appendix D). Anyone wanting to make the 'Pilgrimage to the Seven Churches' should use David Baldwin's concise guide (see Appendix D) which makes a tour of the churches that formed the standard circuit for visitors to Rome in the past – the Basilica di San Pietro, Basilica di Santa Maria Maggiore, Basilica di San Paolo fuori le Mura (St Paul's Outside the Walls), Basilica di San Giovanni in Laterano, Basilica di Santa Croce in Gerusalemme, Basilica di San Sebastiano and the Basilica di San Lorenzo fuori le Mura. To visit all the Sigeric Churches in Rome (and some of the catacombs) on foot, follow the route described in Appendix A. Pilgrims spending longer in the 'Eternal City' who would like to visit the places described in the Einsiedeln Itineraries – the standard tour undertaken by pilgrims visiting Rome at the time of Charlemagne – are directed to Howard Nelson's guide of that name (see Appendix D).

Tips If you are visiting St Peter's Basilica, go there early in the morning (it opens at 7am) to avoid waiting for up to 2hrs in the queue to get in later in the day, when all the tour groups arrive.

If you have walked all the way from Canterbury and been away for three months or more, you may prefer to simply relax for a couple of days, go home and then return later for a more thorough visit to Rome. If so, late autumn is a very pleasant time to go – no longer unbearably hot, and there are fewer tourists about.

St Peter's Basilica, interior

When Sigeric, then Archbishop of Canterbury, arrived in Rome in the year 990, after making his pilgrimage to receive his pallium from the Pope and make his own appointment official, he spent two of his three days there visiting churches. (See Appendix D for Debra Birch's *Pilgrimage to Rome in the Middle Ages*, which tells the story in more detail.) He saw 23 churches altogether – 14 of them within the city walls, the rest without – and 22 are reportedly still extant and can be visited by the diligent 21st-century pilgrim prepared to do a certain amount of 'homework'.

However, all of them have been substantially altered, remodelled and/or extended, particularly during the medieval period and the 16th–17th centuries, so the present-day visitor will not see the churches as they were when Sigeric was in Rome.

Given the geographical dispersal of these buildings, Sigeric's must have been something of a whistle-stop tour – 'checking off' the churches one by one, much as a modern tourist might with sights on his or her 'must-see' list – even though he would have visited at least several of the churches on horseback. Starting at St Peter's on the first day, he went next to Santa Maria in Sassia, and then crossed the river into the city itself to see San Lorenzo in Craticula (= San Lorenzo in Lucina). From there he proceeded clockwise, outside the walls, to visit six basilicas *fuori le mura*: San Valentino, Sant'Agnese, San Lorenzo, San Sebastiano, San Anastasio and San Paolo.

Re-entering the city, probably by the Porta Ostiensis, Sigeric then visited Santi Alessio e Bonifazio, Santa Sabina and Santa Maria in Cosmedin before crossing the Tiber to Trastevere to visit Santa Cecilia, San Crisogono and Santa Maria in Trastevere, ending the day at San Pancrazio on the Via Aurelia, outside the walls. On the second day all the churches he visited were within the city walls – Santa Maria ad Martyres, the Santi Apostoli and the Lateran in the morning, spending the afternoon in the centre of Rome to visit San Croce di Gerusalemme, Santa Maria Maggiore, San Pietro in Vincoli and San Lorenzo in Panisperna.

After completing a long pilgrimage to Rome many modern-day pilgrims may wish to visit the extant Sigeric Churches, particularly those who have followed 'his' route across the Channel, through north and north-eastern France, Switzerland, over the Great St Bernard Pass and down through Italy to their final destination. His circuit of churches is quite difficult to achieve in a two-day visit nowadays, however, in terms of doing

justice to all the churches without suffering from cultural overload and because of the logistics involved in getting from one to another. Quite a juggling act is required to be there when they are open; for although some of the larger churches on the general tourist trail are open all day, most of the others close for an extended lunch break.

As there appears to be no handy guide currently available to lead the modern pilgrim round these churches, what follows are two suggested walking itineraries to take in 18 of them, indicating how to reach the remainder by public transport. Detailed descriptions of the history, construction and interesting features of all these churches are available on notice boards in the buildings themselves, and most of them have a version of the text in English. It is suggested, however, that you equip yourself with a good street plan of Rome; the A3 size of the large 'Charta Roma', the Mappa Ufficiale della Città di Roma handed out in tourist information offices, covers many of the buildings, but for the rest you will need something more comprehensive.

GROUP 1

Starting, as Sigeric did, from **St Peter's Basilica**, from the square in front of it and with your back to the building, go straight ahead across Piazza Pius XII down the Via della Conciliazione. Turn second R into Via dei Cavalieri del Santo Sepulchro to the Largo Ildebrando Gregori and the church of **Santo Spirito in Sassia**. This was built in 717 by the Saxon King Ine of Wessex, who built a church (originally dedicated to Santa Maria) and hospice for pilgrims coming from his homeland – hence the name 'in Saxia'.

Turn R out of the church and continue on Borgo Santo Spirito to the River Tiber (Tevere). Cross it by the Ponte Vitt. Emanuele II, turn L on the other side along Lungotevere degli Altoviti (the Castello San Angelo is now on the other side of the river to your L) and then go along LGT Tor di Nona to the Piazza di Ponte Umberto. Continue ahead here, forking (not turning) R in front of the Museo Napoleonico, and go down some steps to continue along Via di Monte Branzo (still parallel to river). Cross Piazza Nicosia, continue ahead on Via del Clementino, then in Piazza della Fontanella Borghese fork L ahead on Via del Leone to the Piazza and then the **Basilica of San Lorenzo in Lucina**. A *titulus* (one of the parish churches of ancient Rome, distinguished from one another by the name – 'title' – of the founder or proprietor who held the property in custody for the Church), this was built in the fourth century on the foundations of a secular Roman building dating from the third century BC; it had belonged to a Roman lady named Lucina, who sheltered Pope Saint Marcellus (308–309) during Maxentius' persecution.

Turn L out of the church, then L again down Via di Campo Marzio to the end, turn R towards Piazza in Campo Marzio, then immediately L into the Via della Maddelena. Pass the Chiesa della Maddelena, then continue ahead on Via del Pantheon to the Piazza della Rotonda and the **Pantheon/Basilica di Santa Maria ad Martyres**. This was transformed from a pagan temple to a Christian church in 609, when it was given to Pope Boniface IV by the Byzantine emperor Phocas.

Turn R outside into the Via del Seminario and continue to the Piazza San Macuto, then turn R into Via San Ignazio, L into Piazza del Collegio Romano and continue on Via Lata at the end. Cross Via del Corso, continue ahead on Via dei Santi Apostoli, and turn R into the Piazza and then the **Basilica dei Santi Apostoli** (open 7am–12pm and 4–7pm). Sixth-century basilica originally dedicated to Saint James and Saint Philip, but later to all the Apostles. Today it is the headquarters of the Franciscan order in Rome.

Turn L on leaving and R into Via IV Novembre, turning R and then L along it into the Largo Magnanapoli and the Largo Anglicum. Then continue straight ahead on the Via Panisperna to No 90 (on the corner of the Via Milano) and the church of **San Lorenzo in Panisperna**. The first church was built here during the reign of Emperor Constantine and stands on the site of Saint Lawrence's

Relief sculpture of seated Saint Peter holding keys and chains, Chiesa di San Pietro in Vincoli

martyrdom. Its present name refers to the street on which it stands, which in turn probably comes from the tradition of the adjacent convent distributing bread and ham (*pane e perna*) on 10 August, the feast day of Saint Lawrence, and performed in remembrance of his distributing funds from the church to the poor.

From there cross over into the Via Cimarra, turn L into Via Clementina and continue to the Piazza dei Zingari, veer R into Piazza Suburra and turn L up the Salita dei Borgia (stepped) into Via Cavour. Cross over, and turn R and then immediately L up the stepped Via di San Francesco di Paola to the Piazza and church of **San Pietro in Vincoli** (Saint Peter in Chains; open 8am–12.30pm and 3–6pm). Basilica built in the fifth century to house the relic of the chains

298

that bound Saint Peter while he was imprisoned in Jerusalem.

On leaving, turn R in front of church, then R into the Via delle Sette Sale, veering L and then R alongside Parco Traiano, then continue on Viale Monte Oppio. At the end turn L up Via Merulania to the **Basilica di Santa Maria Maggiore** (open 7am–7pm). Patriarchal Basilica. The first church was founded here about 350 by Pope Liberius and financed by a Roman patrician and his wife after the Virgin Mary had appeared to them in a dream, telling them to build a church in her honour. The present building dates from the 18th century.

After visiting, retrace your steps down the Via Merulania for 500m to the **Basilica di San Giovanni in Laterano** (open all day). This was the first building for public Christian worship erected in

Rome – and in the entire world – dating from 313. It is dedicated to Our Saviour and Saints John the Baptist and John the Evangelist.

On leaving the church turn R by the obelisk to the Piazza San Giovanni in Laterano, then fork R to the Piazza di Porta San Giovanni, downhill. At a junction (with the walls to your R) continue L ahead on Viale Carlo Felice (or walk through the gardens, parallel to your R) to the Piazza and church of **San Croce in Gerusalemme** (open 7am–12.45pm and 2–7pm). Dedicated to the True Cross, this church was built to house the Passion Relics brought to Rome by Saint Helena and was first consecrated in 325. The present building dates from the early 1740s.

On leaving turn R and then veer L into Via Eleniana. Go under the walls into the Piazza Porta Maggiore and then go under the walls again on the other side, under the railway line and up the Viale Scalo San Lorenzo. Turn L into Via dei Reti, second R into Via dei Sabelli, then L into Via Verano to the Piazza and the **Basilica di San Lorenzo fuori le Mura**. The first church was built in the fourth century over the tomb of Saint Lawrence. This was done by digging into the catacomb in which he was buried and isolating his shrine, so that a church could be built around it. The reconstructed 13th-century frescoes in the portico depict scenes from the lives of Saint Stephen and Saint Lawrence, both deacons and Roman martyrs.

GROUP 2

Start from the church of **San Pancrazio**, outside the walls on the edge of the Villa Pamphili (a park), between the Via Vitella and the Via San Pancrazio. A sixth-century basilica church was built here by Pope Symmachus (498–514) on the site where the body of the young martyr, Saint Pancratius, had been buried. Below the church there are huge catacombs.

After visiting the church, turn L to the Piazza San Pancrazio and continue along the Via San Pancrazio (watch out for sections with no pavement) to the Piazzale Aurelio. Turn L into the Largo Porta San Pancrazio, continue for a short distance on Via Garibaldi, then at the bend continue straight ahead down the Via Porta San Pancrazio (stepped), veering R at the bottom to go down a few more steps and then veer R into Vicolo Frusta. Turn L into Vicolo Paglia, then turn R into the Piazza and church of **Santa Maria in Trastevere** (open all day). This is one of the tituli and possibly the first church in the city where mass was celebrated openly. It was probably built by Pope Julius I (337–352), although it may have existed as early as shortly after Pope Calixtus' death in 221 (he was martyred near here).

After visiting, and with your back to the church, continue ahead along the Via Lungaretta to the Piazza Tavani Arquati and the Largo San Giovanni de Matha, then turn R into Piazza Sidney Sonnino and the church of **San Crisogono**. The church was probably

View of St Peter's Basilica from Santa Sabina park

built in the fourth century, dedicated to the martyr Saint Chrysogonus, and was also a titulus.

On leaving the church (and with your back to it) fork R down Via Santini, continue ahead (staggered) down Via dei Genovesi, then turn second R along the Via S Cecila to the Piazza and church of **Santa Cecilia**. The first church dates from the fifth century and is said to have been built over the house of the saint. The church (the one which Sigeric would have seen) was rebuilt in 822, and the relics of Saint Cecilia were moved here from the catacombs of Saint Calixtus (further restoration took place in the 18th century).

Retrace your steps, cross the Via Jandolo, and continue straight ahead along Via Vascellari to the Ponte Palatino. Cross the River Tiber

(Tevere), and almost in front of you is the church of **Santa Maria in Cosmedin** (open 4am–4.50pm). This was built during the sixth century as part of a *diaconia*, an institution helping the poor, and was rebuilt by Pope Adrian I in 782. The name indicates Our Lady 'in beauty', probably a reference to the church's rich decoration. Services here are celebrated according to the Greek Catholic rite.

From there turn L out of the church into Via Santa Maria in Cosmedin, continue for a short distance alongside the Tiber on the Lungotevere Aventino, and then turn R uphill (stepped) up the Clivo di Rocca Savella, with the Parco Savello behind the wall on your R. Turn R at the top along the Via di Santa Sabina to the Piazza di Pietro d'Illuria and the church of **Santa Sabina** (open

6.30am–12.45pm and 3–7pm). The church was originally built in the fifth century, probably on the site of the original Titulus Sabane, a church in the home of Sabina, who was martyred about 114. (Below a grating in the floor is a room of a Roman house which has been excavated – possibly the original Christian 'house-church'.)

After visiting continue (R) along Via di Santa Sabina to the Piazza and church of **Sant'Alessio all'Aventino** (nice view over Rome from public garden next door). This church was built in the third or fourth century and originally dedicated to Saint Boniface the Martyr, and so is also referred to as **Santi Boniface e Alessio**. A statue of Saint Alexis in pilgrim attire stands above an altar by the door, the figure clasping the letter which revealed his identity after his death. The church was rebuilt in the 13th century.

THE REMAINING CHURCHES

These are/were all outside the walls. The reason why so many important churches, containing the tombs and/or relics of early Roman martyrs (Saints Valentine, Agnes, Lawrence, Sebastian, Anastasius, Paul and Pancras), lay outside the city walls was that under Roman law Christian burial (in the cemeteries adjoining the churches) was not permitted within the walls. It was only later, due to the theft of bodies and relics from the catacombs and cemeteries outside the city walls, that translation of relics

and reburial was allowed, so that they could then be transferred to more secure settings within.

San Sebastiano lies to the south of Rome, on the Via Appia Antica, and its catacombs are well worth a visit. It is probably most easily reached by the archeobus service that takes in the Roman sites in that area (ask in tourist offices for details). It was one of the *sette chiese* traditionally visited by pilgrims during Holy Years. The original church was built in the fourth century to house the relics of the third-century Roman martyr, whose remains were transferred to the Vatican in 826. The present church dates from the 17th century.

San Paolo fuori le Mura (Saint Paul's Outside the Walls), also to the south of the city, on the Via Ostiense and near the River Tiber, is easily reached by metro (Basilica San Paolo station). It is only some 3km from the 'Tre Fontane', where Saint Paul was martyred and decapitated, and his tomb is located under the high altar. The original church built to house it dated from the time of Constantine (306–337).

Sant'Agnese fuori le Mura and the adjoining catacombs are to the northern side of the city on the corner of the Via Santa Agnese and the Via Nomentana (nearest metro: Bologna). The original church was created from a fourth-century catacomb, hollowed out over Saint Agnes' tomb, and the site became a place of pilgrimage. The current church (a basilica) was rebuilt by Pope Honorius I in the mid-seventh century and stands over this.

The foregoing discussion accounts for 21 out of the 22 reportedly extant churches that Sigeric saw on his visit to Rome. The 23rd, the **Basilica di San Valentino**, was presumably on the Via Valentino (nearest metro: Flaminio), an explanation which coincides with the position marked on Birch's map, but information about it seems hard to come. Zweidler, in the appendix to his *Der Frankenweg*, where he provides a translation of Sigeric's Latin itinerary (see Appendix B), refers to a San Valentino al Ponte Molle – the area north of the Tiber between the Ponte Milvio and the Ponte Flaminio. (The only church today with a dedication to this third-century priest and martyr is San Valentino al Villagio Olimpio, parish church for the Olympic village founded before the 1960 games.)

This leaves us with **San Anastasio**, also something of a puzzle. According to Birch's map, this was located fuori le mura, well to the south of San Sebastiano, between the Via Ardeatina and the Via Ostiense. Zweidler, however, gives a slightly different list of the churches Sigeric went to see, including the abbey church of Santi Vincenzo e Anastasio. This is located near the Via delle Tre Fontane, and is one of three churches built on the site of Saint Paul's martyrdom, the first one being built about 625. Then, in the 'Da Visitare' in Rome section at the end of the second volume of the AIVF's Vademecum, the list of the 22 extant churches mentions not San Anastasio (male) but a female saint, Sant'Anastasia, whose church is located not far from Santa Maria in Cosmedin.

Comments and feedback via the publishers (info@cicerone.co.uk) are welcome from anyone who uses this itinerary to visit the Sigeric Churches, particularly any information which may help to clear up the mystery of San Anastasio and explain what happened to the original Basilica di San Valentino.

APPENDIX B

Sigeric stages in Italy

(Bourg Saint-Pierre Pietrocastel XLIX (49) is the last stage before the Col du Grand Saint-Bernard. See Volume 1 for more information.)

Saint-Rhémy *Sce Remei* XLVIII (48)

Aosta *Agusta* XLVII (47)

Pont Saint-Martin *Publei* XLVI (46)

Ivrea *Everi* XLV (45)

Santhià *Sca Agatha* XLIV (44)

Vercelli *Vercel* XLIII (43)

Tromello *Tremel* XLII (42)

Pavia *Pamplica* XLI (41)

Santa Cristina *Sce Cristine* XL (40)

San Andrea *Sce Andrea* XXXIX (39)

Piacenza *Placentia* XXXVIII (38)

Fiorenzuola d'Arda *Floricum* XXXVII (37)

Fidenza *Sce Domnine* XXXVI (36)

Medesano *Metane* XXXV (35)

Fornovo di Taro *Philemangenur* XXXIV (34)

Berceto *Sce Moderanne* XXXIII (33)

Montelungo *Sancte Benedicte* XXXII (32)

Pontremoli *Puntremel* XXXI (31)

Aulla *Aguilla* XXX (30)

Santo Stefano di Magra *Sce Stefane* XXIX (29)

Luni *Luna* XXVIII (28)

Camaiore *Campmaior* XXVII (27)

Lucca *Luca* XXVI (26)

Porcari *Forcri* XXV (25)

Ponte A Cappiano *Aqua Nigra* XXIV (24)

Fucecchio *Arne Blanca* XXIII (23)

San Genesio *Sce Dionis* XXII (22)

Pieve di Coiano *Sce Petre Currant* XXI (21)

Santa Maria a Chianni *Sce Maria Glan* XX (20)

San Gimignano *Sce Gemiane* XIX (19)

San Martino Fosci *Sce Martin in Fosse* XVIII (18)

Colle di Val d'Elsa *Aelse* XVII (17)

Abbadia a Isola *Burgenove* XVI (16)

Siena *Seocine* XV (15)

Ponte d'Arbia *Arbia* XIV (14)

Torrenieri *Turreiner* XIII (13)

San Quirico d'Orcia *Sce Quiric* XII (12)

Le Briccole *Abricula* XI (11)

San Peitr in Pal (now disappeared; below Radicofani) *Voltole* X (10)

Acquapendente *Acquapendente* IX (9)

Bolsena *Sca Cristina* XVIII (8)

Montefiascone *Sce Flaviane* VII (7)

Bullicame (west of Viterbo) *Valentine* VI (6)

Vetralla *Furcari* V (5)

Sutri *Suteria* IV (4)

Baccano *Bacane* III (3)

La Storta *Johannis* VIIII II (2)

Rome *Urbs Roma* I (1)

APPENDIX C
San Rocco churches and iconography

The listing below is given in route order. (For an account of the life of San Rocco (Saint Roch) and the iconography related to him see 'Pilgrim saints', Introduction.)

Signayes Chiesa di San Rocco. The facade has frescoes with portrayals of Santa Caterina, Saint Bernard de Menton, Saint Grat, the Virgin Mary, Pope Innocent V and Saint Roch (who has two scallop shells on his short shoulder cape and two on a hat slung behind his head, halo, stick, satchel, wound on L, dog and boots – ie a 'pilgrim version'.

Torin Small chapel with fresco of Saint Roch as a pilgrim on RH side of facade with stick, cape with two scallop shells, calf-length boots, but also halo, dog (but no bread), wound on (his) R leg

Felley (Feilley) Cappella di San Rocco, 17th century

Verrès Cappella San Rocco with painting of Saint Roch as a pilgrim over the front door, stick and hat behind his head, and free-standing sculpture of him on the altar, also as pilgrim, with stick and gourd

Balmas Cappella di San Rocco

Borgo Montjovet Chiesa di San Rocco

Ciseran Chiesa di San Rocco

Hône Cappella di San Rocco (built 1665, rebuilt 1901) with statue of Saint Roch over the altar

Pont Saint-Martin Cappella di San Rocco near the entrance to the town. Faded frescoes outside, also inside, but free-standing wooden statue of Saint Roch to R of apse – cape (with shells?), stick, dog

Cappella San Rocco 17th-century votive chapel, 1km before the village of Caremma, built by its inhabitants to thank Saint Roch for protecting them against the plague when it struck in that area; painting of Saint Roch over altar

Cesnola Cappella di San Rocco

Chiesa di San Rocco (3km after Montalto Dora), probably originally 13th century; frescoes inside, including Saint Roch

Burdo Chiesa di San Rocco e Sebastiano, 18th century, built 'per voto durante la pestilenza'

Freestanding statue of San Rocco, Chiesa di Santa Cristina, Bolsena

Bollengo Cappella di San Rocco

Viverone Large brick Oratorio di San Rocco, 16th century, rebuilt 17th, with a relief carving of Saint Roch on the tabernacle door (ie the 'cupboard' where the reserved sacrament is kept)

Roppolo Chiesetta di San Rocco

Cavaglià Circular Oratorio di San Rocco, rebuilt in its present form in 1744, enlarged in 1836; has a depiction of Saint Roch in niche over the door

Alice Castello 16th-century Chiesa dei Santi Fabiano e Sebastiano contains frescoes depicting Saint Roch

Santhià Cappella di San Rocco. The fresco of three figures over the main door (inside the porch) has Saint Roch on L, a saint with a halo and sore, no dog, but also a pilgrim with stick, gourd and scallop shell on (his) LH lapel of cape.

Tromello Chiesa di San Rocco, 17th century

Gropello Cairoli Chiesa di San Rocco, 18th century. Medallion of Saint Roch above front door outside, with saint as pilgrim (stick, gourd, scallop shell on shoulder), but also with halo and dog – portrayal from the knees up only. Inside, to LH side of altar rail, in large glass cubicle, is life-size, free-standing sculpture with worried-looking younger saint (the outside one looks older) in brown Franciscan-type robes, with a short, light greenish shoulder cape with red cross (square) and two scallop shells, staff, gourd, halo, dog (and bread), barefoot.

Chinolo Pô Chiesa di San Rocco has painting of Saint Roch as pilgrim over the altar, with stick, satchel, hat in hand(?)

Pavia Chiesa di Santa Maria in Betlem has painting in RH side aisle with Saints Zenone, Biagio and Rocco, with cupid, in the lower section of the picture

San Rocco al Porto Chiesa di San Rocco

Piacenza Chiesa di San Lazzaro has very large statue of Saint Roch as pilgrim on facade. Chiesa di Santa Maria has free-standing statue of Saint Roch as pilgrim in nave, with stick, bag, boots and dog.

Pietrasanta Cathedral, San Rocco relief sculpture on facade

Gravagna San Rocco Chiesa di San Rocco, modern, stucco

Camaiore Chiesa di San Rocco at very end of Via Roma, with sculpture of the saint in niche over the door, with the dog, a stick in his RH, wearing boots, but, unusually, instead of indicating his wound with LH, it points away to R

Avenza Chiesa di San Rocco

Pietrasanta Relief sculpture of San Rocco on the cathedral facade

Capannori Chiesa di San Rocco, tryptich over altar, has Saint Roch in its centre panel

Altopascio Chiesa di San Rocco, built 1645, recently restored. Served as oratorium for a confraternity which was suppressed, probably in second half of 18th century.

San Miniato Alto Brick Oratorio dei Santi Sebastiano e Rocco near the end of the town; built in 1524, at the time of a plague epidemic, as both Saint Roch and Saint Sebastian were invoked for plague victims

Siena Brick Oratorio di San Rocco, built 1511, with statue of Saint Roch in niche on facade; adjacent Cappella di San Rocco houses polychrome terracotta statue of the saint and cycle of frescoes depicting his life

Torrenieri Chiesa di San Rocco (15th century) has modern sculpture (2000) of two feet outside the building, entitled 'Monumento al Pellegrino'

Acquapendente Chiesa di Santa Caterina has large statue of Saint Roch with halo, stick, dog and two large scallop shells on his shoulders

Bolsena Chiesa di Santa Cristina contains large, free-standing statue of San Rocco, both as saint (with halo) and pilgrim (wearing red 'Wellington boots', with scallop shells on clothing, hat on ground, stick (to which somebody has added a wine gourd) plus dog and loaf of bread

Capranica Chiesa di San Rocco, Fonte di San Rocco

Sutri Chiesetta di San Rocco

Campagnano di Roma Chiesa di San Rocco e San Sebastiano

Rome Chiesa di San Rocco all'Augusteo (in Largo San Rocco, near Ponte Cavour). Completed 1654 and its facade decorated, at the time, with frescoes representing the 'Storie di San Rocco', although the church was, in fact, constructed on the site of a much older one built by the Confraternità di San Rocco and dedicated to San Rocco e San Martino, with adjoining ospedale.

Since the majority of churches in non-touristy places along the route are closed except at service times (and were firmly shut, with no easy means of obtaining the key, when the author passed by) there are no doubt far more examples of San Rocco iconography than are mentioned in this guide, particularly with respect to paintings and sculptures that are located inside the numerous churches and chapels along the way – not only those dedicated to him but, very frequently, to other saints as well.

Interested users of this guide who discover other examples of San Rocco iconography may like to make their findings known to the author via the publishers at 2 Police Square, Milnthorpe, Cumbria LA7 7PY or info@cicerone.co.uk.

APPENDIX D
Further reading

General
Atwood, Donald and John, CR
Penguin dictionary of saints
(Harmondsworth: Penguin, 3rd edn,1995)

Birch, Debra J
Pilgrimage to Rome in the Middle Ages (Studies in the History of Medieval Religion, vol. XIII)
(Woodbridge, Suffolk: Boydell Press, 1998)
A study of pilgrimage to Rome from Late Antiquity to the end of the 13th century, analysing motivation, routes and itineraries, different aspects of the journey such as travel and the dangers inherent in it, accommodation, special privileges granted to pilgrims, letters of recommendation, equipment, the blessing of scrip and staff, safe conduct, hospitality, exemption from tolls, and notes on practical matters such as cost and when to go.

Chaucer, Geoffrey, trans. **Coghill, Neville**
The Canterbury tales
(London: Penguin Classics, 1977)
A collection of stories (mainly in verse) written in Middle English and presented as part of a story-telling contest by a group of pilgrims as they travel together from Southwark (in south London) to the shrine of Saint Thomas à Becket in Canterbury cathedral.

Coleman, Simon and Elsner, John
Pilgrimage past and present in the world's religions
(London: British Museum Press, 1995)

Davies, JG
Pilgrimage yesterday and today: why? where? how?
(London: SCM Press, 1988)
Studies the nature of pilgrimages and motives behind them, from patristic times to the Middle Ages, Protestant condemnation of pilgrimages, and the 19th-century revival of pilgrimages among Protestants, ending with a review of the devotional aspects of modern pilgrimages.

Frey, Nancy Louise
Pilgrim stories
(Berkley & Los Angeles: University of California Press, 1998)
This refers specifically to the experiences of modern pilgrims along the road to Santiago de Compostela – before, during and after their pilgrimage – but the questions

Lavoir (public clothes-washing facility), Etroubles

raised confront any modern pilgrim on a route where the journey itself, rather than the destination, is the real issue at stake.

Robinson, Martin
Sacred places, pilgrim paths: an anthology of pilgrimage
(London: Fount, 1997)
An anthology reflecting the experiences of pilgrims through the ages, dealing with places of pilgrimage, preparation for the journey, the journey itself, the inner journey, worship on the way and on arrival, and the questions raised once the pilgrimage is over.

Spencer, Brian
Pilgrim souvenirs and secular badges (medieval finds from excavations in London)
(London: Stationery Office Books, 1998)
A study, by the former Keeper of the Museum of London, of pilgrim souvenirs and secular badges.

Sumption, Jonathan
Pilgrimage
(London: Faber and Faber, 1975)
A study of the traditions of pilgrimage prevalent in Europe from the beginnings of Christianity to the end of the 15th century, examining major destinations, motivations, the cult of the saints and their relics, medicine and the quest for cures, penitential pilgrimage, the practicalities of the journey and the pilgrims themselves.

Eade, John and Sallnow, Michael J (eds)
Contesting the sacred: the anthropology of Christian pilgrimage
(London: Routledge, 1991)
Contributors examine particular Christian shrines (in France, Italy, Israel, Sri Lanka and Peru), analysing the dynamics of religious expression and belief, but also the political and economic processes at local and global levels, emphasising that pilgrimage is primarily an arena for competing religious and secular discourses.

French, RM (trans.)
The way of a pilgrim
(London: Triangle, 1995)
First published in English in 1930, this book was written by an unknown Russian pilgrim in the 19th century, telling the story of his wanderings from one holy place to another in Russia and Siberia in search of the way of prayer.

Via Francigena
D'Atti, Monica and Cinti, Franco
La Via Francigena cartografia e GPS
(Milan: Terre di Mezzo Editore, 3rd edn, 2012)
A set of 40 maps printed on three very large sheets to be cut up into long strips for each daily stage (back to back) of the route in Italy. Note, however, that the maps do not cover the section from the Great St Bernard Pass to Vercelli, as instead they lead the pilgrim from France into Italy over the Montgenèvre Pass or along the coastal route. They are at a scale of 1.30,000, include heights, distances and GPS coordinates, and are highly recommended.

Chinn, Paul and Gallard, Babette
Walkers', cyclists' and horse riders' lightfoot guide to the Via Francigena
(Arles: EURL Pilgrimage Publications, 4th edn, 2012)
A three-volume route-finding guidebook, mainly for cyclists, to the Via Francigena from Canterbury to Rome, with a fourth volume covering the cultural and historical aspects of this route.

Corvini, Roberto
Abbadia San Salvatore Sena: guide and historical notes
(Genoa: Edizioni d'Arte Marconi no. 97, 1992)
A guide to the abbey – its history, architecture and situation in relation to the Via Francigena.

Grégoire, Jean-Yves
La Via Francigena. Sur la trace des pèlerins de Canterbury à Rome
(Editions Ouest-France, 2010)
A concise introduction to the history and route of the Via Francigena, accompanied by numerous photos.

Magoun Jr, Francis P
'An English pilgrim-diary of the year 990', in *Medieval Studies*, 2 (1940), pp231–52
Examination of the pilgrim-diary associated with Sigeric, Archbishop of Canterbury 990–994, and describing the route he took on his return journey.

Magoun Jr, Francis P
'The Rome of two northern pilgrims: Archbishop Sigeric of Canterbury and Abbot Nikolas of Munkatheverà', in *Harvard Theological Review*, 33 (1940), pp267–89

Mambrini, Stelvio
La Via Francigena e l'Abbazia del S.S.mo Salvatore al Monte Amiata
(Abbazia del S.S.mo Salvatore, Comune di Abbadia San Salvatore e Assozaione Internazionale della Via Francigena, 2010)
Well-researched study of the history and place of the Abbadia San Salvatore in the context of the Via Francigena.

Marques, William
'Why throw your badge away?', in *CPR Newsletter*, 1 (June 2007), pp6–11
Discusses the history of pilgrim badges in Britain, with particular reference to those from Rome.

Ortenberg, Veronica
'Archbishop Sigeric's journey to Rome in 990', in *Anglo-Saxon England*, 19 (1990), pp197–246
Identification of the places Sigeric stayed in on his return journey.

Quaglia, L
La Maison du Grand-Saint-Bernard des origines aux temps actuels
(Aosta 1955 and subsequent editions)

Robins, Peter
'Meaning and usage of the word "francigena"', in *CPR Newsletter*, 9 (April 2010), pp2–9

Robins, Peter
'More on the term "francigena"', in *CPR Newsletter* 17 (Dec 2012), pp6–7

Stopani, Renato
La Via Francigena. Storia di una strada medievale
(Firenze: Casa Editrice Le Lettere, 1998)
Well-illustrated history of the Via Francigena as a pilgrim route.

Touring Club Italiano
Via Francigena. Sulle Orme di Sigerico: dal Gran San Bernardo ai Luoghi Santi di Roma (Guide d'Italia series)
(Milan: Touring Editore, 2006)

Aosta, Arco d'Augusto

Guide to the 'Sigeric Route' from the Great St Bernard Pass to Rome, with detailed information on monuments, landscape, art and architecture along the way. Contains 21 maps and plans and 150 photographs, but it does not provide either walking or cycling instructions or details of accommodation and services, and so is more suitable for a journey along the route by car.

Trezzini, Adelaïde, Terrien, Yvette and Heckmann, Céline
La Via Francigena: le Chemin de Sigéric en Italie
(Grand-Camp: Le Père Editions & Roma: Association International Via Francigena, 2012)
Walkers' guide, in French, to the historic (as opposed to the waymarked) Via Francigena in Italy (although the two routes often coincide). Contains route-finding instructions, details of accommodation, brief details of monuments along the way and sketch maps.

Zweidler, Reinhard
Der Frankenweg – Via Francigena. Der mittelalterliche Pilgerweg von Canterbury nach Rom
(Stuttgart: Konrad Theiss Verlag, 2003)
Discusses the history of the Via Francigena, from Canterbury all the way to Rome, and everyday pilgrim life in the Middle Ages; also describes the places along the way – geography, scenery, art and architecture.

Rome
Baldwin, David
Rome: a pilgrim's companion (CTS Christian Shrines series)
(London: Catholic Truth Society, 2005)
This is an A6-size 'companion' to accompany a conventional guidebook, offering a structure on which to hang a pilgrimage to the Holy City. It covers, briefly, the beginnings and the Early Church, the Vatican and weekly events in Rome today, St Peter's Basilica, Santa Maria Maggiore, plus four more of the 60-plus churches in Rome devoted to Our Lady, as well as the other five places in the 'Pilgrimage to the Seven Churches' tradition of previous centuries. It also includes a section on the saints in Rome and suggested itineraries.

Although this 'companion' is not concerned specifically with the Via Francigena, it would be of interest/help to those seeking to discover 'Pilgrim Rome' at the end of their walking, cycling or riding journey.

Nelson, Howard
Rome: the Early Church. A pilgrim's guide (Pilgrim Guides to Rome 1)
(Confraternity of Pilgrims to Rome, 2011).

This slim volume covers the traces of Peter and Paul in Rome, acknowledging the paucity of evidence for Peter's presence there, but describing the archeological evidence for his burial below St Peter's. It discusses the catacombs, and then the churches built by Constantine: the Lateran and the several basilicas built over martyrs' tombs outside the walls. Later chapters cover the churches built, century by century, by the Popes, after the emperor's move to Constantinople, up to the conversion of the Pantheon to Christian use early in the seventh century. The guide also contains a brief practical section on accommodation, maps and guides, transport and so on.

Nelson, Howard
The Einsiedeln Itineraries: a pilgrim's guide to Rome in Charlemagne's time (Pilgrim Guides to Rome 2)
(Confraternity of Pilgrims to Rome, 2013)
This describes and transcribes a manuscript guide to Rome compiled at about the time of Charlemagne's coronation by Pope Leo III in 800. It then lists and describes each of the sites – mainly, but not exclusively Christian – along each of the routes, and offers a series of walking guides to enable the modern visitor to follow the itineraries.

Both of the above publications are available from the Confraternity of St James' online bookshop (www.csj.org/uk). The 'Itineraries' is also available in Rome from the Crypta Balbi Museum (devoted to medieval Rome and with a good display on this topic) in the Via Botteghe Oscure.

Parker, John Henry
An Englishman in Rome, 1864–1877: the Parker Collection in the Municipal Photographic Archives
(Rome: Artemide Edizione, 1990)

Tweedie, Ian
Saint James in Rome. Some brief notes for visiting members
(London: Confraternity of St James, 1990)

Vidon, Henry
The pilgrims' guide to Rome
(London: Sheen & Ward, 1975)

Personal accounts

Belloc, Hilaire
The path to Rome
(London: Allen & Unwin, 1955)
An account of the author's journey on foot from eastern France to Rome.

Browne, Peter Francis
Rambling on the road to Rome
(London: Hamish Hamilton, 1990)
An account of the author's journey along the road to Rome taken by Hilaire Belloc – travelogue rather than pilgrimage.

Lucca Cathedral, looking up

Detail of façade, Papal Palace, Viterbo

Brunning, Anthony
'Pilgrim to Rome', in *CPR Newsletter* 2 (Dec 2007), pp2–23
An account of the author's walking pilgrimage from Canterbury to Rome in 1990.

Donaldson, Christopher
In the footsteps of St Augustine. The great English pilgrimage from Rome to Canterbury
(Norwich: The Canterbury Press, 1995)
Recreation of the journey from Rome to Canterbury made by Saint Augustine and his 40 companions in the year 597, when he was sent by Pope Gregory the Great to bring Christianity to Britain. Part personal diary of the author's own journey along this route, the book is useful for the historical background to this event and as a guide for the future pilgrim to the 'sights' of Early Christian Rome.

Hughes, Gerard
In search of a way. Two journeys of spiritual discovery
(London: Darton, Longman and Todd, 2nd edn, 1986)
An account of a walking pilgrimage from Weybridge to Rome in 1975, with reflections on two journeys – the first made to find direction in the second. The physical travel, on foot, lasted 10 weeks, but the accompanying spiritual journey still continues.

Lambert, Christopher
Taking a line for a walk: 1000 miles on foot from Le Havre to Rome
(Woodbridge, Suffolk: Antique Collectors' Club Ltd, 2004)
A colour facsimile of the author's journal when he walked from Le Havre to Rome in 2000, via Lausanne and the Via Francigena. This book reproduces, on a double-page spread for each day, his handwritten text and several hundred colour-wash pen-and-ink drawings.

Mooney, Brian
A long way for a pizza – on foot to Rome
(London: Thorogood Publishing, 2012)
An account of the author's 1300 mile journey on foot from his home in Essex to Rome. A sequel is in preparation, describing the return journey he made more recently.

Warrender, Alice
An accidental jubilee
(York: Stone Trough Press, 2012)
A description of the author's journey on foot from Canterbury to Rome following a very serious road accident.

Other
Peressini, Rossella and Andrews, Robert
Get by in Italian
(London: BBC Books, 2007)
A brief introductory course on the Italian language accompanied by a 60mins CD.

APPENDIX E
Italian–English glossary

affittacamere — rooms for rent

alimentari — grocery shop (more like a corner shop/delicatessen and normally more expensive than a supermercato)

attenti al cane! — beware of the dog (Attenti ai cani! = there are more than one of them!)

bancomat — cash dispenser

basulato — paved (refering to roads, including Roman roads, whose surface consists of very large, slightly curved stone slabs)

bivio — fork, bifurcation

borgo — (big) village, district, suburb

campeggio — campsite

capella — chapel, side chapel

capolougo — chief place in a comune

casa cantoniera — road-builders' house, always painted dark red

cascina — (large) farm (its buildings)

cavalcavia — flyover

chiesa — church

chiesetta — small church, chapel (but not side chapel)

Siena, 'Pilgrim Street'

circonvallazione — ring road

comune — smallest autonomous political and administrative unit

corso — main street, avenue

corte — court yard (also used in street names)

distributore — petrol station

divieto di... — it is prohibited to... (eg divieto di accesso – no entry)

317

edicola mariana	niche, small (roadside) shrine with a statue of the Virgin Mary	*menu fisso*	fixed-price meal
fabbrica	factory	*municipio*	town hall
fattoria	farm	*naviglio*	(navigable) canal
fiume	(large) river	*osteria*	pub, bar (usually old)
foresteria	guest quarters (in convent, etc), hostel	*paese*	place, village, country
frazione	hamlet	*passagio a livello*	level crossing
guado	ford	*pese pubblico*	public weighbridge
IAT (Informazione ed Accoglienza Turistica)	tourist information office	*piazza*	square (public place)
Io sono de guardia qui!	'beware of the dog!' (literally means 'I'm on duty here!')	*piazzale*	large square
		pieve	parish church
letti di castello	bunk beds	*podere*	farm, estate (its lands, as opposed to buildings)
località	locality	*rallentatori*	'sleeping policeman' (road humps)
locanda	inn	*ristorante*	restaurant
loggia	loggia, lodge	*rotatoria*	(traffic) roundabout
		ru	medieval irrigation channel
		sacco a pelo	sleeping bag
		sali e tabacchi	a kiosk selling cigarettes, stamps, bus tickets, etc (literally 'salt and tobacco', referring to the fact that salt, like tobacco today, was once licensed to be sold only in state outlets)
		strada	road, street
		strada bianca	gravel/unsurfaced road
		strada privata	private road
		strada provinciale (SP)	provincial/main road

Sign for Abbazia SS. Salvatore

strada regionale (SR)	local (B-class) road
strada statale (SS)	national (A-class) road, trunk road
tenuta	estate, domain, (large) property (both buildings and land)
torrente	(smaller) river
trattoria	(small) restaurant
via sterrata	rough unsurfaced road
vicolo	alley
vietato ingresso	no entry
vigili del fuoco	fire brigade

Pilgrim ostello, Monteriggioni

APPENDIX F
Useful contacts

Confraternity of Pilgrims to Rome
(+44) 7739 647426
www.pilgrimstorome.org.uk
pilgrimstoromesecretary.@yahoo.com

Association Internationale Via
Francigena (AIVF)
12 Route de Bagnes
1943 Vollèges
Switzerland
www.francigena-international.org

Associazione Europea delle Vie
Francigene (AEVF)
Piazza Duomo 16
43036 Fidenza
Italy
www.viefrancigene.it

The Map Shop
15 High Street
Upton-upon-Severn
Worcestershire WR8 0HJ
Tel: 01684 593146
www.themapshop.co.uk
themapshop@btinternet.com

Stanfords
12 Long Acre
Covent Garden
London WC2E 9LP
Tel: 020 7836 1321
www.stanfords.co.uk
sales@stanfords.co.uk

Instituto Geografico Centrale
Via Prata 2
10121 Torino
Italy
www.istitutogeograficocentrale.it
(for hiking maps)

Italian State Tourist Board
1 Princes Street
London W1B 2AY
info@london.enit.it

Via Francigena del Sud

Pilgrims who have walked to Rome may be
interested in discovering other routes, such
as those to Rome from the south of Italy:
www.romaefrancigena.eu

In order to qualify for the Testimonium Peregrinationis ad Limina Petri (certificate of pilgrimage) – similar to the 'Compostela' for those who have walked, cycled or ridden to Santiago – you must be in possession of a credenziale (pilgrim passport), have had it stamped each day, and have walked to Rome from at least Acquapendente or cycled there from at least Lucca. A Testimonium can be obtained from the following two places in Rome.

Opera Romana Pellegrinaggi, Piazza Pio XII 9, just off the Piazza di San Pietro, is an organization that arranges group pilgrimages. They are open Mon–Fri 9am–6pm, Sat–Sun 9am–4pm (06.69896384), and on presentation of your stamped credenziale will provide you with a certificate of pilgrimage.

Uffici della Canonica di San Pietro, in the Vatican City. This is open on Mon–Tues, Thurs–Sat, 9.30am–12.30pm. To get there go to first to the Piazza del Sant'Uffizio (on the opposite side of the Piazza di San Pietro from the one where you entered) and go through the Ingresso del Petriano (entrance), where the Swiss guards on duty will ask you what you want and direct you to the police booth next to it to scan any bags you have with you. You will then be directed to an office on the right, where your details will be recorded, your passport handed over and a visitor's badge given to you before you are directed to the Palazzo della Canonica (now to your left). (Be prepared for some of the officials, guards or policemen on duty not to be familiar with the Testimonium, so a certain level of Italian is useful.)

Once inside you will be invited to sit down at a table and write any comments/reflections you may wish in the pilgrim book, and then be asked to fill in the details of yourself, your journey and the reason(s) for undertaking the pilgrimage in the Via Francigena ledger. In the meantime the official will take your credenziale, stamp it for the last time and issue you with your parchment Testimonium. (As you leave do not forget to return the visitor's badge to the security office and collect your passport.)

Pilgrims who cannot apply for their Testimonium in person while in Rome may request it by post. Write to the

Fabbrica di San Pietro, 00120 Città del Vaticano, enclosing

- a photocopy of your identity card or passport
- a photocopy of your credenziale with all its stamps
- your full address
- your date of birth
- the starting place of your pilgrimage
- the starting date and arrival date Also state
- whether you walked or cycled
- your motivation – religious/ spiritual, cultural, other
- what organisations assisted you before or during your pilgrimage (AIVF, St James' associations/ confraternities, AEVF, CPR or other).

APPENDIX H
Index of Maps

APPENDIX I
Index of principal place names

Looking out over Lucca

APPENDIX J
Summary of the route

Looking up to Castelnuovo Fogliari

Vineyard near Torrenieri

NOTES

LISTING OF CICERONE GUIDES

Rocky Rambler's Wild Walks
Scrambles in the Lake District
  North & South
Short Walks in Lakeland
  1 South Lakeland
  2 North Lakeland
  3 West Lakeland
The Cumbria Coastal Way
The Cumbria Way and the
  Allerdale Ramble
Tour of the Lake District

DERBYSHIRE, PEAK DISTRICT AND MIDLANDS

High Peak Walks
Scrambles in the Dark Peak
The Star Family Walks
Walking in Derbyshire
White Peak Walks
  The Northern Dales
  The Southern Dales

SOUTHERN ENGLAND

Suffolk Coast & Heaths Walks
The Cotswold Way
The Great Stones Way
The North Downs Way
The Peddars Way and Norfolk
  Coast Path
The Ridgeway National Trail
The South Downs Way
The South West Coast Path
The Thames Path
Walking in Essex
Walking in Kent
Walking in Norfolk
Walking in Sussex
Walking in the Chilterns
Walking in the Cotswolds
Walking in the Isles of Scilly
Walking in the New Forest
Walking in the Thames Valley
Walking on Dartmoor
Walking on Guernsey
Walking on Jersey
Walking on the Isle of Wight
Walks in the South Downs
  National Park

WALES AND WELSH BORDERS

Backpacker's Britain – Wales
Glyndwr's Way
Great Mountain Days
  in Snowdonia
Hillwalking in Snowdonia

Hillwalking in Wales: 1&2
Offa's Dyke Path
Ridges of Snowdonia
Scrambles in Snowdonia
The Ascent of Snowdon
The Ceredigion and Snowdonia
  Coast Paths
Lleyn Peninsula Coastal Path
Pembrokeshire Coastal Path
The Severn Way
The Shropshire Hills
The Wye Valley Walk
Walking in Pembrokeshire
Walking in the Forest of Dean
Walking in the South
  Wales Valleys
Walking on Gower
Walking on the Brecon Beacons
Welsh Winter Climbs

INTERNATIONAL CHALLENGES, COLLECTIONS AND ACTIVITIES

Canyoning
Canyoning in the Alps
Europe's High Points
The Via Francigena
  (Canterbury to Rome): 1&2

EUROPEAN CYCLING

Cycle Touring in France
Cycle Touring in Ireland
Cycle Touring in Spain
Cycle Touring in Switzerland
Cycling in the French Alps
Cycling the Canal du Midi
Cycling the River Loire
The Danube Cycleway
The Grand Traverse of the
  Massif Central
The Moselle Cycle Route
The Rhine Cycle Route
The Way of St James

AFRICA

Climbing in the Moroccan
  Anti-Atlas
Kilimanjaro
Mountaineering in the Moroccan
  High Atlas
The High Atlas
Trekking in the Atlas Mountains
Walking in the Drakensberg

ALPS – CROSS-BORDER ROUTES

100 Hut Walks in the Alps

Across the Eastern Alps: E5
Alpine Points of View
Alpine Ski Mountaineering
  1 Western Alps
  2 Central and Eastern Alps
Chamonix to Zermatt
Snowshoeing
Tour of Mont Blanc
Tour of Monte Rosa
Tour of the Matterhorn
Trekking in the Alps
Trekking in the Silvretta and
  Rätikon Alps
Walking in the Alps
Walks and Treks in the
  Maritime Alps

PYRENEES AND FRANCE/SPAIN CROSS-BORDER ROUTES

Rock Climbs in the Pyrenees
The GR10 Trail
The GR11 Trail – La Senda
The Mountains of Andorra
The Pyrenean Haute Route
The Pyrenees
The Way of St James – France
  & Spain
Walks and Climbs in the Pyrenees

AUSTRIA

The Adlerweg
Trekking in Austria's Hohe Tauern
Trekking in the Stubai Alps
Trekking in the Zillertal Alps
Walking in Austria

EASTERN EUROPE

The High Tatras
The Mountains of Romania
Walking in Bulgaria's
  National Parks
Walking in Hungary

FRANCE

Chamonix Mountain Adventures
Ecrins National Park
GR20: Corsica
Mont Blanc Walks
Mountain Adventures in
  the Maurienne
The Cathar Way
The GR20 Corsica
The GR5 Trail
The Robert Louis Stevenson Trail
Tour of the Oisans: The GR54

For full information about all
our guides, books and eBooks,
go to: www.cicerone.co.uk.

Walking – Trekking – Mountaineering – Climbing – Cycling

Over 40 years, Cicerone have built up an outstanding collection of 300 guides, inspiring all sorts of amazing adventures.

Every guide comes from extensive exploration and research by our expert authors, all with a passion for their subjects. They are frequently praised, endorsed and used by clubs, instructors and outdoor organisations.

All our titles can now be bought as **e-books** and many as iPad and Kindle files and we will continue to make all our guides available for these and many other devices.

Our website shows any **new information** we've received since a book was published. Please do let us know if you find anything has changed, so that we can pass on the latest details. On our **website** you'll also find some great ideas and lots of information, including sample chapters, contents lists, reviews, articles and a photo gallery.

It's easy to keep in touch with what's going on at Cicerone, by getting our monthly **free e-newsletter**, which is full of offers, competitions, up-to-date information and topical articles. You can subscribe on our home page and also follow us on **Facebook** and **Twitter**, as well as our **blog**.

Cicerone – the very best guides for exploring the world.

CICERONE

2 Police Square Milnthorpe Cumbria LA7 7PY
Tel: 015395 62069 info@cicerone.co.uk
www.cicerone.co.uk